Sports Law in Austria

Sports Law in Austria

Gert-Peter Reissner
Nicole Windisch

This book was originally published as a monograph in the International Encyclopaedia of Laws/Sports Law.

Founding Editor: Roger Blanpain
General Editor: Frank Hendrickx
Volume Editor: Michele Colucci

Wolters Kluwer

Published by:
Kluwer Law International B.V.
PO Box 316
2400 AH Alphen aan den Rijn
The Netherlands
E-mail: lrs-sales@wolterskluwer.com
Website: www.wolterskluwer.com/en/solutions/kluwerlawinternational

Sold and distributed by:
Wolters Kluwer Legal & Regulatory U.S.
920 Links Avenue
Landisville, PA 17538
United States of America
E-mail: customer.service@wolterskluwer.com

ISBN 978-94-035-2376-7

e-Book: ISBN 978-94-035-2696-6
web-PDF: ISBN 978-94-035-2706-2

The Authors

University Professor Mag. Dr Gert-Peter Reissner is head of the Labour Law, Social Security Law and Legal Informatics Department of Karl-Franzens University Graz and member of the Ph.D. programme 'Sports and Law' in Innsbruck which aims to comprehend the interdisciplinary legal implementations of sport.

He is one of the leading experts on labour law in the Austrian market and has published numerous monographs, commentarics and articles regarding this subject. He has also published various articles on sports law.

Gert-Peter Reissner is co-editor of the *Series of Publications Regarding Sports Law at the University Innsbruck*' and *Scriptures on Sports Law* as well as co-author of the publication *Introduction to Austrian Sports Law*. He is also a member of various associations, including the Austrian Association for Labour and Social Security Law and the International Labour and Employment Relations Association.

Mag. Nicole Windisch is a university assistant at the institute for Labour Law and Social Security Law of Karl-Franzens University Graz. Currently, she is writing her Ph.D. thesis in the field of labour law for media employees.

The Authors

Table of Contents

Table of Contents

List of Abbreviations

ABGB	Allgemeines bürgerliches Gesetzbuch JGS 946 (Austrian General Civil Code)
AngG	Angestelltengesetz BGBl 1921/292 (Austrian Employee Act)
Arb	Sammlung arbeitsrechtlicher Entscheidungen (Collection of labour law decisions)
ArbAbfG	Arbeiter-Abfertigungsgesetz BGBl 1979/107 (Austrian Labourer Severance Act)
ArbG	Arbeitsgericht (German Labour Court)
ArbVG	Arbeitsverfassungsgesetz BGBl 1974/22 (Labour Constitution Act)
ARG	Arbeitsruhegesetz BGBl 1983/144 (Austrian Rest Periods Act)
ASG	Arbeits- und Sozialgericht (Labour and Social Security Court)
ASGG	Arbeits- und Sozialgerichtsgesetz BGBl 1985/104 (Labour and Social Security Court Act)
ASKÖ	Arbeitsgemeinschaft für Sport und Körperkultur in Österreich (Austrian Working Group for Sport and Physical Culture)
ASoK	Arbeits- und Sozialrechtskartei (Index for Labour and Social Security Law)
ASVG	Allgemeines Sozialversicherungsgesetz BGBl 1955/189 (Austrian General Social Insurance Act)
ASVÖ	Allgemeiner Sportverband Österreichs (Austrian Sports Association)
AuslBG	Ausländerbeschäftigungsgesetz BGBl 1975/218 (Austrian Employment of Foreign Nationals Act)
AUVA	Allgemeine Unfallversicherungsanstalt (General Accident Insurance Institution)

List of Abbreviations

AZG	Arbeitszeitgesetz BGBl 1969/461 (Austrian Working Time Act)
BAG	Bundesarbeitsgericht (German Federal Labour Court)
BAO	Bundesabgabenordnung BGBl 1961/194 (Austrian Federal Fiscal Code)
BGBl	Bundesgesetzblatt (Federal Law Gazette)
BGH	Bundesgerichtshof (German Federal Supreme Court)
BKS	Bundeskommunikationssenat (Federal Communication Senate)
B-KUVG	Beamten-Kranken- und Unfallversicherungsgesetz BGBl 1967/200 (Austrian Public Official Illness and Accident Insurance Act)
BLGBl	Landesgesetzblatt für Burgenland (Regional Legal Gazette of Burgenland)
BlgNR	Beilagen zu den stenographischen Protokollen des Nationalrats (Supplements to the Stenographic Protocols of the National Council)
BMF	Bundesminister(ium) für Finanzen (Austrian Federal Ministry of Finance)
BMSVG	Betriebliches Mitarbeiter- und Selbständigenvorsorgegesetz BGBl I 2002/100 (Austrian Federal Act on Corporate Staff and Self-Employment Provision)
BMWA	Bundesminister(ium) für Wirtschaft und Arbeit (Austrian Federal Ministry of Commerce and Labour)
BSFG	Bundes-Sportförderungsgesetz 2005 BGBl I 64 (Federal Sports Promotion Act)
BSO	Bundessportorganisation (Federal Sports Organization)
BVerfG	Bundesverfassungsgericht (German Federal Constitutional Court)
B-VG	Bundes-Verfassungsgesetz 1920 idF von 1929 (Austrian Federal Constitution)
CAS	Court of Arbitration for Sport
DRdA	Das Recht der Arbeit (Austrian Journal on Labour Law)
ECHR	European Convention on Human Rights
ECtHR	European Court of Human Rights
EEA	European Economic Area
EFZG	Entgeltfortzahlungsgesetz BGBl 1974/399; Entgeltfortzahlungsgesetz (deutsch) (Austrian and German Continuation of Wage Payments During Sickness Act)

EG	Vertrag zur Gründung der Europäischen Gemeinschaft (Treaty establishing the European Community; prior to 1999: EGV bzw EWGV); Europäische Gemeinschaft(en) (European Communities)
EisbG	Eisenbahngesetz 1957 BGBl 60 (Austrian Railway Act)
EpiG	Epidemiegesetz 1950 BGBl 186 (Austrian Epidemic Law Act)
ErbStG	Erbschafts- und Schenkungssteuergesetz 1955 BGBl 141 (Austrian Inheritance and Donations Tax Act)
EStG	Einkommensteuergesetz BGBl 1988/400 (Austrian Income Tax Act)
EU	Vertrag über die Europäische Union (Treaty on the European Union; prior to 1999: EUV); Europäische Union (European Union)
EvBl	Evidenzblatt der Rechtsmittelentscheidungen in der ÖJZ (Evidence Sheet of the decisions of appeal published in the Journal for Austrian Lawyers)
FIFA	Féderation Internationale de Football Association (International Football Association)
FIS	Féderation Internationale de Ski (International Ski Federation)
ForstG	Forstgesetz 1975 BGBl 440 (Austrian Forest Act)
FS	Festschrift (Commemorative Publication)
FSVG	Freiberuflich Selbständigen-Sozialversicherungsgesetz BGBl 1978/624 (Austrian Social Insurance Act for Self-Employed)
GDPR	General Data Protection Regulation, Regulation (EU) 679/2016 (DSVGO)
GewO 1859	Gewerbeordnung 1859 RGBl 227 (Austrian Code of Trade and Commerce)
GrStG	Grundsteuergesetz 1955 BGBl 149 (Austrian Real Estate Tax Act)
GRUR	Gewerblicher Rechtsschutz und Urheberrecht (German Journal for Intellectual Property and Copyright)
GS	Gedenkschrift (commemorative volume)
GSVG	Gewerbliches Sozialversicherungsgesetz BGBl 1978/560 (Austrian Social Insurance Act for Self-Employed Persons in Trade and Industry)
H	Heft (Issue)
h	Stunde (Hour)

List of Abbreviations

IESG	Insolvenz-Entgeltsicherungsgesetz BGBl 1977/324 (Austrian Insolvency Remuneration Guarantee Act)
IIHF	International Ice Hockey Federation
infas	Informationen aus dem Arbeits- und Sozialrecht (Information for Labour and Social Law)
IOC	International Olympic Committee
JAP	Juristische Ausbildung und Praxis (Journal for Legal Training and Practice)
JBl	Juristische Blätter
KLGBl	Landesgesetzblatt für Kärnten (Regional Legal Gazette of Carinthia)
KSchG	Konsumentenschutzgesetz BGBl 1979/140 (Austrian Governing Provisions to Protect Consumers)
KStG	Körperschaftsteuergesetz 1988 BGBl 401 (Austrian Corporation Tax Act)
KuKuSpoSiG	Kunst-, Kultur- und Sportsicherungsgesetz BGBl I 2020/40 (Art, Culture and Sports Protection Act)
K-WBG	Gesetz über die Wegfreiheit im Berglande LGBl 1923/18 (Law on the Freedom of Way in the Mountain Country)
leg cit	Legis Citatae
LFG	Luftfahrtgesetz BGBl 1957/253 (Austrian Aviation Act)
LG	Landesgericht (Regional Court)
lit	litera (letter)
LMG	Lebensmittelgesetz BGBl 1975/86 (Austrian Federal Law on the Marketing of Foodstuffs)
LSO	Landessportorganisation (Regional State Sports Organization)
LVwG	Landesverwaltungsgericht (Regional Administrative Court)
Miet	Mietrechtliche Entscheidungen (Judgments on Tenancy Law)
MR	Medien und Recht (Austrian Journal on Media and Law)
MRG	Mietrechtsgesetz BGBl 1981/520 (Austrian Tenancy Law Act)
NADA	Nationale Anti-Doping Agentur (National Anti-Doping Agency)
NJW	Neue Juristische Wochenschrift (deutsch) (German Legal Weekly Magazine)
NÖLGBl	Landesgesetzblatt für Niederösterreich (Regional Legal Gazette of Lower Austria)
NOC	National Olympic Committee

Nr	Number
ÖBSV	Österreichischer Behindertensportverband (Austrian Disabled Sports Federation)
ÖEHV	Österreichischer Eishockey-Verband (Austrian Ice Hockey Federation)
ÖFB	Österreichischer Fußball-Bund (Austrian Football Federation)
ÖISS	Österreichisches Institut für Schul- und Sportstättenbau (Austrian Institute for School and Sport Facilities Development)
ÖJZ	Österreichische Juristen-Zeitung (Journal of Austrian Lawyers)
ÖOC	Österreichisches Olympisches Comitè (Austrian Olympic Committee)
ÖSH	Österreichische Sporthilfe (Austrian Sport Development Foundation)
ÖStZB	Österreichische Steuerzeitung Beilage (Supplement to the Austrian Tax Journal)
ÖTV	Österreichischer Tennisverband (Austrian Tennis Federation)
ÖZW	Österreichische Zeitschrift für Wirtschaftsrecht (Austrian Journal for Commercial Law)
OGH	Oberster Gerichtshof (Austrian Supreme Court)
OLG	Oberlandesgericht (Austrian Regional Court of Appeal)
OÖLGBl	Landesgesetzblatt für Oberösterreich (Regional Legal Gazette of Upper Austria)
ORF	Österreichischer Rundfunk (Austrian Broadcasting Corporation)
RdW	Recht der Wirtschaft (Austrian Journal for Commercial Law)
RGBl	Reichsgesetzblatt ('Reich' Legal Gazette)
RL	Richtlinie (Directive)
Rs	Rechtssache (Legal Case)
RZ	Österreichische Richterzeitung (Austrian Judges' Journal)
Rz	Randzahl (margin note)
S	Austrian Shilling
SeilbG	Seilbahngesetz 2003 BGBl I 103 (Austrian Cableway Act)

Slg	Sammlung; Sammlung der Rechtsprechung des Gerichtshofes und des Gerichts erster Instanz (der EG) (Collection of the Decisions of the European Court for Justice and the Court of First Instance of the European Communities)
SLGBl	Landesgesetzblatt für Salzburg (Regional Legal Gazette of Salzburg)
SMG	Suchtmittelgesetz BGBl I 1997/112 (Addictive Drugs Act)
SpuRt	Zeitschrift für Sport und Recht (deutsch) (German Journal for Sports and Law)
SSV-NF	Entscheidungen des Obersten Gerichtshofes in Sozialrechtssachen, Neue Folge (Decisions of the Austrian Supreme Court in Social Matters)
Stb	Der Staatsbürger (Beilage zu den Salzburger Nachrichten, 1948–1985)
StGB	Strafgesetzbuch BGBl 1974/60 (Austrian Criminal Code)
StGG	Staatsgrundgesetz RGBl 1867/142 (Basic Law on the General Rights of Nationals)
StPO	Strafprozessordnung BGBl 1975/631 (Republication) (Austrian Code of Criminal Procedure)
StLGBl	Landesgesetzblatt für Steiermark (Regional Legal Gazette of Styria)
StVO	Straßenverkehrsordnung 1960 BGBl 159 (Austrian Code on Road Traffic Regulations)
SWI	Steuer- und Wirtschaftskartei International
SZ	Entscheidungen des OGH in Zivilrechtssachen (Decisions of the Austrian Supreme Court in Civil Matters)
TAS	Tribunal Arbitral du Sport
TLGBl	Landesgesetzblatt für Tirol (Regional Legal Gazette of Tyrol)
TSchG	Tierschutzgesetz BGBl I 2004/118 (Austrian Protection of Animals Act)
USSR	Union of Soviet Socialist Republics
UEFA	Union of European Football Associations
UNCITRAL	United Nations Commission on International Trade Law
UNESCO	United Nations Educational, Scientific and Cultural Organization
UrhG	Urheberrechtsgesetz BGBl 1936/111 (Austrian Copyright Act)
UrlG	Urlaubsgesetz BGBl 1976/390 (Austrian Vacation Act)
US	United States

UStG	Umsatzsteuergesetz 1994 BGBl 663 (Austrian Turnover Tax Act)
VAT	Value-Added Tax
VerG	Vereinsgesetz 2002 BGBl I 66 (Austrian Act on Associations)
VersR	Versicherungsrecht (deutsch) (German Journal on Insurance Law)
VfGH	Verfassungsgerichtshof (Austrian Constitutional Court)
VfSlg	Sammlung der Erkenntnisse und wichtigsten Beschlüsse des VfGH (Collection of the Decisions and important resolutions of the Austrian Constitutional Court)
VLGBl	Landesgesetzblatt für Vorarlberg (Regional Legal Gazette of Vorarlberg)
VwGH	Verwaltungsgerichtshof (Austrian Administrative Court)
WADA	World Anti-Doping Agency
WADC	World Anti-Doping Code
WLGBl	Landesgesetzblatt für Wien (Regional Legal Gazette of Vienna)
WoBl	Wohnrechtliche Blätter
WRG	Wasserrechtsgesetz BGBl 1959/215 (Republication) (Austrian Water Resources Act)
WrK	Wiener Kommentar zum Strafgesetzbuch, hrsg von *Höpfel/Ratz*
Z	Ziffer; Zahl (Clause; Number)
Zak	Zivilrecht aktuell (Journal for Civil Law)
ZAS	Zeitschrift für Arbeitsrecht und Sozialrecht (Journal for Labour and Social Security Law)
ZellKomm	Zeller Kommentar zum Arbeitsrecht (2018), edited by *Neumayr/Reissner*
ZfG	Zeitschrift für Gesundheitsrecht (Journal for Health Law)
ZfS	Zeitschrift für Schadenersatzrecht (deutsch) (German Journal for Tort Law)
ZPO	Zivilprozessordnung RGBl 1895/113 (Austrian Code of Civil Procedure)
ZVR	Zeitschrift für Verkehrsrecht (Journal for Traffic Law)
ZZP Int	Zeitschrift für Zivilprozess International (deutsch) (German Journal for International Civil Procedure)

List of Abbreviations

General Introduction

§1. General Background and Specificity of Sport

1. The term '*sports*' includes a number of aspects of various sociological dimensions. Therefore, specific additional terms applied in order to differentiate mass sports, high-performance sports, top-class sports, junior sports, old people's sports, and disabled sports may serve as examples.

I. High-Performance Sport: Top-Class Sport – Mass Sport

2. In certain areas, *high-performance sport* has been shifted to a grey zone between voluntary participation in sports and games on the one hand and activity for an income on the other hand. This development has been influenced by *top-class sport*, which is controlled by strong economic interests and is seen as high-paid work performance.

3. Even though *mass sport* derives stimulus and models from high-performance sport, it develops its own internal dynamics. These dynamics can best be observed in mass sport such as jogging or nordic walking.

4. Mass sport as well as high-performance sport contains an element of both game and performance. An incentive is a crucial element of mass sport.

II. Economic Relevance

5. The drive to fitness and recreational activities has produced a large market in the last couple of years. In this process, new branches have evolved which equip the athlete from tip to toe. The various products are constantly improved and modernized. The attention which is given to a number of sports in the media causes a flow of earnings/returns due to broadcasting rights. Usually, high-performance sport serves as an advertising medium in the mass media and is instrumentalized to open the market for products of everyday life as well as sports equipment, sports nutrition, practice literature, etc. Therefore, the process of professionalization is inevitably accompanied by the commercial relevance of top-class sport and its effects as a multiple for mass sports and high-performance sports. In the long run, it would be impossible to commit the sportsman to ideals and substitutional expenses, whereas amounts of several millions are invested by sponsors and the media in events in which the sportsman or athlete takes centre stage.

Part I. The Legal Framework

Introduction

6. Due to diverse involved interests, the initial economic situation calls for the discussion of *legal relationship between the concerned parties.*

7. First and foremost, the *legal status of the athlete* has to be examined. The questions of employee characteristics and the application of regulations based on employment law have to be raised. Furthermore, the legal position of athletes within structures of voluntary sports associations and sports unions has to be discussed without consideration of legal relations between employer and employee. Besides the legal position of the athlete within the voluntary association, the *internal structures of voluntary associations or unions* need to be pursued.

8. The economic dimensions of modern sports naturally raise competitional legal issues.

9. Sports activity requires adequate facilities and areas; this fact entails *problems concerning law of property.*

10. Due to the enormous increase of sports activities and often inexperienced participants in sports exercises, sports accidents have evolved into a mass phenomenon. The uninjured body presents a legally protected interest, and unalloyed joy of life and job performance have got a legal status worthy of protection which can be expressed in monetary value. Therefore, the issue of *liability concerning criminal and civil law* for teammates, sportsmen who are accidentally engaged in sports activities with the injured sportsman, organizers of sports events as well as operators of sports facilities needs to be discussed.

11. Apart from the system of continued payment of wages on behalf of the employer as *social security for the sportsman* in case of an accident, the sportsman is also protected by the complete system of social law, especially of social insurance.

12. Furthermore, one economically relevant problem concerns the position of voluntary sports associations and athletes in *fiscal law.*

13. Therefore, sports activities are bound to legal regulations which cover nearly every single field of law (constitutional law, administrative law, civil law, criminal law, employment law, social law, competitional law, fiscal law). Viewed in the light of the current COVID-19 crisis, the constitutional law perspective gains also special significance in the field of sports. The essay at hand tries to organize the most relevant issues of sports law according to classic criteria and classification of law.

§1. Public Law and Fundamental Rights

14. First of all, it is necessary to treat the allocation of rights and obligations in sports law in order to subsequently analyse the relevant constitutional and personality rights. In Articles 10 et seq. of the Federal Constitution of 1920 and 1929 (B-VG), the rights and obligations within legislation and execution are divided between the federal republic and the states. The concept of the competence articles entails a complete list of federal rights and obligations, whereas the rest is assigned to the states (cf. especially Article 15 B-VG).

15. Due to the fact that the field of sports is not mentioned in the B-VG, the issues of legislature and execution in sports are – under Article 15 B-VG – assigned to the *states*.

16. Apart from this, the federal republic only has competence in the area of promotion of sports. In doing so, it acts within the framework of private sector administration according to Art 17 B-VG. For this purpose, the Federal Sports Promotion Act (BSFG) was enacted (cf. §2.II.A).

I. Right to Practise Sport

17. In general, the constitutional law does not entail a right to practise sport or to participate in sporting competitions. In the light of the introductory considerations, the following executions distinguish between *high-performance sport* and *top-class sport* on the one hand and *mass sport* or *hobby sport* on the other.

18. During the COVID-19 pandemic, various legal provisions also prohibited or restricted the access to sports facilities (cf. in detail Part VI). Therefore, the VfGH[1] was recently faced with an alleged violation of the right to respect for private and family life according to Article 8 ECHR. Among other things, the applicant claimed an infringement because of an impact on her social life by the exclusion from entering sports facilities in the mentioned case. In view of the fact that the VfGH denied an interference in the quoted fundamental right, he must have previously considered the scope of the provision to be opened. In summary, in the field of *hobby* and *mass sports*, a violation of the right to respect for private and family life is conceivable.

1. VfGH 29.4.2022, V 23/2022, Rz 63.

19. Besides this, professional athletes in the *high-performance* and *top-class sports* area can plead an infringement of their right to freedom of acquisition in accordance with Art 6 StGG. Accordingly, prohibitions on the practice of *top-class sports* were under certain conditions not subject to the COVID-19 regulations[2] (cf. Part IV, §1.II).

20. Apart from this, the ECtHR[3] stated regarding a search of a lawyer's office that the scope of Art 8 ECHR is not limited to an 'inner circle'. Therefore, professional or business activities should not be excluded from the protection. The ECtHR[4] assumes a broad term of the private and family life. In order to establish relationships outside of one's home, Art 8 ECHR also includes a right to 'private social life' so that professional activities or activities taking place in a public context are also part of the scope of protection. In this context, it is, for example, conceivable that the professional sportsman complains about the strict doping controls during training and competitions (cf. Part IV).[5]

II. Freedom of Association

21. The right of freedom of assembly and association is enshrined in Art 11 ECHR and at national level in Art 12 StGG. This right also came to the fore during the COVID-19 crisis. Initially, gatherings with a certain number of participants were generally prohibited. Later on, such events could take place subject to compliance with certain protective mechanisms. The prohibition applied, for example, not only to sporting events but also to certain training sessions of sports associations. Regarding the latter aspect, there was a ban on entering public sports facilities anyway (*see* Part VI, §1.II). However, an exception existed, e.g., regarding gatherings for professional purposes, which are necessary for the maintenance of the professional activity.[6] This aspect probably also gained relevance in terms of the field of professional sports. At the level of simple laws, attention must be paid in further sequence to the Act on Associations 2002 (VerG, cf. Part II, Chapter 1, §2I).

---

2. Cf., for example, § 11 Clause 2 Z 1 5.COVID-19-Notmaßnahmenverordnung BGBl II 2021/475.
3. ECtHR 16.12.1992, 13710/88, *Niemietz*, Rz 29.
4. ECtHR 18.4.2018, 8151/11 and 77769/13, *National Federation of Sportspersons' Associations and Unions*, Rz 153.
5. See in this sense in more detail *Rietiker*, Die Perspektive des Europäischen Gerichtshofs für Menschenrechte zur Sportsgerichtsbarkeit – unter besonderer Berücksichtigung des Verfahrens vor dem internationalen Schiedsgericht für Sport, in *Balthasar/Cornu* (ed.), Internationaler Sport – Eine rechtliche Herausforderung für Verwaltung und Gerichtsbarkeit? (2015) 53 (62).
6. *See, e.g.*, § 10 COVID-19-LV BGBl II 2020/197.

III. Personality Rights

A. *The Athlete's Right to His Picture*

22. *In general*, the athlete has the right to his own picture in the sense of § 78 UrhG. According to the OGH,[7] this protection of one's picture is part of the personal rights in accordance with § 16 ABGB. Consequently, the publication of portraits of persons is not permitted if legitimate interests of the person depicted are violated.[8] Therefore, athletes may prohibit others from *taking* and *publishing* pictures.

23. However, famous persons – and athletes are part of this group – who are well known to the public may not prohibit others from taking or publishing pictures as long as the informational interest of the general public is satisfied. Therefore, the athlete has to permit the coverage of a sports event (also on TV) without explicitly giving his consent. After all, the object of protection is not the image itself, but certain interests associated with the image.[9] Nevertheless, if the organizer of a sports event markets this event to a mass medium, he has to ensure the consent of the participating athlete.

24. Anyway, in no case does an athlete have to accept that his picture is used for promotional purposes without his consent. In this context, the OGH[10] stated that the consensus-free publication of images of prominent athletes in connection with self-promotion of the media company does not pursue any public interests. Accordingly, besides legal consequences under the law of unfair competition (cf. Part V, §2), there is an indirect violation of § 78 UrhG. The OGH[11] followed up on this legal opinion in another decision and added that no claims for injunctive relief by third parties can be derived from the athlete's right to his picture.

§2. The National Sports Legislation

25. Naturally, in consequence of the missing legislative jurisdiction on behalf of the federation, legislative rights and obligations by the states have got priority (cf. §2I). In the field of sports, the federation can generally only act by means of private law (cf. §2II).

7. OGH 6.12.1994 ecolex 1995, 272.
8. On the current legal development of § 78 UrhG, cf. *Haybäck*, Aktuelle Rechtsentwicklung zum Bildnisschutz nach § 78 UrhG, wbl 2020, 53.
9. Cf. OGH 11.3.2008 MR 2008, 123 (*Korn*).
10. OGH 17.9.2014 MR 2014, 314 (*Frauenberger*).
11. OGH 28.3.2017 ecolex 2017, 789 (*Hofmarcher*).

I. Sport Law and Sport Funding of the States

26. On state level, the *State Sport Codes* form the legal baseline for the various *Regional State Sports Organizations* (LSOs), which are thus a corporate body under public law.[12] The LSOs are usually composed of the clubs which exist within the respective state and which are mainly or completely targeted towards sports activities or sports promotion in combination with preservation of their characteristics, identity, and independence. It is also the task of the LSO to represent and promote the matters and interests of sport as well as to advise all the national bodies in all matters referring to sport.

27. Among the sports laws of the states, the sports law of Vorarlberg deserves special attention. On the one hand, the *sports law of Vorarlberg* includes regulations on the safety of sports activities. Based on these regulations, the 'Pistenwächter' (ski slope police) in Vorarlberg is established by law. This police squad is entitled to file action with the responsible authorities in case of violation of recognized rules of safety in skiing as a regulatory offence. Furthermore, the array of penalties in § 16 of this sports law contains administrative penalties in terms of a doping offence.

28. Furthermore, it is notable that some states have got *statutory provisions for protection of sports facilities*[13] which provide a certain constituent protection for specific sports facilities. Thus, § 3 of the Styrian Act on Protection of Sports Facilities regulates that the closing down of sports facilities can only be permitted with the consent of the community. In terms of competencies, this regulation may be supported by the legal authority of the states on issues of regional development. On a case-by-case basis, its application will be compared with the constitutional protection of property. Consequentially, as provided by law anyhow, significant public interest in maintaining the concerned sports facilities has to be proven.

29. Except for the states of Vienna and Burgenland, each state has its own *ski school law*.[14] In Upper Austria, the Schischulgesetz 1990[15] expired with the enactment of the Sportgesetz.[16] According to the current legal situation, regulations concerning the operation and monitoring of ski schools are included in tourism law.[17]

---

12. The following state laws regulate issues of sports, e.g., *Burgenland*: Sportförderungsgesetz 2004 BLGBl 2004/26; *Carinthia*: Sportgesetz 1997 KLGBl 1997/99; *Lower Austria*: Sportgesetz 1997 NÖLGBl 5710-9; *Upper Austria*: Sportgesetz OÖLGBl 2019/56; *Salzburg*: Landessportgesetz 2018 SLGBl 2018/38; *Styria*: Landessportgesetz 2015 StLGBl 2015/53; *Tyrol*: Sportförderungsgesetz 2006 TLGBl 2006/97; *Vorarlberg*: Sportgesetz VLGBl 1972/15; *Vienna*: Landessportgesetz WLGBl 1972/17.
13. *Lower Austria*: §§ 11 ff. Sportgesetz; *Upper Austria*: § 11 f Sportgesetz; *Styria*: Sportstättenschutzgesetz 1991 StLGBl 1991/11; *Vienna*: Sportstättenschutzgesetz WLGBl 1978/29.
14. *Carinthia*: Schischulgesetz KLGBl 1997/53; *Salzburg*: Salzburger Schischul- und Snowboardschulgesetz SLGBl 1989/83; *Styria*: Schischulgesetz 1997 StLGBl 58; *Tyrol*: Schischulgesetz 1995 TLGBl 1995/15; *Vorarlberg*: Schischulgesetz VLGBl 2002/55.
15. OÖLGBl 1991/1.
16. OÖLGBl 1997/93.
17. Cf. Part III, especially § 64 of Tourismusgesetz 2018 OÖLGBl 3.

Besides this, measures against doping and for the processing of personal data are enshrined in the new Sportgesetz.[18] Furthermore, in Lower Austria, the Sportgesetz[19] entails provisions about ski schools in general, especially the requirement of an official permit, and about the education and examination of ski instructors. Originally, ski school laws were based on monopoly-like certifications. However, this monopoly has been broken up by the VfGH[20] in 1989 as it is contrary to fundamental right.

30. In terms of sport promotion, single states offer specific promotion measures. We need to refer to the radio tax in Lower Austria, which is collected in combination with the radio licence fee and is partly allocated to sports promotion,[21] or the 'sports penny' in Vienna.[22] Besides, sports promotion by the states is basically conducted within the frame of promotion of tourism.

II. Federal Sports Promotion and Anti-Doping Code

31. Despite the lack of federal competence, the federation is not completely abstaining concerning sports promotion in Austria. Besides the promotion effect which results in a large part from nationally funded school and university sports as well as various educational institutions for trainers and tutors, the BSFG (cf. §2.II.A) and the Federal Sports Facilities Ltd (cf. §2.II.B) should be emphasized as instruments of sports promotion on behalf of the federation. Recently, the federal sports promotion has been bound to compliance with the Anti-Doping Act of 2021 as part of efforts in order to fight doping (cf. §2.II.C).

A. Federal Sports Promotion Act 2017

32. The BSFG differentiates between top-class sport and high-performance sport promotion on the one hand and mass sport promotion on the other hand. The sports promotion funds should enable the associations and clubs to fulfil their mission in popular sports as well as in top sports.

33. The particular federal sports promotion funds are distributed according to a complicated key which is regulated in §§ 5 et seq. of the law. Apart from the ÖFB (Austrian Football Federation), the main beneficiaries of these funds are the association of Alpine Clubs, the BSO (Federal Sports Organization), the ÖOC (Austrian Olympic Committee) and the disabled sports associations. Furthermore, the umbrella organizations ASKÖ, UNION, ASVÖ and the 'Fachverbände' (sports federations which are responsible for their respective type of sport) are funded.

---

18. OÖLGBl 2019/56 in connection with the Sportartenverordnung 2022 OÖLGBl 40.
19. Cf. Chapter 4 Sportgesetz 1997 NÖLGBl 5710-9.
20. VfGH 30.11.1988 VfSlg 11.910.
21. Rundfunkabgabegesetz NÖLGBl 2015/69.
22. Sportförderungsbeitragsgesetz 2012 WLGBl 2012/22.

34. 50% of the top-class sport and high-performance sport promotion funds go to the 'Fachverbände'. Those funds are distributed according to the capability of each 'Fachverband', which is evaluated using the following criteria:

- international proof of success;
- international and specific national significance of the sport;
- quality and extension of the junior work;
- sportive development prospects;
- quality of the 'Fachverband's' structure and work.

35. The promotion of the 'Fachverbände' is determined for the aspects referred to in the law, i.e., expenses for staff and infrastructure, the posting of athletes to competitions or the promotion of junior athletes.

36. Furthermore, 71% of the mass sport promotion funds go to the three umbrella organizations in equal parts. The umbrella organizations pledge themselves to develop and maintain service offering for their members. They also are obliged to pass a grave part of the funds to their member associations for specific purposes.

37. The legal qualification of the BSFG is not particularly unproblematic. As already mentioned above, the federation acts due to the lack of competence in sport within the framework of private sector administration. In this regard, the federation as regional administrative body utilizes its *legislation competence in regard to private law ref Article 17 B-VG* and thus gets involved as private agent subject to civil law. This is carried out on a legal basis; therefore, it is called '*Innenbindungsgesetz*' (an act which solely binds the federal entity). Based on such a law, it is not possible to derive any legal claims for promotion from the federation. However, the federation is obliged to ensure equal treatment of the promotion applicants within the framework of *fiscal validity of fundamental rights*. If a promotion applicant is discriminated in the subsidy procedure, he is entitled to direct benefits even if there is no legal claim to a subsidy.[23]

B. The Federal Sports Facilities Ltd

38. Effective 1 January 1999, all federal sports facilities have been separated from federal administration and have been integrated into the Federal Sports Facilities Ltd.

39. The federal sports and leisure centres Kitzsteinhorn, Faaker See, Maria Alm/Hintermoos, Obertraun, Schloss Schielleiten and Südstadt are managed operatively by the Federal Sports Facilities Ltd itself. The federal sports facility St. Christoph has been entrusted by way of a lease contract to the Austrian Ski Federation.

---

23. Cf. OGH 26.1.1995 ÖZW 1996, 51 (*Kalss*).

40. The federal sports facilities and leisure centres offer state-of-the-art sports facilities including accommodation and meals at an affordable price especially to associations and clubs for their training camps, etc.

C. *Federal Anti-Doping Act 2021*

41. In the course of Salzburg's failed application for the 2014 Olympic Winter Games, federal legislature has put the regulations concerning doping controls, which until then had been only anchored in law of association, on legal foot and has provided the relating rules with legal force. In order to implement the World Anti-Doping Code (WADC), elaborated by the World Anti-Doping Agency (WADA), the first Federal Anti-Doping Act[24] was enacted in 2007. Thereby, Austria fulfilled its obligation to implement applicable provisions by means of policies, statutes, rules or regulations.

42. The mentioned act entailed provisions which have been substantially contained in the BSFG 2005 (cf. §2.II.A). However, due to systematic reasons, they were comprised in a separate law. Thereby, the civil law nature of the regulations, which have to be complied with in order to receive federal sports funds, has not been changed.

43. Due to the modification of the WADC by 2021, the signatories are obliged to amend their national regulations. In view of that, a new Anti-Federal Act[25] was enacted in 2021. The amendment focuses on the following points: restructuring of anti-doping prevention, of data protection provisions and of the Austrian Anti-Doping Legal Commission (ÖADR) respectively the independent arbitral commission. Besides that, the new act aims to enhance the national testpool, to accelerate the procedure and to implement statutes of limitations.

44. The Federal Anti-Doping Act 2021 is strongly based on the previous regulation. The content can be summarized as follows:

45. On the basis of a description of the term 'doping' (cf. § 1 Clause 2 Federal Anti-Doping Act), the law contains doping prevention by a specifically trained anti-doping officer, who is authorized by anti-doping organizations or the independent doping control institution (cf. § 5 of the law). As already mentioned above, the catalogue of *doping prevention measures* (cf. § 3 Federal Anti-Doping Act) had been enhanced in the course of the new legal regulation. Within the area of prevention work, the WADC 2021 entails international standards, e.g., for education, laboratories, result management or testing and investigations. In this context, the independent doping control institution is assigned to conduct awareness programmes and to elaborate an annually audited doping prevention plan, which shall be implemented

24. BGBl I 2007/30.
25. BGBl I 2020/152.

by the respective sport organizations (cf. § 2 Clause 27 of the law). If these organizations disregard their duty of implementation, subsidies have to be reimbursed. Thereby, as stated in Art 18 WADC 2021, the prevention measures primarily intend to protect and promote the health of the athletes.

46. The various data protection provisions have been summarized in § 6 Federal Anti-Doping Act in the course of the amendment. In order to perform their task, the independent doping control institution is authorized to process health data and data relevant to criminal law. As noted in the legislative materials,[26] the health protection of the athletes pursues an important public interest – therefore, the processing of personal data is lawful in the light of the GDPR.[27] In order to select athletes for doping controls outside of competitions, a national test pool has been provided (cf. § 9 Federal Anti-Doping Act). By the Federal Anti-Doping Act 2021, the division between top, basis and team segments has been added. In order to handle the segmentation, the independent doping control institution is obliged to carry out an individual and a sport-related risk assessment. While the top segment comprises athletes with high risks, the basis one refers to the others. The allocation of team sports to the latter segment is conducted with reference to a sport-related risk assessment.

47. Additional provisions of the law refer to medical certificates of exemption, the directive of doping controls, the content of the doping control order, general provisions on doping controls, doping controls during competitions and championships as well as pool training, and provisions on analysis of samples as well as disciplinary sanctions. Moreover, an independent arbitral commission is established (cf. § 8 of the law).

48. Due to the newly inserted case resolution agreement (cf. Article 10.8.2 WADC 2021), the person concerned by a request for review has the possibility to admit the anti-doping violation within ten days from delivery of the examination request. Thereby, the athlete can obtain a reduction in the duration of the disciplinary measures based on a decision of the chairman of the ÖADR with the consent of the WADA (friendly settlement according to § 19 Federal Anti-Doping Act). As stated in the materials,[28] this regulation was made for reasons of procedural economy. Furthermore, the newly enacted statutes of limitations (cf. § 22 of the law) provide that the affected party must be notified within ten years of the alleged violation – otherwise, a persecution is no longer possible. Finally, the law regulates specific obligations of the athletes, special provisions for animals which take part in competition, and the obligation of doctors, dentists and veterinarians to inform.

49. § 28 Federal Anti-Doping Act[29] contains a criminal offence. According to this provision, a person is punished if he is trafficking prohibited substances – provided that these substances are not addictive drugs under the Addictive Drugs Act

26. Explanatory notes on 482 BlgNR 27. GP 2.
27. Also *see* Art. 6 Clause 1 lit e GDPR.
28. Cf. explanatory notes on 482 BlgNR 27. GP 22.
29. This rule replaces the penal provisions of § 5a Medical Products Act.

(SMG) – for the purpose of doping in sport, or if he is using these substances on others or if he is using methods of artificial increase of oxygen transfer (blood doping) which are banned or genetic doping on others. According to qualifications, the scale of penalties goes up to imprisonment for five years.

50. On the contrary, the punishment of self-doping is still only rarely included in state laws as an administrative offence, such as in § 16 Clause 1 lit o of the Vorarlberg Sports Act.

51. Furthermore, the Federal Anti-Doping Act works to implement commitments that are binding under international law. In 1991, the *Anti-Doping Convention of the European Council* for Austria entered into force.[30] In addition, Austria has joined the *UNESCO Convention against Doping in Sport*, the National Council having ratified this convention.[31] The emphasis of this convention is focused on the obligation of the signatory states to act accordingly, in coordination with the principles of the WADC, on international cooperation in order to protect the athletes and sporting ethics, as well as promoting the exchange of results of research and cooperation between the signatory states and leading organizations in the field of combating doping in sport, especially the WADA.

52. The *constitutional framework* of the Federal Anti-Doping Act is still in many respects *Article 17 B-VG.*[32] Consequently, to a certain extent, this is a so-called *Innenbindungsgesetz* (*see* above 1.) which cannot have a normative effect on the interested parties as it can only bind the federation within the framework of its private sector administration. The criminal offence of § 28 leg cit is based on the constitutional competence of the *criminal justice* (Article 10 Clause 1 Z 6 B-VG).

30. BGBl 1991/451.
31. BGBl III 2007/108.
32. Cf. Explanatory notes on the motion of the sports committee, 105 BlgNR 23. GP 2.

Part II. Private Sports Organizations and Their Regulations

Chapter 1. Public Regulation

§1. Introduction

53. The organization of sport in Austria is almost exclusively using the organizational form of the sports club or sports association. This does not only account at the grassroots for the simple sports club but also for associations on state level as well as on federal level, the ÖOC and the BSO.

54. Only the LSOs – as explained above – are based on state law and are therefore corporate bodies under public law.

§2. Regulation of Sports Organizations

I. The Association

55. The fact that the organization of Austrian sport is almost exclusively presented by the legal institute of the association makes it necessary to highlight some essential foundations of sports associations from the point of view of sport. As sports associations appear regularly as non-profit making associations, the applicable legal basis for them is the *Act on Associations 2002 (VerG).*[33] This act is the result of long years of reform efforts which have especially led to a stronger legal regulation of big athletic associations, which may well manifest in sport.[34]

56. From the legal point of view, an *association* is a permanent voluntary union of individuals which is designed to reach a common admissible ideal purpose. The association corresponds to the attributes of a *corporate entity* (cf. § 2 Clause 1 VerG).

33. BGBl I 2002/66.
34. Cf. *Krejci*, Neuer Start der Vereinsrechtsreform? RdW 2001, 206.

57. *Federations* are also associations (§ 1 Clause 5.1 VerG). Their members are mainly sports associations but at the same time natural persons as well. An organization which represents common interests of associations is called umbrella association according to § 1 Clause 5.2 VerG. Within the Austrian sport, the term 'umbrella association' has been coined as the generic term for sports associations such as ASKÖ, UNION and ASVÖ, whereas the term 'Fachverband' covers the associations which represent a specific type of sport.

58. Before commencing business, the proponents of the association formally have to *notify* the intended formation of the club by means of presenting the association's statutes with the competent association authority (§ 11 VerG). Since the beginning of 2022 the association authority is obliged to provide the statutes to the chancellor if the purpose of the association is the practice of a cultus. Thereby, it should be ensured that there is no interference in internal affairs of a legally recognized church or religious society. If no *prohibition* is issued within four weeks or if the authority declares already before the end of the four weeks term that the association is not prohibited, the association can start its work as a legal entity (§ 13 VerG). Reasons for prohibition could be the fact that the association is illegal in its purpose, its name or its organization (§ 12 VerG).

59. The managing body of the association must *register* the *members of this body* including their function according to statutes, their names and their physical addresses within four weeks of their appointment with the authority. If the headquarter of the association is changed, the respective authority has to be informed about the new address within the same term (§ 14 VerG).

60. If demanded, the association authority has to pass on *information available in the association register* concerning the address of the association as well as the members who are authorized to represent the association to everybody (§ 16 VerG). Furthermore, the association authority has to certify who is authorized to act and represent if the association or persons or institutions submit such a request (§ 17 VerG).

A. Managing Body of the Association

61. The properly constituted club is a corporate entity, thus entailing full *legal capacity. The ability to act* is contained by means of the organs of the association.[35]

62. For any kind of actions in relation to outside institutions, organizations and bodies which are performed according to association statutes by the authorized organs, only the association is liable (§ 23 VerG). Furthermore, *only the association is obliged* to *legal contract and related issues* which are concluded by the *organs within the association statutes*. However, sports associations are not considered to

35. *Gelbmann*, Die Organe des ideellen Vereins, JAP 2003/2004, 86.

be debtors who are financially sound to be eligible. Therefore, business partners often demand a personal declaration of liability from the association organs in their role as bailsman.

63. In case of *insolvency* of the association, the organs are *obliged* to *institute insolvency proceeding* – otherwise, they were liable for protraction of bankruptcy filing.[36] If these proceedings are not complied with, a punishment due to fraudulent bankruptcy (§ 156 StGB) as well as personal liability of association organs to creditors due to protraction of bankruptcy filing may arise.

64. Anyway, the representation liability according to § 9 BAO for taxes and dues and § 67 Clause 10 ASVG for social security contributions (cf. Part III, Chapter 1, §1.III.E.B) should also be pointed out here beforehand.

65. The *association* itself is entitled to demand *damages* from *individuals who have acted on its behalf* when they have culpably caused damage by exceeding their range of activity which is defined by statute or decisions of the association (§ 24 VerG).[37] Indeed, in relation to outside institutions, legal acts of the organs are valid (§ 6 Clause 3 VerG). The 'ultra vires' doctrine ('beyond the powers'), which would lead to an opposing result, is generally not applied to corporate entities of civil law in Austria.[38]

66. The *dissolution* of the association may be carried out by the superior authority (§ 29 VerG) or by means of members' resolution (§ 28 VerG) in case of acts contrary to the law or the by-laws.

67. As far as civil liability claims for damage are concerned, the activities of the association are *controlled by ordinary courts*. Thus, disputes concerning the payment of membership fees, the validity of resolutions of all kinds or contested elections are all subject to civil proceedings. Provisions in the statutes which intend to prohibit the right to apply to the courts are void.[39]

B. Legal Status of the Members of the Association

68. The rights and obligations of the members of the association result primarily from the *by-laws* of the association. If the association violates its obligations to members, the association is liable to damages to the member.[40]

---

36. OGH 22.10.1997 ARD 4943/23/98.
37. Cf. *Gelbmann*, Zivilrechtliche Haftung der Vereinsorgane im VereinsG 2002, JAP 2002/2003, 184.
38. OGH 26.4.2001 ZAS 2002, 46 (*Vonkilch*); in general *Koziol/Welser*, Grundriss des bürgerlichen Rechts I[15] (2018) Rz 250 ff.
39. Cf. *Holzer*, Arbeits- und sozialversicherungsrechtliche Konsequenzen der Mitarbeit von Vereinsmitgliedern im Rahmen wirtschaftlicher Vereinstätigkeit, in *Korinek/Krejci* (ed.), Der Verein als Unternehmer (1988) 365; *Rechberger/Frauenberger*, Der Verein als 'Richter', ecolex 1994, 7.
40. OGH 18.4.2001 JBl 2001, 585.

69. Considering the list of *obligations on behalf of the members*, especially the obligation to payment of a membership fee has to be pointed out. Additional payment obligations may result from use of specific facilities or institutions such as courts and the sauna of a sports association. Furthermore, the members are encouraged to comply with the rules which have been specified by the association in order to regulate the use of sports facilities. Eventually, the association may well expect loyalty from its members. Breaches of the membership obligations may be sanctioned in accordance with the disciplinary authority of the association, a topic to be dealt with. The ultimate sanction of the association is exclusion from the association. Due to the severity of this sanction, statute provisions regarding exclusion reasons are to be interpreted in a narrow sense.[41]

70. Concerning the *rights of the members* of a sports association, the association has to promote the development of its members in the field of sport. Furthermore, the association is obliged to treat its members equally when sending them to sports competitions, nominating them for teams, or supplying them with access to sports facilities. The relevant decisions of the association are subject to a judicial review. In addition, claims for damage on behalf of the discriminated member may be considered.

C. Jurisdiction of Associations

71. § 8 VerG states the demand for a regulation on how to resolve disputes resulting from association relations – this regulation is to be included in the by-laws. Both the extent of this legally unspecified *jurisdiction* and the legal nature of the *respective penalties* are debatable.[42] The association jurisdiction is under no circumstances entitled to interfere with the competence of the courts. In fact, six months after disputes have been submitted to an arbitration body, means of redress at the ordinary court are available (§ 8 Clause 1 VerG). In this context, the OGH[43] recently stated that the dispute about a bias of a nominated member of an arbitration body does not postpone the commencement of this period. Such conflicts are already part of the arbitration procedure. Therefore, the first request (e.g., for the constitution of an arbitration body or the nomination of arbitrators) is decisive for the beginning of the period. The use of legal action before the expiry of this period is precluded by the *inadmissibility* of legal action as a procedural obstacle. Apart from this, non-members of the association may be bound by contract to the by-laws. Accordingly, means of redress at the ordinary court are not legally inadmissible, but they have to be rejected on the basis of the *prior substantive unenforceability*.[44] In order to exclude an application to the ordinary courts, an arbitration agreement under §§ 577 et seq. ZPO would need to be concluded. Moreover, the decisions of

41. OGH 10.5.2006 ecolex 2006, 844.
42. Cf. *Rechberger/Frauenberger*, ecolex 1994, 5; *Rummel*, Privates Vereinsrecht im Konflikt zwischen Autonomie und rechtlicher Kontrolle, in FS Strasser (1983) 838.
43. OGH 28.9.2020 ecolex 2021, 120 (*Höhne*).
44. OGH 27.6.2019 EvBl 2019/169 (*Rohrer*).

the association court can be subject to judicial review.[45] In case of disciplinary proceedings, the association court ought to respect the principle to be heard (§ 8 Clause 2 VerG) as well as the principle of equal treatment of the members.[46] Its composition must guarantee unbiased judicature (§ 8 Clause 2 VerG).

72. In the given context, typical '*association disputes*' are disputes between the individual members of the association or with the executive body of the association concerning extent and exercise of rights and obligations of the members, in particular disciplinary sanctions against association members due to violation of obligations regulated in the by-laws. Thus, violations and breaches relating to discipline in sport, regulations on use of sports facilities and courts, fairness in sport or loyalty – if they are included in the by-laws – may lead to internal suspensions limited to a period of time or even to exclusion from the association. However, it has to be pointed out explicitly that this possibility (which will be discussed in detail further on) is governed by specific framework conditions if the relationship between association and association member is an employer-employee relationship in which the member is obliged to exercise sport in exchange for payment (cf. Part III, Chapter 1, §1.III).

73. The disciplinary law of an association is based on the legal relationship between the members in consideration of private law. Membership implies the subjugation to the statutory disciplinary authority of the association. The Supreme Court accepts this power of sentence as a reaction of a social group to one of its members whose behaviour and conduct is opposed to the requirements and demands of the group.[47] The power of sentence of the sports associations is especially extensive towards the individual sportsman. It is disputable whether the mere indirect membership of the individual to a federation – by means of membership to an association which itself is part of a federation – is sufficient to subjugate the individual to the federation's power of sentence in civil law. Most of the federations solve the problem by demanding an explicit declaration of submission from each individual sportsman in exchange for granting licences. In regard to the fact that the individual sportsman is not entitled to take influence on these regulations, an effective legal control over the content is extremely important. In this context, particularly doping suspensions of sportsmen have been presented to the courts for the purpose of revision.

II. 'Dachverbände': Umbrella Organizations

74. Umbrella organizations are an Austrian peculiarity. These are organizations founded on ideological bases which root back to the interwar period and partly even further. Thus, the historical development of the *ASKÖ* is linked to the workers'

45. OGH 20.1.1993 EvBl 1993/117; 9.2.1995 JBl 1995, 649; 3.7.2007, 5 Ob 84/07z ao; 26.3.2020, 1 Ob 42/20p; 29.5.2020 RdW 2020/529, 767.
46. OGH 30.7.1987 JBl 1988, 445; 27.2.2020, 8 Ob 128/19k.
47. Cf. OGH 10.2.1981 JBl 1982, 41.

sports movement. In contrast, the *UNION* continues the tradition of the Christian-German gymnastics movement. However, the *ASVÖ* was founded no earlier than in 1949 in order to host those associations which differed in ideology from both ASKÖ and UNION.

75. The main incentive for an accession to one of the three umbrella organizations is the participation of the very same in the distribution of funds from the *specific federal sports funding* (cf. Part I, §2.B.1.).

76. The umbrella organizations mainly address mass sport and leisure sport and offer a variety of services. They are a contact point for all matters and represent the interests of around 14,000 sports associations which are currently registered with them[48] and are the foundation of Austrian sport. In terms of operating and maintaining sports facilities, they are substantially responsible for the provision of infrastructure for mass sport as well as professional and top sports.

III. 'Fachverbände'

77. 'Fachverbände' are federations which represent their specific type of sport and which focus on professional as well as top sports in their respective type of sport. They are responsible for the organization and realization of the national championships. Furthermore, they are members of international federations for specific types of sport such as International Ski Federation (FIS), Union of European Football Associations (UEFA) or International Football Association (FIFA), and they decide on the composition of the Austrian team in international competitions. Currently, the BSO contains more than fifty approved 'Fachverbände' as well as the Austrian Disabled Sports Federation (ÖBSV) as a federation with specific purpose.[49]

78. In principle, associations remain free to define their conditions for membership in their by-laws. However, a *monopoly association is obliged to accept members*. Thus, it is subject to contractual obligation.[50] 'Fachverbände' are monopoly associations due to the fact that participation in competitions of a respective sport is only possible under their patronage.

79. As mentioned before in regard to the association in general, all decisions of the federal organs are naturally subject to judicial review.[51] In addition, regulations

48. *See* in detail *Sport Austria*, Vollmitglieder, https://www.sportaustria.at/de/ueber-uns/mitglieder/vollmitglieder/ (17.8.2022).
49. Cf. *Sport Austria*, Vollmitglieder https://www.sportaustria.at/de/ueber-uns/mitglieder/vollmitglieder/ (17.8.2022).
50. Cf. OGH 24.9.1998 DRdA 1999, 117 (*Holzer*) as well as OGH 19.11.2003 SpuRt 2004, 154 on the problem of jersey advertising; *Salcher*, Kontrahierungszwang in der Sportverbandspyramide, ÖJZ 2017, 706.
51. Cf., e.g., OGH 9.2.1995 JBl 1995, 649.

in the federal by-laws which prohibit access to the courts are void.[52] As outlined before, the *nomination* of a competitive athlete or top athlete for *national or international competitions* rests in the hands of the respective sports federation. Based on the economic relevance for the athlete, the practice of nomination raises the question of whether the athlete is entitled to a nomination. Repeatedly, athletes have tried to enforce the nomination for participation in championships in national courts.[53] By all means, it can be stated that a 'Fachverband' insofar is obliged to strict equal treatment of the athlete as it holds a nomination monopoly. Furthermore, the 'Fachverband' has to meet all of the established nomination criteria. Frequently, suspended athletes aim to have their *doping suspension* judicially reviewed.[54]

80. Beyond that issue, the question has been raised as to which extent punishment for breaches of sports regulations on behalf of the federations may be judicially reviewed in general. In this context, *Pfister*[55] wants to distinguish between rules of sport and rules of law in the German law. Whereas the *rule of sport* is rather sport-specific (e.g., colour of the jersey of the home team, duration of half-time break, etc.), the rule of law always tends to have an impact on the financial situation of the parties concerned. According to that, in contrary to the rule of law, a rule of sport cannot be judicially reviewed. However, despite this distinction between rules of sport and rules of law, the verifiability of nearly all the decisions taken by the federation still remains due to the fact that rules such as the sports rules mentioned above will probably not be subject to a dispute. Normally, conflicts may arise where interests in sport are accompanied by economic and financial interests. Anyway, this constellation of interests is almost always present in legal disputes.

81. One of the most spectacular court decisions, which corrected the decision of a sports federation, concerned the Ice Hockey Championship of 1987 in Vienna. In the course of this world championship, on 22 April 1987, the International Ice Hockey Federation (IIHF) decided by its executive committee that the games of the Federal Republic of Germany FRG against the Union of Soviet Socialist Republics (USSR) were to be changed to a score of 0:7 in favour of the USSR, and all the other games which the German team had already played also were to be changed to a score of 0:5 for the opposing teams as the German team supposedly had played with a player (Miroslaw S) who was – according to the executive committee – not entitled to participate in world championships. Due to this decision of the executive committee of the IIHF, the team of the FRG would have lost four points which they had honestly won and would have been prematurely eliminated from the world

52. Cf. *Holzer* in *Korinek/Krejci*, Verein 365; *Rechberger/Frauenberger*, ecolex 1994, 7.
53. Cf., e.g., OGH 24.9.1998 DRdA 1999, 117 (*Holzer*) in reference to the nomination of a professional ice hockey player into the national team.
54. Cf. OGH 9.2.1995 JBl 1995, 649 in reference to the doping suspension of a swimmer; LG Wien 23.2.1996 SpuRt 2000, 194 on the abolition of a doping suspension of a sprinter; furthermore, thus *Eisenberger*, Ist der ÖSV immun gegen Bosman? Der 'Fall Goldberger' im Lichte des Gemeinschaftsrechts, RdW 1997, 642.
55. Sportregeln vor staatlichen Gerichten, SpuRt 1998, 221; on revision of sports rules for football penalty shooting at a German court cf. LG Chemnitz 24.4.1997 SpuRt 1998, 41.

championship. Beforehand, the German federation had sent a letter of request to the IIHF dated 27 February 1987. The IIHF confirmed to the German federation in a letter of 20 March 1987 that the player Miroslaw S was entitled to participate in the world championship. Nevertheless, on 22 April 1987, the decision mentioned above was taken by the executive committee. By motion on behalf of the German federation, the Regional Court of Vienna[56] granted a preliminary injunction (24 April 1987) in which the IIHF was assigned to grant the FRG team further participation in the world championship of 1987 under consideration of the results so far scored. The court found that the IIHF had violated its own by-laws by changing the scored results and taking away the deservedly won points from the FRG. An application issued by the IIHF for suspending the preliminary injunction was rejected by order of the very same court (27 April 1987), and the world championship was played to the end with the FRG participating in it.

82. In addition to that, *transfer rules* stated in the by-laws have also been subject to a judicial review several times. Thus, the Supreme Court[57] has to apply Article 204.4 to the by-laws of the IIHF. According to this regulation, a player who has already played for the national team of a country and has thereby participated in an IIHF championship or in Olympic Games is not entitled to play for the national team of another country and participate in these major sports events. The Supreme Court actually concedes that the prevention of a 'national team tourism' is a legitimate concern; therefore, it cannot be illegal to invoke the statutory regulations which try to prevent such tourism. However, in this specific case, this kind of 'tourism' was not the issue, as the concerned player had participated in the world championship of 1985/86 as a member of the Canadian team, afterwards he had played in Austria for five seasons, and had gained the Austrian citizenship in 1996. If such a long period of time has passed since the last game for a foreign national team and if a sufficiently close link to the 'new' nation is established, then the invocation of statutory regulations which prohibit a member of the Austrian national team from participating in international competitions is objectively not justified and, thus, illegal.

83. Furthermore, the Supreme Court[58] has confirmed the final decision of the Regional Court Graz – in its function as the Employment and Social Court,[59] it had granted the release to a professional ice hockey player by means of preliminary injunction. The defendant association had refused to release the player after his contract had been terminated. This decision was confirmed on appeal.[60] The contractual relationship which had to be evaluated was based on the respective by-laws and registration regulations of the Austrian Ice Hockey Federation (ÖEHV) at that time. According to these by-laws and registration regulations, players who were employed by an association were registered with the ÖEHV as 'players associated

56. LG Wien 24.4.1987, 26 Cg 94/87.
57. OGH 24.9.1998 DRdA 1999, 117 (*Holzer*).
58. OGH 27.3.1996 ARD 4820/34/97.
59. LG Graz 2.8.1995, 33 Cga 135/95.
60. OLG Graz 30.11.1995, 7 Ra 95/95.

with their club', and therefore they required a release from their association if they wanted to play for another association of the ÖEHV. Otherwise, according to § 13 Clause 2 of the registration regulations, the players were suspended for eighteen months. For the period of suspension, neither an Austrian association (being a member of the ÖEHV) nor any comparable umbrella association abroad was entitled to employ the player. However, the Supreme Court stated that the main issue was not the illegality of the registration regulations of the ÖEHV but the aspect that – according to certified and accepted facts of the case – the accused association was trying to force the player to play under conditions which were assigned by the association, by using and abusing the registration regulations, and refusing to release the player after termination of the fixed-term contract *contra bonos mores*.[61]

IV. Austrian Olympic Committee

84. The re-foundation of the Olympic Games in modern times initiated by *Pierre de Coubertin* marks the beginning of a development which proved to be a story of economic success without parallel especially at the end of the twentieth century. The International Olympic Committee (IOC), founded in 1896 in Paris, entrusts the National Olympic Committees (NOC) with the responsibility of nursing the Olympic idea/spirit. The ÖOC was founded in 1935. The ÖOC is a private association. All those 'Fachverbände' which represent sports that are part of the Olympic Games programme are ordinary members. The three umbrella associations as well as the BSO are additional ordinary members. Furthermore, the ÖOC has a number of honorary members and associate members. The members of the ÖOC executive board are elected every four years – after the Olympic Summer Games.

85. The main task of the ÖOC is to prepare, ensure and accomplish the participation of Austrian teams in the Olympic Games. Thus, in this context, the ÖOC is committed to ensure compliance with guidelines and rules of the Olympic Charter, in particular compliance with sponsorship and advertising regulations and additional rules for participation for athletes, supervisors and coaches. Furthermore, the ÖOC is the respective organization which is entitled to represent Austria in the Olympic Games as well as in other international sports events, which are carried out under the patronage of the IOC. It heads the delegation and is responsible for the demeanour of the team members. In addition, the ÖOC is entitled to nominate cities within their respective areas as candidates for future Olympic Games. In case of a successful candidature, the ÖOC has to take care of organizational matters. In addition to that, the ÖOC has to promote the Olympic idea throughout Austria as well as encourage and support the development of sport for all.

61. *See Holzer*, Freigabe eines Eishockeyprofis durch einstweilige Verfügung des Arbeits- und Sozialgerichts, DRdA 1996, 528.

V. Federal Sports Organization

86. The BSO was founded in 1969 in order to coordinate the Austrian sports activities and events and to represent sport on an overall platform throughout Austria. Due to insufficient legal foundation, the BSO has been constituted as an *association* and thus as an entity of civil law – opposed to the LSO which is a corporation under public law. Since 2019 the BSO operates under the name 'Sport Austria'.

87. The ordinary members of the BSO are the umbrella associations (ASKÖ, UNION, ASVÖ), the recognized and established 'Fachverbände', the ÖBSV, the ÖOC, the Austrian Paralympic Committee (ÖPC) and the Special Olympics Austria (SOÖ). Quite a number of federations, facilities and institutions which are of particular importance for the Austrian sport, such as the Austrian Army Sports Association and the nine LSOs, are associate members of the BSO.

88. The BSO preserves the interests of the Austrian sport on the international stage. Therefore, it is represented by delegates in the following *international boards and committees*:

- European Non-Governmental Sports Organization
- European Non-Governmental Sports Organization Youth
- European Olympic Committees (EOC)
- European Union (EU)-Sport Forum
- European Sports Conference
- The Association for International Sport for All.

89. Within the scope of its *tasks as a representative of interests*, the BSO is dedicated to consultations of legislative bodies as well as the supreme authorities of federal administration in matters of sport. It promotes sports events of national or international importance, plus in connection to that, the construction and maintenance of sports facilities. It propagates sport by means of publications and performance badges. Furthermore, it promotes vocational training for coaches and trainers. An annual recurrent activity of the BSO, which is well known, is the organization of 'fit-runs' and 'fit-marches', running or walking events which take place on the Austrian national holiday on 26 October.

90. The BSO consists of various *authorities* such as the general assembly and the executive board, the extended executive board including representatives of the umbrella federations, the 'Fachverbände' and nominees of ÖBSV, SOÖ, ÖOC and ÖPC. Apart from the advisory boards for finance and legal matters, mass sport respectively high-performance and top-class sport, such institutions are also established for the sport promotion of women and digital media platforms. Furthermore, besides an arbitrating body and an auditor, there are also several working groups which are concerned with individual issues such as safety in sport.[62]

VI. Further Relevant Institutions of Austrian Sports

91. The *Austrian Sport Development Foundation 'Sporthilfe' (ÖSH)*, an association, is dedicated to the promotion, funding and sponsorship of top Austrian athletes. This organization was already founded in 1972. In the year 2000, a total of 156 summer sports athletes from twenty-four federations and 107 athletes of snow and ice sports from thirteen federations were sponsored. Ninety-five athletes were sponsored due to their achievements in the category of 'world elite', thirty-one were sponsored for achievements in the high-performance category, ninety-nine for achievements in the top-grade category, and twenty-eight in the young talent category. Among other procedures, the funds are raised by means of revenues resulting from events such as the 'LOTTERIEN Sporthilfe-Gala', where the athlete of the year is chosen.

92. The foundation *Austrian Institute for Construction of Schools and Sports Facilities*, whose members consist of the Austrian federation and the nine states of Austria, has a broad range of functions, which include planning, construction and operation of schools, sports facilities and recreation centres as well as the development of respective norms and regulations.

93. In 1958, the *ÖBSV* was constituted. In the last couple of years, this association has been recognized for outstanding services in terms of promotion and integration of disabled athletes. In 1998, the Paralympic Committee was founded to cover the competitive sport section. Its primary task contains the collection of funds in order to finance the participation of disabled athletes in the Paralympic Games, and to promote competitive sports performance of disabled athletes in the media.

94. The *National Anti-Doping Agency Austria (NADA Austria)* ensures the implementation and control of anti-doping regulations. It is the supreme body in Austria in regard to doping. As a legal body, the NADA is a non-profit limited liability company. It is the successor organization of the Austrian Anti-Doping Committee. The basis for the reconstruction is § 5 Clause 5 Federal Anti-Doping Act. The tasks of the NADA include the organization of anti-doping measures and provisions according to the European Anti-Doping Convention, detecting doping transgressions, and initiating the appropriate sanctions for the athletes or other responsible parties concerned and associated with the athlete through the respective 'Fachverband'. On behalf of the WADA, NADA has to conduct doping controls in training periods. Furthermore, it compiles the current list of illegal doping substances, doping procedures and methods (Index of Banned Substances and Procedures), which

62. *Sport Austria*, Jahresbericht 2021, https://publikation.sportaustria.at/p/sport-austria-und-bso-jahresberichte/2021-12-20/r/1/1/4425/479781 (Version of 20.12.2021).

has to be enforced in regard to the Anti-Doping Programme of WADA. In addition, the anti-doping leaflet entails all the drugs and medications which contain doping substances.

95. With the entry into force of the 'International Standard for Education' in the course of the new WADC 2021, the cooperation between NADA and national sport organizations was once again intensified. In this context, NADA takes on an important role in the preventive area of the anti-doping control. Thereby, as also prescribed in § 3 Clause 1 Federal Anti-Doping Act, the emphasis lies on awareness programmes, information and educational work.

VII. International Sports Organizations

A. Continental and International Sports Federations

96. Most of the sports federations have already teamed up on continental as well as on the international level. Thus, for example, for football, there is UEFA on the European level, and FIFA on the global scale.

97. Apart from that, the IOC plays a central role in international sports organization due to the organization of – alternating – Summer and Winter Games, in particular because the Olympic Games have developed into an enormous success and an outstanding event, not only in the range of sports but also in the commercial field. So, associations and federations form associative pyramids which are horizontally and vertically structured. They are headed by the international sports federations. The structure can be graphically illustrated as follows:

International 'Fachverband' for Sport – IOC

Umbrella Association – National 'Fachverband' for Top Sports – NOC

Regional 'Fachverband' for Sport

Association

Athlete

VIII. International Sports Jurisdiction

98. On the initiative of the IOC, the 'Internationale Sportgerichtshof' in Lausanne was founded in 1983. The court is referred to as 'CAS' (according to the official English name 'Court of Arbitration for Sport') or as 'TAS' (in regard to the French name 'Tribunal Arbitral du Sport'). In order to guarantee its independence from IOC – especially in trials in which the IOC is involved – the TAS underwent a number of reforms in order to make itself more independent of the IOC, resulting in the creation of the International Council of Arbitration for Sport. This initiative which is supported by most of the international federations is targeted towards keeping national jurisdiction as far outside of sport as possible and, thus, submitting disputes in sport exclusively to the CAS.

99. The TAS recognizes the jurisdiction of the court if the parties which specify recourse to the CAS have included an arbitration clause in their by-laws in order to refer disputes to it or if similar contractual recognition is presented.[63]

100. The arbitration court consists of two decision-making bodies. One chamber is responsible for private law disputes between federations and their members (associations and athletes alike – so-called appeals procedures), the second chamber is concerned with economic disputes, for example, with sponsors and licensees (so-called ordinary proceedings).[64] Apart from these two proceedings, an ad hoc procedure is possible in order to allow quick decisions during a competition (e.g., during the Olympic Games).

101. In appeals procedures, the TAS claims competence to grant preliminary injunctions. According to arbitrary regulations, by admitting to an appeals procedure, the party waives the right to request preliminary legal protection from national courts. However, legal protection on behalf of the state may not be excluded in regard to Austrian law as this opposes the ordre public.[65] Nevertheless, in § 593 Clause 1 ZPO, the courts of arbitration are provided with the legal jurisdiction to order all *means of security* if this possibility has not been excluded by the parties concerned. The option to appeal to national courts for preliminary legal protection remains unaffected according to § 585 ZPO.

102. The *enforcement* of preliminary injunctions remains in the hands of national courts under the condition that they ex officio examine and review this preliminary measure of an arbitrary court at request for grounds of non-enforcement. The court has to dismiss the enforcement of preliminary injunctions if they are inconsistent with formerly adopted measures (cf. § 593 Clause 4 Z 3 ZPO).[66]

103. In general, the TAS is enormously important due to the fact that almost all the international sports federations as well as the WADA have recognized the jurisdiction of TAS as an appeal court. The TAS also offers the option to appeal against the imposition of sanctions on behalf of the national federations.

---

63. Cf. *Pfister*, Die Doping-Rechtsprechung des TAS, SpuRt 2000, 133 (137).
64. Further details in *Wyler*, Die Schiedsabrede im Sport, in *Röhricht* (ed.), Sportgerichtsbarkeit (1997) 43; *Netzle*, Das Internationale Sport-Schiedsgericht in Lausanne. Zusammensetzung, Zuständigkeit und Verfahren, in *Röhricht* (ed.), Sportgerichtsbarkeit (1997) 9.
65. *Von Saucken*, Die Reform des österreichischen Schiedsverfahrensrechts auf der Basis des UNCITRAL-Modellgesetzes über internationale Handelsschiedsgerichtsbarkeit (2004) 187.
66. *Koller*, Das neue österreichische Schiedsrecht, JAP 2005/2006/30, 186.

104. From the Austrian point of view, it has to be noted that – given the prevailing view – up to the year 2006,[67] in which the Arbitrary Law Amendment Act came into force, the mere membership of an athlete in an association or a federation was insufficient to subject him to the arbitration court, even if the arbitration procedure was stated in the by-laws. On the contrary, all formal regulations and requirements presented in §§ 577 et seq. ZPO were to be met.[68]

105. Despite the fact that nowadays it is frequently stated that basically also association statutes may be sufficient to the formal requirements of § 583 Clause 2 ZPO,[69] the sufficiency has to be questioned if the arbitration clause is only applied by means of a referral cascade. This may be the case when an association statute only generally refers to the by-laws of a federation and these again refer to the statutes of an international federation which finally contain the arbitration clause. However, it would suffice if the declaration of enrolment to a sports association explicitly referred to the arbitration clause in the respective association statutes. In addition to that, federations tend to sign individual arbitral agreements with each athlete – especially in the context of licensing procedures.[70]

106. In accordance with Article V Clause 1 a of the New York Convention on recognition and enforceability of international arbitral decisions[71] – which is also significant for Austria – the statute of the arbitral agreement, thus, for the case given the Swiss law, has to be applied in order to ensure the validity of the arbitration agreement. Nevertheless, the subjective arbitrability of a legal dispute is to be evaluated according to the personal statute of the federation and the athlete. As a consequence, the focus mainly lies on the barriers which limit the arbitration law in regard to issues of Austrian labour law. Fact is that § 9 Clause 2 ASGG regulates that – concerning issues of labour law – arbitration agreements may only be signed for disputes which have already existed at the time of the conclusion of this agreement but definitely not for future disputes.[72] In regard to the generally typical employee status of the athlete in team sports (cf. Part III, Chapter 1, §1.III), this circumstance ought to be considered by TAS as well. If the TAS takes a decision which ignores this specific Austrian legal position, its recognition and enforceability have to be seriously questioned in Austria.[73]

---

67. BGBl I 2006/7.
68. *Rechberger/Hofstätter* in *Rechberger/Klicka* (ed.), Kommentar zur ZPO[5] (2019) § 577 Rz 11; *Rechberger/Frauenberger*, ecolex 1994, 5; on the parallel discussion in Germany, cf. *Schwab/Walter*, Schiedsgerichtsbarkeit[7] (2005) Rn 4 ff, *Oschütz*, Probleme der Schiedsgerichtsbarkeit im Sport: arbeitsrechtliche Streitigkeiten und einstweiliger Rechtsschutz, in *Haas* (ed.), Schiedsgerichtsbarkeit im Sport (2003) 43.
69. *Oberhammer* in *Kloiber/Oberhammer/Rechberger/Haller* (ed.), Das neue Schiedsrecht. Schiedsrechtsänderungsgesetz (2006) 186.
70. Cf. *Heß*, Sportschiedsgerichte im Lichte der New Yorker Konvention, ZZP Int 1998, 463.
71. BGBl 1961/200.
72. In regard to the parallel discussion in Germany, cf. *Heß*, ZZP Int 1998, 467.
73. *König*, Sind Schiedsabreden auf den CAS/TAS wirksam? SpuRt 2004, 137; cf. furthermore on the case *Kimoni v.* GAK *Holzer*, Punkteabzug in der Fußball-Bundesliga und Anmeldung im Konkursverfahren, Zak 2007, 186; *Holzer/Herzeg*, Aufhebung von Punkteabzügen in der T-Mobile Bundesliga im Konkursverfahren, SpuRt 2007, 197.

§3. Taxation of Associations

107. As it has been shown before (cf. 2.), Austrian sport generally relies on the association or club as the legal system for organization. In regard to taxation of such an association, it is important to know whether the association is entitled to tax privileges, which will be presented and discussed in detail further on, as the association may or may not be considered a *non-profit* organization. It has to be assumed that in general Austrian sports associations tend to gain these tax advantages, that is to gain the non-profit status. Therefore, the prerequisites for non-profit status have to be addressed beforehand (cf. §3.I), and subsequently the fiscal consequences will be discussed in detail (cf. §3.II).

108. The Austrian Federal Ministry of Finance (BMF) has stated the *principles on taxation of associations* in a decree, namely the *'Vereinsrichtlinien' or association regulations of 2001*. Due to the fact that this decree is no regulation and therefore is not legally binding, the VwGH as well as Independent Financial Senates did not always follow the legal interpretations of the decree – which mostly favour the associations – but often directly rely on legal regulations in order to justify a more rigorous interpretation.

However, it has to be noted that the Independent Financial Senates were transformed into a special administrative court, the Federal Fiscal Court, in the course of the creation of a two-tier administrative jurisdiction by 2012.

I. Prerequisites of Non-profit Status

109. No specific official notification is issued in regard to non-profit status, but the respective tax office decides in the course of the taxation procedure if the association is entitled to privileges.[74] However, the tax authorities have to issue a statement in unbinding form on requests referring to the issue of privilege. This statement is not a notification. However, protection of confidence in regard to the assessment of the statement is given if the facts have been correctly and properly presented to the authority.[75]

110. The non-profit status requires the condition that an association – according to its statutes and its actual management – exclusively and immediately pursues a *non-profit agenda*, which also entails '*body sport or physical sport*'.[76] In Austria, the term 'body sport' carries a broad meaning, thus including mental exercise, such as chess which has also acquired non-profit status.[77] Nevertheless, according to this definition of non-profit status, aero-modelling sport is normally not included,[78] as it definitely cannot be viewed as a body sport at all. Even though physical exercise is

74. VwGH 24.4.1953, 337/52; 2.7.1953, 2019/51.
75. Vereinsrichtlinien 2001 Rz 11.
76. Vereinsrichtlinien 2001 Rz 72.
77. Vereinsrichtlinien 2001 Rz 478.
78. Vereinsrichtlinien 2001 Rz 62.

not at the centre of these sports, glider sport, shooting sport and motorsport among others are in practice recognized as privileged.[79] In terms of motorsport, this classification has also been criticized.[80]

111. Umbrella federations or 'Dachverbände' and 'Fachverbände' contain non-profit status if their sub-federations or associations have acquired non-profit status as well.

112. The pursuit of a non-profit agenda has to be accompanied by *support and promotion of the general public*. This aspect may be realized in two different directions: If the association consists of a determinate number of members due to its statutes, it has to promote sports to the outside in order to sustain its non-profit status. If an association exclusively promotes its members, it has to be open to everybody. However, promotion of a complete indeterminate number of persons is not required. Especially those restrictions which result from limits in regard to capacity of the sports facilities remain permissible.

113. Nevertheless, the non-profit status of an association may well be compromised by the rates of membership contributions. Thus, the VwGH[81] decided that due to the fact that the members of a golf club had to pay a registration fee of ATS 56,000, (EUR 4,069.68), an annual membership fee of ATS 3,500 (EUR 254.35) and an annual user fee of ATS 11,612 (EUR 843.88), the rate of these contributions was considered too high in order to still entail support and promotion of the general public. Therefore, the non-profit status of the club had to be negated. On the contrary, the court[82] has recently held the view that tax evasion does not compromise the non-profit status because of not changing the purpose of the association. Therefore, a loss of the privileged status does not automatically follow from the disregard of tax law provisions (possibly negligently out of ignorance of the current legal situation).

114. An association is *by no means entitled to pursue profitability*. A distribution of profits to the members of the association is absolutely impermissible. In case of dissolution of the association, the members are only entitled to get a refund on their current contribution. The rest has to be returned to a non-profit agenda. A respective regulation on this issue already has to be included in the statutes. Moreover, in order to pursue an agenda, the association may only use those material resources which are prescribed for this explicit agenda in the statutes.

115. The *functionaries of the association* may only receive *adequate compensation* by the association. However, staff of the association may also be employed with higher remuneration without compromising the non-profit status of the association. This aspect is especially relevant for the employment of professional athletes.

---

79. Cf. Vereinsrichtlinien 2001 Rz 478; *Ebner*, Allgemeines steuerliches Gemeinnützigkeitsrecht, in *Ebner/Hammerl/Oberhuber* (ed.), Die Besteuerung der Vereine: Handbuch für die Praxis, Beratung und Wissenschaft[11] (2022) Rz B043.
80. Cf. *Bichler*, Überlegungen zur Gemeinnützigkeit mancher Sportvereine, ÖStZ 1992, 105.
81. VwGH 26.6.2000 ARD 5213/31/2001.
82. VwGH 14.9.2017 ÖStZ 2018, 141.

116. Besides the principles of non-profit status which are contained in the by-laws, the association particularly has to make sure that the actual management also corresponds to the non-profit status. Nevertheless, the *pursuit of the association's agenda* has to be separated from the means which are used to attain its objectives. In order to *provide the necessary means*, the non-profit association has access to a variety of *economic activities*. These activities may be defined as management of assets (cf. §3.I.A), special-purpose operations (cf. §3.I.B) and auxiliary operations which compromise privileges (cf. §3.I.C).

A. *Administration of Assets*

117. The mere administration of association assets does in no way compromise the non-profit status of the association. Only the systematic speculation with association assets is considered to impair the privilege.[83] However, interest income is still subject to deduction by means of the capital yields tax. Value-added tax (VAT) does not have to be paid according to § 6 Clause 1 Z 14 UStG. Income resulting from rent and lease is also part of asset management.[84]

B. *Special-Purpose Operating Bodies*

118. These operations are linked to the statutory agenda of the sports association in a more or less close relationship. Special-purpose operations are therefore separated into two groups, one being the special-purpose operations in the narrow sense, also called '*indispensable auxiliary operating bodies*', or 'operations to realize the agenda'. In this scope, the activities of the association directly support the achievement of the non-profit purpose of the association. Contrary to that, there are special-purpose operations in the wider sense, also called '*dispensable auxiliary operating bodies*'. The adopted means is clearly separated from the purpose stipulated in the statutes but does not impede with its priority and is still closely linked to it.[85]

1. The Indispensable Auxiliary Operating Body

119. First of all, sports activities which are targeted towards collecting revenues are allocated to indispensable auxiliary operations of the association. These *sports activities* are not only any kind of revenues such as proceeds from sport and fitness events, advertising revenues, revenues resulting from the transfer of a player, membership fees and fees for hosts on the one hand but also expenses such as tax write-off of acquisition and manufacturing costs of sports facilities or sports equipment, expenses for maintenance and repair, expenses for coaching of players and teams as

---

83. Vereinsrichtlinie 2001 Rz 232, 323.
84. Cf. *Doralt/Ruppe*, Grundriss des österreichischen Steuerrechts II[8] (2019) Rz 154.
85. Cf. *Doralt/Ruppe*, Steuerrecht II[8] Rz 153.

well as costs which arise in the course of a sports event on the other hand. In addition to that, remunerations for athletes as well as coaches, payments for rent and lease and operation costs for the sports facilities are included.[86]

120. Furthermore, *sponsoring revenues* of an association which result from the respective advertising activity of the association – for example, bearing the sponsor's name in the association's name or printing the name of a sponsor on the jerseys of the players – are also included as revenues from these sports activities.[87]

121. Any kind of activity which is directly related to the sport, such as games and competitions, sports lessons, sports courses and seminars or travels to and from the location of competitions are part of the *sports events*.

122. From a tax point of view, *liability for tax is completely inapplicable* if an indispensable auxiliary operation is present. As a result, the revenues from sports activities which are related to the indispensable auxiliary operating body are considered irrelevant in terms of corporate tax and VAT.[88]

123. The characteristics of the indispensable auxiliary operation are sustained as long as not more than 25% of the turnovers are dispensable or compromise the privilege. This limit is called the 'Verschmutzungstoleranz'.[89]

2. The Dispensable Auxiliary Operating Body

124. Dispensable auxiliary operations include all those profit-oriented operations which are presented as a means to achieve the privileged purpose stated in the by-laws, but which are at the same time either not indispensable for its realization or which compete with operations liable to taxation to a larger extent than could be avoided in order to achieve the privileged goals.[90] The nature of the indispensable auxiliary operation is sustained as long as not more than 50% of the turnovers compromise the privileges. This limit is the 'Verschmutzungstoleranz' in dispensable auxiliary operations.[91]

125. The *importance* of dispensable auxiliary operations *in regard to fiscal law* is stated by the fact that the common legal requirement of exclusive non-profit activity is ignored by law. The association's non-profit status is maintained. Only the activity of the auxiliary operation in regard to income and assets is subject to tax

86. Vereinsrichtlinie 2001 Rz 367.
87. Vereinsrichtlinie 2001 Rz 157.
88. Vereinsrichtlinie 2001 Rz 324, 366, 480; *see also* regarding the prerequisites of an indispensable auxiliary operating body § 45 Clause 2 BAO.
89. Vereinsrichtlinie 2001 Rz 165–167.
90. Vereinsrichtlinie 2001 Rz 173 f; cf. also § 45 Clause 1 BAO.
91. Vereinsrichtlinie 2001 Rz 178.

liability. In the case of VAT, it is assumed that the activity is performed as a hobby without any tax liability. In regard to corporate tax, a tax allowance of EUR 10,000 is relevant. [92]

126. The dispensable auxiliary operations of an association include any kinds of small *sociable and social events* of the association which are open against payment, for example, festivities of any kind, balls, parties, joke events and other entertainment sports events. The festivity of an association which may be attended against payment does not really directly promote the ideal purpose of sports exercise. Nevertheless, it may at least support the relationship between its members in regard to the common ideal agenda and may serve as a means of recruiting new members, which justifies the assumption of a dispensable auxiliary operation. In addition to that, the *sale of emblems, badges and other signs of membership* (flags, pennants, stickers), which are connected to the association, are also normally considered as dispensable auxiliary operations. In this context, *specific cash benefits offered in return by the members*, which go beyond the membership contribution such as additional fees for fitness areas, sauna, and indoor lessons have to be mentioned.

3. Operations Which Compromise the Privileges

127. If the association is involved in profit-oriented activities which exceed the scope of operations to realize the agenda as mentioned before, then the association may not be entitled to privileges in terms of tax liability and the various tax laws have to be applied. Moreover, in general, the association is subject to *unlimited tax liability*.

128. Such operations which might compromise the non-profit status of the association are, for example, sociable and social *events which* assume the *nature of an institution of independent significance* and which by far go beyond the interests of the association, e.g., large club festivities.[93] Apart from that, various operations may compromise the privileges, for example, the operation of a shelter or hut in competition to gastronomic facilities which are liable to taxation.[94] This aspect also accounts for cafeterias, buffets or other *gastronomic facilities* of an association, unless they are part of either an indispensable or a dispensable auxiliary operation.[95] Anyway, especially the sale of goods, foods and beverages is a typical activity which is performed in full competition with operating bodies of the free economy. The operating body will always be considered to compromise the privileges if it *exclusively or largely* – with more than 50% of its annual revenue – *pursues its economic interests*, even as a source of fundraising for the achievement of the privileged purpose.[96]

92. Vereinsrichtlinie 2001 Rz 176 with further references.
93. Cf. § 45 Abs 3 BAO; Vereinsrichtlinie 2001 Rz 180, 306.
94. Vereinsrichtlinie 2001 Rz 376.
95. Vereinsrichtlinie 2001 Rz 380.
96. Vereinsrichtlinie 2001 Rz 178.

4. Exceptional Preservation of Non-profit Status

129. However, the association may apply for a *certificate of exemption* in order to maintain non-profit status. Basically, the tax offices which are responsible for collecting the VAT are entitled to abstain either completely or partly from enforcement of tax liability by means of approval if the association submits an application. The certificate of exemption is granted under the condition that the privileged purpose which is pursued by the legal entity might be foiled or significantly at risk if the tax liability were not to be abstained. Moreover, the surpluses resulting from the operations which compromise the privilege have to be assigned to privileged purposes. A written certificate of exemption is only required if the amount of the association's surpluses resulting from agricultural and forestry operations, commercial operations and economic operations exceed the annual amount of EUR 40,000. For any kind of surpluses below this limit, an automatic exemption is provided in § 45a BAO.[97]

130. The certificate of exemption may contain conditions or obligations if this seems necessary in order to achieve the privileged purpose. It often includes the requirement to eliminate certain deficits in statutes or by-laws within a given time period. In this way, the certificate is immediately effective, but may be obsolete in retrospective if the requirements are not met in time. Nevertheless, in this case, a new application for a certificate of exemption is possible.[98]

131. If the certificate of exemption has been granted, the tax liability in regard to the operation which compromises the privileges remains in force, but – contrary to that – the tax liability privilege for the remaining activities of the association is active, and the non-profit status of the association is preserved.

II. Basic Fiscal Privileges for Non-profit Sports Associations

132. These privileges are to be found in the field of VAT (cf. §3.II.A), of corporate tax (cf. §3.II.B) and other taxes and charges (cf. §3.II.C).

A. Value-Added Tax

133. Within the scope of asset administration, the *non-genuine tax exemption* according to § 6 Clause 1 Z 14 UStG is relevant. Thus, no VAT has to be paid, but on the contrary, input tax deduction is not possible either. This aspect also accounts for non-profit activities within both dispensable and indispensable auxiliary operating bodies.[99]

---

97. Vereinsrichtlinie 2001 Rz 186 ff.
98. Cf. *Hammerl*, Wirtschaftliche Tätigkeiten von Vereinen, in *Ebner/Hammerl/Oberhuber* (ed.), Die Besteuerung der Vereine: Handbuch für die Praxis, Beratung und Wissenschaft[11] (2022) Rz C245.
99. Vereinsrichtlinie 2001 Rz 463.

134. For revenues up to the amount of EUR 7,500 by operations which compromise the privileges, the so-called *Liebhabereivermutung* is applied (the assumption that the revenues result from a hobby); therefore, no VAT has to be paid, but again no input tax deduction is possible.[100] This result is relevant up to an annual turnover of EUR 30,000. Up to this extent, the association is viewed as a small business. Beyond this limit, full VAT liability is applied in combination with the possibility of input tax deduction.

135. If the annual turnover exceeds the limit of EUR 40,000, the non-profit status can only be preserved by means of a certificate of exemption, as mentioned above.

136. The external part of revenues, especially revenues by membership fees or subsidies, is not liable to tax in the first place.

B. Corporate Tax

137. Revenues resulting from membership contributions, indispensable auxiliary operations and administration of assets – if the latter is not liable to capital yields tax (e.g., interest on savings) – are *not subject to corporate tax liability.*[101] However, if the administration of assets is liable to capital yields tax, the liability for corporate tax is covered by liability for capital yields tax.

138. Nevertheless, the *tax liability* remains for both dispensable auxiliary operations and operations which compromise the privileges. In this context, § 23 Clause 1 KStG accepts a *tax allowance* of EUR 10,000, for non-profit associations.[102]

C. Additional Fiscal Privileges

139. § 15 Clause 1 Z 14 ErbStG exempts gifts and subsidies to non-profit associations from *inheritance and gift tax.*[103]

140. Additional privileges consist of the exemption from *advertising tax* according to a decree of the BMF[104] and from *property tax* according to § 2 Z 4 in connection with § 7 GrStG in regard to any property allocated to the sports activities.

---

100. Liebhabereirichtlinie 2012 Rz 178.
101. Vereinsrichtlinie 2001 Rz 323 f.
102. Vereinsrichtlinie 2001 Rz 394.
103. For tax cases after 1.8.2008 this tax has generally expired.
104. Decree dated 14.3.2001, RdW 2001, 383; cf. also Vereinsrichtlinien 2001 Rz 757–761.

III. The Role of Professional Sport

141. Since 2016, provisions concerning the tax treatment of a *professional operation for non-profit sports associations in team sports* are applicable.[105] Thereby, the distinction between team sports on the one hand and individual sports on the other has to be noted. In the first case, tax effects typically arise for the sports associations itself because they usually employ professional athletes on a permanent basis. Moreover, the advertising revenues generated are to a significant extent related to the higher publicity resulting from professional operation. In view of this, sports associations with a professional team basically compromise the privilege.[106] In this context, a *professional operation* is considered if the number of professional athletes, who can be used in matches, is higher than half of the total number of deployable players according to season match reports.[107] According to the concretization by the maintenance decree in 2017, a professional sportsman can be assumed if he receives a remuneration or other benefit of more than EUR 21,000 gross per season.[108]

142. In order to preserve the non-profit status and therefore the mentioned privileges despite a professional team, the sports association is obliged to transfer the professional operation into a branch association or to set up an own accounting area. In addition to that, it is possible to outsource the professional sector to a corporation or cooperative.[109]

143. Apart from this, a sports association with a professional team may still have non-profit status even if professional athletes practise the respective sport within the association as long as the professional sports activities are not targeted towards profitability and possible revenues are assigned to the promotion and support of youth and amateur sport. However, the outsourcing of professional operation is also necessary in this constellation, even if the establishment of a branch association or own accounting area suffices. On the contrary, a transfer into a cooperation or cooperative has to be chosen if the professional operation comes to the fore.[110]

144. Therefore, professional operations are *subject to corporate tax liability and to VAT*. This also applies after the outsourcing, regardless of the variant chosen.[111]

---

105. Cf. thereon remarks concerning the period of application Vereinsrichtlinie 2001 Chapter 10.5; in detail, *see Lummerstorfer*, Voraussetzungen für die Erlangung der steuerlichen Begünstigungen, in *Höhne/Jöchl/Lummerstorfer* (ed.), Das Recht der Vereine[6] (2019) 610 and *Hargassner*, Haftungen, Versicherungen, Steuern, Registrierkassenpflicht, Datenschutz, in *Hargassner* (ed.), Handbuch für Vereinsfunktionäre[4] (2021) 139 (182).
106. Vereinsrichtlinie 2001 Rz 881 f.
107. Vereinsrichtlinie 2001 Rz 882.
108. Vereinsrichtlinie 2001 Rz 879.
109. Vereinsrichtlinie 2001 Rz 884; cf. *Lummerstorfer* in *Höhne/Jöchl/Lummerstorfer*, Begünstigungen[6] 611.
110. Vereinsrichtlinie 2001 Rz 885.
111. Vereinsrichtlinie 2001 Rz 888 f.

145. Besides this, individual sports like tennis, skiing or swimming do not affect the non-profit status of the sports association. Merely the professional athlete himself is obliged to tax requirements.[112] Rather, he does not pursue any beneficiary purpose, but acts out of his own economic interest.[113]

146. Under the premise of the non-profit status of a sports association (even after the outsourcing), the entrance fees, transfer fees for players and revenues resulting from advertisement contracts are included in the sports activities and justify an indispensable auxiliary operation.[114] Regarding a professional operation, transfer fees and advertising revenues are in general subject to tax liability.[115]

IV. Liability of Association Functionaries

147. According to § 9 BAO, representative organs of the association are liable as indemnity bondsmen for payable taxes if the uncollectibility of these taxes is attributed to the representative's culpable behaviour.[116] If a number of representatives are assigned to the executive board of the association, the organ which is primarily responsible for fiscal issues is liable; nevertheless, other organs may also be affected by tax liability if they are accused of having neglected their obligation to inspection.[117] No specific type of fault is required. Slight negligence already results in liability.[118]

§4. Aspects of Tort Law in Sports

I. Liability of the Athlete Towards Other Athletes

148. A common source of injury besides the rather high number of sports injuries – which is the athlete's own responsibility – is the behaviour of other athletes or competitors.

A. Contractual Liability or Tort Liability

149. It is entirely indisputable that causal infringements of sports competitors objectively correspond to the definition of physical assault or homicide in regard to civil law. However, it has to be questioned whether there are constellations in which

112. Vereinsrichtlinie 2001 880.
113. Vereinsrichtlinie 2001 Rz 72, 878.
114. Cf. Vereinsrichtlinien 2001 Rz 157, 269, 297, 367.
115. Vereinsrichtlinie 2001 Rz 890, 901 with further references.
116. Cf. *Doralt/Ruppe*, Steuerrecht II^{8} Rz 142.
117. Cf. VwGH 29.4.1994 ÖStZB 1994, 674.
118. Cf. VwGH 18.10.1995, 91/13/0037.

the infringement may also be viewed as a breach of contract. This aspect is especially relevant in regard to liability law, in reference to sharing the burden of proof and helpers' liability.

150. In *individual sports*, it is obvious that normally there is no legal relation whatsoever between the individual athletes. This aspect is also valid when two athletes take part in the same competition. The legal relation of both sportsmen to the organizer can hardly be interpreted as a contract which offers protection to the other participants. This concept may well be applied to *team sports* without any restrictions on validity. Even in professional sports, it cannot be stated that the contractual relation between athlete and association should present a protective effect on the opponents in the contest.[119] However, a special problem, which requires its own account, results from the specific situation in professional sport that the infringer and the injured person are part of the same team and, thus, are contractors of the same association. In this constellation, the employer liability privilege according to § 333 ASVG or the co-workers' liability privilege according to § 332 Clause 5 ASVG may be applied. Apart from that, a fault-based liability within tort liability may be assumed without restrictions if a sportsman injures or kills another sportsman in the course of exercising sport. Moreover, it is not relevant for the evaluation of illegality whether the infringement occurs in amateur sport or professional sport.[120]

B. Classification of Sports

151. Concerning aspects of liability, a differentiation between contact sports, also 'sports against each other', and parallel sports ('sports next to each other') has become established.

1. Contact Sports

152. In order to characterize contact sports, a certain – however different – element of use of force in the competition is essential. According to the intensity of this element, contact sports may be further subdivided into *duel sports*, such as boxing, wrestling, and judo, in *game sports* such as football, handball, and ice hockey, and in *return sports*, in which physical contact between the participants is rather unusual. Examples for return sports would be tennis, squash, volleyball, fistball, etc.[121]

---

119. Cf. *Seebacher*, Haftungsfragen bei Körperverletzung im Sport (1997) 14.
120. Cf. *Gschöpf*, Haftung bei Verstoß gegen Sportregeln (2000) 94.
121. Cf. *Harrer/Wagner* in *Schwimann/Kodek* (ed.), Praxiskommentar zum ABGB VI^4 (2016) § 1295 Rz 98 ff.

2. Parallel Sports

153. Parallel sports are characterized by the fact that any kind of physical contact with other athletes – even if they are competitors in the competition – ought to be avoided as far as possible. Examples of these sports are disciplines of athletic sports, swimming, skiing, cycling, etc.[122]

3. Dangerous Parallel Sports

154. Similar to contact sports, which differentiate between certain levels of risk to be injured by a competitor, parallel sports differentiate between various levels of security. Parallel sports which are carried out by means of individual start and as a 'race against the clock' have to be evaluated differently from the same kind of sport with a mass start. In this context, certain parallel sports are pointed out as dangerous parallel sports as there is an immanent risk for injury.

C. The Sports Liability Privilege

155. Jurisprudence and jurisdiction both agree that an infringement which lies within the risk that is connected to the specific sport is not illegal. Thus, a liability for damages on behalf of the infringer is not possible.

1. Dogmatic Foundation

156. The *illegality* of sport infringements regularly results from *infringement of a – in general – legally protected right,* basically the physical integrity of competitors. However, in this connection, an *extensive weighing of interests* is essential, in which the social interest in mass sports exercise also has to be appreciated, just as much as the circumstance that the injured person has agreed to the typical risk of the sport which he has practised.

157. In addition to that, *breaches of rules* do not automatically lead to illegality of the infringement. Moreover, slight breaches of rules are part of normal behaviour in various sports games. Anyway, the defence in indoor handball may be considered in terms of breaches – the defence is characterized by the fact that in most cases it is only possible to prevent a goal by the opponent by means of breaching the rules.

158. Furthermore, in terms of the issue of illegality, the *severity of the infringement* may not play a role in the currently prevailing concept in Austria in view of

122. Cf. *Harrer/Wagner* in *Schwimann/Kodek* VI[4] § 1295 Rz 91 ff.

behavioural injustice. Naturally, an infringement in sport may be illegal even when there is no explicit breach of rules.[123] Sports rules often only refer to typical risks in sport.

159. If the illegality of the infringement is stated because it is not covered in the typical risk of the sport – but on the contrary – increases the very same, a *verification of fault* has to be carried out. The widely prevailing principle that only a seriously negligent infringement leads to liability for damages may be related to the fact that the concept of illegality is seriously confused with the concept of fault. The level of negligence of an infringement has to be considered in objective-abstract terms in order to determine whether a sports injury lies within the frame of the typical risk for the respective sport. Infringements which are caused by objectively deliberate or seriously negligent behaviour are excluded from this aspect a priori. Therefore, they are considered illegal if they are not related to sports activity in duel sports. Nevertheless, in the specific individual cases, the accusability ought to be examined, but the aspect of slight negligence is already sufficient for the justification of liability – this applies in general to assault in tort law.

2. Conditions for Application

160. The basic condition for application of the sports liability privilege is comprised in the fact that the casualty has taken part in the competition *out of free will.*[124] Another condition is the fact that the *rules* according to which the competition is carried out are either rules which are generally acknowledged and practised within the respective sport or which have been mutually agreed upon among the participants. The latter is especially relevant in connection with sports games[125] as the participants often tend to simplify the rules of the respective sport in order to reduce the permitted physical contact between the participants. Thus, bodychecks in ice hockey as leisure sport are regularly proscribed due to inadequate protective gear of the participants.

161. In this context, the sports liability privilege is also applied to sports games of children and juveniles. However, in regard to this issue, it has to be considered that the child may only be held responsible for civil wrongs after having reached the age of 14 years. Due to the widely common liability, insurance for children within the household insurance judicature of the Supreme Court may be applied because the liability insurance – regarded as wealth – may present a reason for liability according to § 1310 ABGB.

---

123. In reference to a mixed double in tennis OGH 13.6.1978 SZ 51/79 = EvBl 1979/16.
124. In reference to scrimmaging OGH 15.3.1979 EvBl 1979/169; in reference to a shove into the pool OGH 7.6.1984 RZ 1984/76; on paintball OGH 5.7.2006 Zak 2006, 376; 5.6.2008, 6 Ob 104/08z; on a tradition run with the companions of St. Nicholas (‘Klaubauf’) OGH 21.2.2018 ZfG 2018, 80.
125. In reference to a snowball fight OGH 19.4.1984 ZVR 1985/127; in reference to a scrimmage OGH 8.9.2000 ZVR 2001/95; in reference to a collision during ice skating OGH 14.7.2005 JBl 2006, 249 (*Resch*).

3. Burden of Proof

162. In tort law, the facts which supply the baseline for the *judgment of illegality* have to be proven by the aggrieved party.[126] Thus, the aggrieved party has to prove a damage resulting from an infringement which has increased the typical risk of the respective sport. The aggrieved party has to present proof that – as it has been literally stated in a decision by the Supreme Court – the behaviour of the infringer 'has exceeded the common and usual breach of rule and behaviour of fighting for the ball'.[127]

163. Furthermore, the burden of proof in regard to *fault* has to be presented by the aggrieved party as well – as generally common in tort law. The reversal of the burden of proof – as it is assumed by judicature against jurisprudence in case of violations of protective measures[128] – can definitely not be applied because even in cases where the infringement occurs by means of breaching a sport rule it has to be stated that these rules primarily try to reduce any interference with the sports event. These rules only try to protect the physical integrity of the athletes as a secondary aspect.[129] For example, 'tripping somebody up' in ice hockey is not prohibited because it may lead to an injury but because it should prevent an advantage in the game which the infringer may gain by breaching the rules.

D. The Application of the Sports Liability Privilege in Particular

164. Subsequently, the practical application of the sports liability privilege to various sports will be presented as far as Austrian jurisdiction is concerned. However, a comprehensive analysis of application varieties for all possible sports would definitely go beyond the possible scope.

1. Combat Games

165. In practice, the most important combat games are football, handball, ice hockey, and basketball.

a. Football

166. Several times the Supreme Court already had to deal with the issue of liability for injuries resulting from sliding in. In these cases, it is important to consider whether it is predictable for the athlete who is sliding in that he would not be

126. *Koziol*, Österreichisches Haftpflichtrecht I: Allgemeiner Teil[4] (2020) Rz 16/14.
127. OGH 22.9.1987 SZ 60/176 in reference to the high leg in football.
128. Especially *Koziol*, Haftpflichtrecht I[4] Rz 16/17.
129. Cf. *Gschöpf*, Haftung 151.

able to play the ball anymore.[130] Furthermore, in order to assess the illegality, it is relevant to examine the circumstance of whether the athlete has hit the opponent close to the ground or – as it has been viewed quite often – at knee level. In addition to that, the direction of the assault has to be considered as well. Especially assaults from behind always have to be qualified as illegal because – from the very beginning of this situation – there is normally no chance whatsoever to play the ball according to the rules, the opponent has no chance to react to the attack, and the injuries of the Achilles tendon are extremely serious. The foul 'high leg' has been correctly qualified by the Supreme Court as typical and therefore not illegal.[131] Committing an offence such as a tactical, so-called professional foul is assessed controversially. However, even this definitely deliberate foul cannot be qualified a priori as illegal. What is significant is to which extent the attack may be objectively considered to increase the risk. The attack does not increase the risk, for example, when the deliberate tactical foul play against the opponent is committed by holding the opponent back on the shirt.

b. Indoor Handball

167. Indoor handball is characterized by the fact that certain body contacts such as 'Freisperren' (offence player is physically blocking the defence player of the other team in order to enable his teammate to throw) are explicitly permitted as offence strategy. Even though the 'jamming' or 'clinging' to the opponent is against the rules, it is typical for defence strategies. Therefore, it is not surprising that German judicature – Austrian judicature is not present as far as this issue is concerned – has rejected liability of the infringer even in severe cases of injuries.[132] At the same time, severe breaches of rules such as punches with the fist or karate chops as well as pushing or shoving the player when he is jumping are definitely qualified as illegal actions.[133]

c. Ice Hockey

168. In regard to ice hockey, the Austrian Supreme Court has indeed decided on two issues, which affect only plays of juveniles in their leisure time and which are legally relevant to the extent that the Supreme Court has affirmed the basic application of the sports liability privilege in both cases, but has only approved of the infringer's release from liability in one of the two cases.[134] In its second decision, the Supreme Court found that due to 'high-sticking', an increased risk behaviour on behalf of the infringer is present and therefore he was indeed liable.[135] Ice hockey

130. In reference to hitting the opponent by means of straight leg OGH 22.9.1994 JBl 1996, 786 (*Sprung*); cf. furthermore OGH 28.10.1994, 9 Ob 1604/94; 30.11.2006, 3 Ob 81/06t; 25.6.2020, 9 Ob 27/20s and on criminal law OGH 22.12.1959 SSt 30/131. Summarizing *Häckel*, Schadenersatz für Verletzungen infolge Foulspiels beim Fußball, Zak 2008, 183.
131. OGH 24.9.1981 JBl 1983, 101; 22.9.1987 SZ 60/176.
132. Cf. OLG Frankfurt 22.3.1990 ZfS 1990, 255; LG Marburg 19.5.1988 VersR 1989, 94.
133. Details in *Seebacher*, Haftungsfragen 116.
134. OGH 15.7.1987 JBl 1988, 114 on a collision.
135. OGH 1.9.1982 EvBl 1983/118; 24.10.2019, 6 Ob 136/19x.

is characterized by a wide admissibility of physical fouls. Especially the 'body-check' against the player who is controlling the puck is rule-consistent. Nevertheless, the bodycheck is prohibited if the player is pressed against the boards in the course of the check. In this context, the Austrian Regional Court of Appeal (OLG) Munich[136] judged a bodycheck against the boards with a run-up of 5m carried out against a player who was not controlling the puck not as a minor infringement but as an illegal offence.

d. Basketball

169. In accordance with the character of basketball as a 'non-contact' sport, pushing the opponent with both hands while he is performing a jump shot is against the rules and viewed to substantiate liability.[137]

2. Duel Sports

170. So far, Austrian jurisdiction has only had a chance twice to comment on illegality of infringements in these types of sports.

171. One of the decisions referred to the applicability of the sports liability privilege in the case of *scrimmaging*, but it failed in the first place due to the fact that the casualty had not agreed to scrimmaging.[138] Apart from that, it has to be stated that rule-consistent infringements in these types of sports should not be viewed as illegal in regard to the approval of the casualty, despite the fact that they may have been deliberately inflicted,[139] as long as the respective sport is not in general considered to be *contra bonos mores*. However, the Supreme Court[140] has classified the injury which was inflicted on a child in training by a coach during a *judo training session* as illegal, even though it was conceded that the behaviour of the coach could not have been qualified as illegal if the injury had occurred in a competition amongst competitors of the same level. The Supreme Court postulates in general that during a mere training session of combat sports, a higher level of consideration is required than during a real competition.[141]

3. Return Sports

172. In regard to return games, Austrian jurisdiction has mainly been concerned with *tennis*. The Supreme Court stated that it is part of the risk in mixed double that

136. OLG München 22.3.1988 VersR 1989, 598.
137. OGH 19.9.1996, 2 Ob 2255/96y.
138. OGH 15.3.1979 EvBl 1979/169.
139. Cf. *Burgstaller*, Zum Standort des erhöhten Risikos, ÖJZ 1970, 385.
140. OGH 23.9.2004 SpuRt 2005, 106.
141. Cf. thereon with reference to a sailing regatta as a parallel sport OGH 26.11.2020 Zak 2021, 38.

a player is hit on the head by the partner's racket when trying to play the ball.[142] Nevertheless, German judicature decided that the eye injury of a tennis player during warm-up, which was inflicted because he was bending down to pick up a ball and was hit by a ball that had been played by the opponent, was indeed classified as illegal.[143] However, an eye injury inflicted by one of the players in a *squash* game in the course of a backswing movement was not classified illegal in German judicature,[144] but an injury due to 'backswing in a break' without a ball was considered to be illegal.[145] In regard to *volleyball* the OGH[146] stated that a hobby player is liable if she plays the ball into the net and – out of frustration – hits it again and subsequently inflicts an eye injury to her co-player who has been trying to keep the ball in play according to the rules.

4. Dangerous Parallel Sports

173. In dangerous parallel sports, the sports liability privilege is applied if a typical risk within the respective type of sport is present. In regard to *horseback riding*, such a risk was assumed because a rider was injured by a kicking horse in the warm-up/cool-down area.[147] In addition to that, the bite of a stallion during a trail ride was also classified as such.[148] However, a riding manoeuvre in which a riding instructor came close to one of his riding students, who was consequently bitten by his stallion, was qualified as dangerous.[149] In *cycle racing,* the Supreme Court assessed an accident due to riding in a slipstream as a typical risk for the respective sport,[150] whereas the procedure of 'closing or cutting' a corner in order to block or impede a competitor who tries to overtake has been qualified as a reason for liability.[151] Besides this, the OGH[152] stated according to riding on a motocross track that it is not the task of the court to formulate abstract due diligence standards for each sport. A motocross track is ridden by people with different skills. Therefore, it cannot be expected that a certain driving line is adhered to by the rider in front. The defendant was obliged to choose a non-threatening driving line. Naturally, car racing is considered part of the dangerous parallel sports.[153]

---

142. OGH 13.6.1978 SZ 51/89 = EvBl 1979/10.
143. OLG München 23.4.1970 NJW 1970, 2297.
144. OLG Hamm 22.5.1984 VersR 1985, 296.
145. OLG Köln 13.7.1994 SpuRt 1994, 200.
146. OGH 30.5.2006 Zak 2006, 297; 27.2.2008, 3 Ob 40/08s.
147. OGH 16.12.1990 JBl 1992, 44.
148. OGH 27.3.1995, 1 Ob 646/94.
149. OGH 3.12.1981 ZVR 1982/266.
150. OGH 14.1.1999 ZVR 2000/6.
151. Cf. OGH 29.5.2008, 2 Ob 7/08f.
152. OGH 18.12.2020 EvBl-LS 2021/33 (*Painsi*).
153. In reference to an overtaking manoeuvre OGH 22.3.1983 ZVR 1984/92; cf. furthermore OGH 8.8.1989 ZVR 1989/204.

5. Parallel Sports

174. The sports liability privilege is not applied to those parallel sports which are not dangerous as the competitor does not take any risk in relation to exercising the respective sport. In this field, any kind of infringement which causes a damage regularly leads to liability.

175. In this context, the Supreme Court has come to a decision in regard to a collision between two yachts during a *sailing regatta.*[154] Nevertheless, the classification of regatta sport as a mere parallel sport is not completely indisputable. The question has been raised whether any kind of physical contact between the boats – although against the rules – should also be against the law.[155] In general, the specific form of sports venue of the respective sport has to be considered. In many types of sports, competitions 'against the clock' are just as common as the competition with a mass start. In the quoted decision regarding a sailing regatta, the OGH[156] denied the sports practice within the framework of a competition because the accident occurred during the preparation period for a race. In the present case, the claimant has been injured by the uncontrolled overturning of the mainsail from one side of the ship to the other. As the court stated, no risk inherent in the nature of a sporting competition has materialized. Because of the fact that the mutual duty of consideration is higher outside the competitive situation, the OGH finally affirmed the liability of the boat crew member. In regard to the latter case, *cross-country skiing* with the highly popular mass starts (which doubtlessly include a certain kind of injury risk) is allocated to dangerous parallel sports.

176. Besides, in reference to *collisions in cross-country skiing* FIS-Rules may be applied (in regard to the FIS-Rules in alpine skiing *see* §4.I.D.5.a). The rules, for example, prescribe:

- keep to the provided running direction;
- yield to the cross-country skier who is going downhill;
- use the right-most cross-country track, if possible;
- overtake on the left.

a. Alpine Skiing and Snowboarding

177. Alpine skiing and snowboarding on ski runs as well as in alpine areas are absolutely included in parallel sports. The skier (snowboarder) does in no way agree to any kind of risk of injury through his mere participation in skiing.[157]

---

154. OGH 24.3.1994 ZVR 1995/10; 26.11.2020 Zak 2021, 38.
155. Cf. *Gschöpf*, Haftung 99.
156. OGH 26.11.2020 Zak 2021, 38.
157. Cf. *Gschöpf*, Haftung 108 with further references.

178. Anyway, it has to be questioned who has behaved illegally in case of a *collision,* for example.[158] In this context, the OGH[159] recently affirmed the liability of a skier because of driving between two pausing skiers in a squatting position instead of passing them on the left or right side. Apart from this, lower standards of due diligence are applied according to timed routes. Such special race courses, separated from the general ski slope, are available to skiers willing to perform with their skis in a less controlled manner.[160] There are no regulations with force of law (exception: Vorarlberger Sports Law; *see* below). However, rules have been developed which regulate how a careful skier ought to ski. The legality of the skiers' behaviour is regulated by the so-called piste rules of conduct. These significant rules of skiing are expert recommendations in regard to the care and precaution which a skier should undertake in order to avoid collisions with other skiers. The most important list of rules are the FIS-Rules and the Ski Run Regulations Draft of the Austrian Board of Trustees for Alpine Safety. In regard to content, the two sets of rules are basically the same.[161]

179. Important *piste rules* are:

- secure sports equipment by means of stoppers or leash;
- follow priority rules between skiers (yield to slower skiers before you, yield to skiers on the lift);
- commit yourself to moving in control[162] and in sight;[163]
- follow the rule for emergency fall (however, this rule is often criticized);[164]
- keep safety margins;
- free neuralgic points;
- mind the signs on the ski run.[165]

Jurisdiction regularly applies these rules as a summary of principles of due diligence in regard to proper conduct on the ski runs. However, their quality as customary law remains undecided as it may be difficult to justify.[166]

---

158. OGH 22.9.2020, 4 Ob 111/20g; 26.2.2019, 3 Ob 226/19k; 30.4.2019, 1 Ob 59/19m; 15.5.2018, 5 Ob 11/18f; 25.11.2015, 8 Ob 90/15s; *see also* regarding FIS-rules and collisions *Mahler-Hutter*, Der Sachverständige für Schisport. Kollisionen – FIS-Regeln, in *Pilgermair* (ed.), Skisport und Recht (2021) 195.
159. OGH 25.6.2021 Zak 2021, 298.
160. OGH 22.9.2020, 4 Ob 111/20g; *see also* concerning the stricter due diligence of the maintainer for such race runs OGH 19.10.1989 JBl 1990, 458 and OGH 20.4.2010 ZVR 2010, 399 (*Kathrein*).
161. Cf. thereon *Pichler/Holzer*, Handbuch des österreichischen Skirechts (1987) 133; *Gschöpf*, Haftung 44 with further references.
162. *See* in reference to choosing a risky driving line on a ski piste known to the plaintiff, OGH 19.2.2016 Zak 2016, 98.
163. Cf. in reference to skiing in a snowpark, OGH 12.10.2021, 1 Ob 169/21s; *see also* OGH 30.4.2019, 1 Ob 59/19m.
164. *See* OGH 27.9.1988 ZVR 1989/29.
165. Cf. thereon according to the sign of a piste closure OGH 24.5.2018 Zak 2018, 238.
166. OGH 26.2.1997 ZVR 1997/17.

180. Nevertheless, these rules have already gained force of law if they are valid within § 2 Vorarlberger Sports Law[167] and if they have been included in a regulation according to Clause 2 or 3 in regard to safe sports exercise. In such a case, any violation of the regulation is prosecuted as an administrative offence by the so-called ski run guards.

b. Excursus: Private Right to Arrest

181. The so-called private right to stop or arrest a person, especially on the ski runs, is a practically important case of self-help in connection with collision accidents in sports. Is the injured skier – if he is actually able to do so – or another person, who is incidentally present, entitled to stop and arrest another skier, who has caused a collision accident, against his will and at least force him to display his identity?

182. It has to be assumed that the negligent injury of another person in parallel sport is a criminal offence. If *sufficient grounds* may be assumed that a *person* has *directly beforehand committed an offence* which *results in legal prosecution,* then *every person* is entitled to *properly stop and arrest* this person in accordance with § 80 Clause 2 StPO; nevertheless, he is obliged to report this arrest immediately to the next security organ. If these conditions are complied with, the arrest of the sportsman is not considered illegal and therefore not liable to prosecution. If the arrested sportsman finally turns out to be innocent or only partly guilty, the person who has arrested him does not have to fear prosecution. Fact is that whoever assumes such a circumstance – which would exclude the illegality of such an act – by mistake cannot be convicted for wilful tort; he has to be convicted for a negligent act if the error is based on negligence and the negligent act is liable to prosecution (§ 8 StGB). However, according to § 99 StGB in connection with § 7 StGB, deprivation of liberty is only liable to prosecution in case of an intentional act, but not in case of a negligent act.

E. Carelessness of the Injured in His Own Matters

183. The mere participation of an athlete in a combat sport or in a dangerous parallel sport can in no case be viewed as carelessness on behalf of the injured athlete.[168] The casualty's consent as a contributor may only be considered in case of infringements which are related to the verdict of *contra bonos mores*. This assessment cannot be applied to any of the currently common sports. Carelessness or negligence of the injured person in his own matters may only be considered if the casualty has suffered an injury due to his own improper conduct in sport exercise. One of these aspects may refer to negligence in regard to appropriate protective gear.[169] For example, in general sportsmen who wear glasses should be directed to

167. VLGBl 1972/15 in the version of VLGBl 2022/4.
168. Cf. *Seebacher*, Haftungsfragen 138; *Gschöpf*, Haftung 143.
169. *See* in detail *Schwaighofer*, Schutzbekleidung und Mitverschulden im Sport (2019).

wear sports glasses.[170] Moreover, in certain types of sport it is either mandatory or at least common practice to wear a helmet. According to the Supreme Court[171] it has become such a common practice in the area of 'sporty ambitious' cycling. Thereby, the following circumstances have to be taken into account: the use of a racing bike, the wearing of racing clothes and a high driving speed. Regarding the last aspect, the OGH assumed such a speed level in the present case at 35 km/h, and negated a level at 15 to 20 km/h in another decision.[172] This also accounts for the use of shin pads. In terms of combat sport, continuous verbal provocative comments to the competitor may also be viewed as carelessness or negligence. It may also be based on overestimation of the sportsman's own abilities[173] and skills or lack of concentration on behalf of the injured sportsman. In this context, the OGH[174] affirmed a carelessness in own matters if the plaintiff got injured because of a stay in the swivel area of the large boom during the break of a sailing regatta. Because of her sailing education, she ought to have known better. Nevertheless, the fact that she was not given any special task (e.g., as a helmsman) has also to be taken into account. In skiing, negligence is often related to improper or wrongly adjusted ski bindings.[175] Apart from this, the OGH[176] recently negated a carelessness in his own matters when the skier does not stop at the edge but in the middle of the ski slope, at a point visible from a distance of 30m.

II. Liability of the Organizer

184. The organizer of a sports event is the person who directly influences the event in regard to course and organization. For example, this may be an association which is organizing the respective sports competition. This aspect does not change even if a licence on behalf of the respective sports federation is essential for the organization of the competition. By means of merely granting the licence the federation is not automatically the organizer of the event. If the organizer is not at the same time the property owner of the sports facility, the proprietor is either partly or completely liable for certain kinds of risks.

A. Liability for Safety of the Sports Facility

185. This type of liability primarily affects the property owner of the sports facility. He is responsible for the sports facility meeting all the safety provisions regulated by public law, for example, the building regulations, as well as corresponding to the provisions of the respective sports federations and the sports which

170. *See* OGH 1.9.1982 EvBl 1983/118; for more examples *see* 16.12.2019, 8 Ob 42/19p; 19.12.2016, 2 Ob 223/15f; 25.11.2015, 8 Ob 90/15s.
171. OGH 27.8.2014 ZVR 2014, 391 (*Karner*).
172. Cf. OGH 27.11.2020 JBl 2021, 385.
173. Cf. in this context, e.g., OGH 12.10.2021, 1 Ob 169/21s.
174. OGH 26.11.2020, 4 Ob 148/20y.
175. Cf. thereon *Pichler/Holzer*, Skirecht 128.
176. OGH 25.6.2021 Zak 2021, 298.

are practised in the facility.[177] Basically, the owner of the sports facility is only obliged to take hazard prevention measures, which generally apply to the intended type of use. To this, the OGH[178] negated an obligation of the owner of a swimming pool to set further precautions regarding a water slide. Signs indicating the permitted slide stops suffice. So, a permanent supervision by lifeguards is not necessary. Apart from this, jurisdiction came to the conclusion that besides compliance with official approvals, the owner of a sport facility (or the organizer of an event) can also be obliged to take additional measures. In doing so, predictable and identifiable sources of danger should be prevented.[179]

186. Furthermore, jurisdiction[180] considered the protection of a football field with an aluminium railing to be sufficient. In the present case, the plaintiff wanted to run around the opponent's defender in the course of an attack. When he lost the duel, he tried to stop outside the side-out line. In doing so, he fell down and crashed into a pillar at the aluminium railing. As the Supreme Court already stated in another decision[181] concerning the protection of a wall bar in indoor football, the player does not have to expect dangers within the field, but increased attention on the sidelines (as well as in indoor football) is required. Based on this, an organizer or owner of a sport facility is entitled to trust that a football player will pay attention to where he is going at full speed, even in competition. In this context, liability for buildings according to § 1319 ABGB has to be emphasized in particular. This liability for fault with reversal of burden of proof affects the 'owner' of the building. The owner is considered to be a person who has had the legal possibilities to reduce the resulting danger by means of provisions.[182] Anyway, the safety obligations may well be contractually conveyed to the organizer as the lessee of the facility in such a case. However, primarily, the property owner is still liable for building safety of the facility. For example, the collapse of a stand would definitely still result in liability in accordance with § 1319 ABGB.[183]

187. In this context, the OGH[184] negated the liability of the owner of a golf course for an accident caused by a defective manhole cover according to § 1319 ABGB. The court held that the deficiency cannot be recognized with the naked eye.

---

177. Cf. thereon *Joeinig*, Fitness-Center, Kletterwände, Sporthallen – Die Haftung des Betreibers, in *Hinteregger/Reissner* (ed.), Sport und Haftung (2006) 145. In reference to an accident on a climbing wall OGH 15.2.2007, 6 Ob 17/07d.
178. OGH 11.8.2008 Zak 2008, 418.
179. *See* thereon with reference to the security of the participants of a race on a ski hill OGH 27.1.2022, 9 Ob 85/21x.
180. OGH 20.2.2020 Zak 2020, 217.
181. *See* thereon OGH 28.2.2012, 4 Ob 172/11i.
182. Cf. *Terlitza*, Die Bauwerkehaftung – § 1319 ABGB (2000) 26 and 94; *see also Danzl* in *Koziol/Bydlinski/Bollenberger* (ed.), Kurzkommentar zum ABGB[6] (2020) § 1319 ABGB Rz 4.
183. Cf. OGH 20.10.1964 EvBl 1965/48.
184. OGH 23.1.2019 EvBl-LS 2019/100 (*Weixelbraun-Mohr*).

188. Besides this, it has to be noted that the qualification of a manhole located on a motor racing track as a building has to be criticized. Unlike the previously mentioned case, the deficiency in this situation concerns the racetrack and not the manhole itself. [185] In the present case, the plaintiff fell during the training session, slid along the track and finally crashed into a steel-covered manhole. Nevertheless, the court[186] affirmed the liability of the organizer of the motor racing event according to § 1319 ABGB.

B. Liability for Safety of the Event

189. The liability of the organizer to the paying spectators as well as to the active athletes is defined by *contractual liability*. This aspect is also relevant when the injured athlete is a member of the organizing association due to the fact that the relationship between member and association may be viewed as a contractual relationship.

190. The organizer is obliged to provide safety for the spectators as well as the athletes within reasonable limits and has to follow the respective provisions of the authority. He is subject to the helpers' liability according to § 1313a ABGB and the reversal of burden of proof according to § 1298 ABGB. This issue is important as the property owner of the facility is also viewed as the agent of the organizer, and the organizer is subsequently liable to his contractual partners for construction defects of the facility.

191. Therefore, it is not necessary in the case of paying spectators and active athletes to refer to the legal institute of *safety obligations*. This aspect consists due to launching an activity in public space or due to causing risks against participants or endangered persons. Any infringement results in tort liability of the person who is liable in regard to safety. If spectators watch an event without paying an entrance fee, safety obligations have to be applied. Likewise, the organizer is only liable to a non-participant third party within the scope of safety obligations.

192. One aspect which both safety obligations and contractual protective obligations have in common is the fact that *due diligence* may not be overstretched. The measures which are expected of the person who is obliged to safety are limited by what is *reasonable in the individual case.*[187] However, the level of reasonable measures is also determined by the closeness of relationship between the safety provider and the endangered person. In the case of contractual obligation for protection,

185. Cf. in detail *Harrer/Wagner* in *Schwimann/Kodek* VI^4 § 1295 Rz 81.
186. OGH 12.10.2004, 1 Ob 216/04b.
187. Cf. thereon *Hinteregger*, Sportevents – Die Haftung des Veranstalters, in *Hinteregger/Reissner* (ed.), Sport und Haftung (2006) 3.

the precautionary measures of the safety provider will be evaluated by a more rigorous standard than in the case of non-paying spectators. Nevertheless, the organizer is also subject to due diligence in reference to the non-paying spectators according to § 1299 ABGB.[188]

1. Liability to Spectators

193. The liability of the organizer to paying spectators also results from an infringement of *contractual protective obligation and due diligence*, therefore it is part of contractual liability as the spectator and the organizer are linked by means of a contract for work[189] due to the fact that the spectator has paid for the ticket for the sports event.[190] The contract entails the performance of the respective competition. Based on this contractual obligation, a secondary obligation results which covers the physical integrity of the contractual party.[191] Therefore, the organizer has to undertake any reasonable precautions in order to make a safe visit of the event possible.[192] The infringement of this obligation for protection is liable to prosecution due to breach of contract.

194. It can definitely *by no means* be assumed that the *spectator has agreed* to an endangerment of his personal safety because he is visiting a sports event.[193] Nevertheless, if spectators or other persons who are not participating in the competition enter a clearly marked race track or enter and linger in the area which has been assigned to the competition or if they leave designated areas – a circumstance which is especially relevant in motorsports (rally) – they are definitely responsible if they cause an accident with their behaviour, no matter whether the accident occurs due to a collision with a competitor or as a consequence of the obstruction of the competitor. If they suffer a damage due to their own lack of discipline, the organizer cannot be held liable for this damage.[194]

195. The individual measures which have to be undertaken in order to protect the spectators of a sports event depend on how high the risk of danger associated with the event is calculated.[195] Nevertheless, the amount of expected spectators is also relevant as the risk of danger constantly increases with the increasing amount of spectators. The closer the source of danger is to the spectator, the sooner and the more respective measures of protection have to be undertaken. Only the risk of

---

188. *Pichler/Holzer*, Skirecht 259; *Reischauer* in *Rummel* (ed.), Kommentar zum Allgemeinen bürgerlichen Gesetzbuch II^3 (2007) § 1297 Rz 9.
189. The contract may also be considered a mixed contract as the given contract is not a contract for work in the conventional sense (self-contained work performance, obligation to provide 'success').
190. Cf. OGH 21.10.1953 SZ 26/255; 4.12.1957 JBl 1958, 126; 26.5.1970 EvBl 1970/344; *Gaisbauer*, Zur Haftung des Veranstalters eines Autorennens gegenüber Zuschauern, VersR 1975, 500.
191. Cf. *Koziol*, Österreichisches Haftpflichtrecht II: Haftung für eigenes und fremdes Fehlverhalten^3 (2018) 215 ff with further references.
192. Cf. OGH 13.1.1960 SZ 33/5; *Gaisbauer*, VersR 1975, 501.
193. Cf. *Reischauer* in *Rummel* II^3 § 1297 Rz 9b.
194. In reference to a go-kart training OGH 22.9.1983 ZVR 1984/139.
195. OGH 7.12.1976 SZ 49/154.

extraordinary events – damage which results from incidents which could not have been foreseen by the organizer and are not part of the usual course of the event – has to be covered by the spectator of dangerous sports himself.[196]

196. The scope of safety measures should correspond with any constituent provisions by public law as well as with the required authorization of the official authorities.[197] In this context, it has to be noted that the authority which has imposed conditions is also obliged to monitor the compliance with them. Otherwise, the acting organs of an authority can also be held liable for damages to the spectators. In the present case, the injury of the spectator was caused by the overturning of the wooden gang and a 400 kg LED wall when other visitors moved in the direction of the playing field. As stated by the court, the authority was obliged to ensure the fulfilment of the condition (operationally safe installation) by obtaining an expert opinion.[198] In addition to that, the regulations of the respective sports federations have to be considered as well. However, even if the organizer follows all the mentioned provisions, he is not relieved of undertaking additional protective measures if he knows about the risks due to his experience and if measures for risk prevention are reasonable within the scope of his obligation to contractual liability. This might be the case in particular when circumstances arise which require additional protective measures and which have to be noticed by the organizer due to his obligatory attention to the course of the event.[199] In another decision, the OGH[200] followed up on this opinion and affirmed the liability of the organizer of a football game; despite an approval by the building authorities. Moreover, in this sense jurisdiction came to the conclusion that the compliance with the relevant ÖNORM standards and the commissioning of a football field by a sports association does also not release the organizer from his obligation to take further safety measures.[201]

197. The organizer is also liable for any kind of injuries and damages to the spectator which result from lack of safety measures and which are inflicted by the athletes as the latter is considered an agent to the organizer in relation to the spectator.[202] In these cases, the competitor normally is not liable to the spectator as there is no faulty or illegal behaviour involved. He may only be liable if he has noticed the lack of safety measures beforehand and subsequently has refused to acknowledge the safety interests of the spectator – thereby causing damage by fault.[203]

196. OGH 21.10.1953 SZ 26/255.
197. OGH 22.9.1983 ZVR 1984/139.
198. OGH 7.9.2021 Zak 2021, 358.
199. Cf. OGH 9.4.1970 JBl 1971, 249; OGH 6.10.1982 JBl 1983, 324; in reference to a flight show OGH 30.11.1987 JBl 1988, 318.
200. *See* OGH 31.3.2020 Zak 2020, 217.
201. Cf. OGH 20.2.2020 Zak 2020, 217: the court referred to this before going into the specific facts of the case concerning the liability towards an athlete.
202. Thus OGH 4.12.1957 JBl 1958, 126 = ZVR 1958/252; in Germany already RG 4.3.1930 RGZ 127, 313.
203. OGH 9.10.1930 ZBl 1931/3; *Pichler/Holzer*, Skirecht 260; *Reischauer* in *Rummel* II[3] § 1297 Rz 9b.

198. In particular, there are some typical sources of risk which accompany sports event and which have to be met by the organizer: If the organizer offers a package including *transport* to the sports facility in combination with the entrance ticket, he is liable for the safety of transport. If he does not organize the transport himself, he is liable for the transport company as his helper. The safety of *entrance and exit areas* of sports facilities is especially relevant. For these areas, adequate lighting, skid resistance of the grounds and sufficient dimensioning are required. In regard to *ticket sale*, the organizer has to make sure that the amount of available tickets corresponds with the capacity of the sports facility. By means of *ticket check* he has to guarantee that no dangerous items can be taken to the stand. In general, the organizer is required to supply sufficient security services in relation to size and importance of the sports event. These services must keep the escape routes, routes for rescue teams and emergency routes passable at any time, and must make sure that the spectators take their seats and do not try to, for example, rush into other sectors of the stand during the course of the event. The security services definitely have to be rendered in cooperation with the organs which are officially prescribed by the authority or which the organizer may have requested himself. A special focus lies on thc issuc of *beverage sale*. It is rather problematic and may only be decided case-by-case whether drinks in glasses or glass bottles may be considered. Without doubt, it has to be differentiated between the VIP area of a golf tournament and the standing area of a regional football match. Apart from these general safety measures and obligations of the organizer – which have to be substantiated for each individual case – he also has to meet the specific measures and obligations which relate to the specific type of sport.

a. Football

199. According to the OGH,[204] the organizer has to protect the spectators on the stand behind the goal from balls being shot beyond the goal by means of a lattice or a net even if such a protective measure has not been requested by the football federation or the authorities. The circumstance that a spectator who had been injured by a ball had not been watching the match on the field has not been acknowledged as carelessness on behalf of the spectator because the spectator had been hit by the ball while he was on his way to the restrooms. However, the German 'lower courts'[205] have decided that during the course of the game, a spectator should watch the proceedings on the field in order to be able to react to balls flying towards the spectator area.

200. Apart from this, the OGH[206] affirmed the liability of the organizer of a football game towards a spectator who had purchased a VIP ticket in a recent decision. When leaving the VIP area, the plaintiff tripped over a steel staircase, fell and injured himself. Although an official approval existed, the organizer would have been obliged to take appropriate precautions (e.g., fall protection). In the present

204. OGH 2.4.1997 ZVR 1998/91.
205. Cf. OLG Schleswig-Holstein 10.11.1994 SpuRt 1999, 244; LG Trier 14.7.1960 VersR 1964, 879.
206. *See* regarding the protection of a trip hazard OGH 31.3.2020 Zak 2020, 217.

case, the court also acknowledged a carelessness on behalf of the spectator because he did not look ahead, but to the right of the football field and moreover the source of danger was detectable.

b. Ice Hockey

201. In connection with ice hockey, the courts have been discussing the issue to which extent the spectator area on the long side of the rink has to be protected from pucks regularly flying beyond the protective nets which are generally applied on the broadside of the rink behind the goal due to prescription of the federation. The OGH[207] has considered such a safety measure as necessary and reasonable. The compliance with safety provisions by authority or federation would only supply a minimum standard of obligation to maintain safety. Measures which exceed these provisions have to be undertaken by the organizer if it is obvious to him that the provided measures are insufficient for the protection of the spectators. However, the organizer of a junior ice hockey game is not obliged to set up an acrylic glass wall and warning notices in order to comply with his obligation to maintain safety.[208] Apart from this, the OGH[209] recently denied the liability of the operator of an ice sports facility. In the present case, the spectator stayed in the area next to the players' benches without wearing any protective equipment. Besides this, the plaintiff knew the usual course of an ice hockey game and the dangers associated with it because of his experience as a hockey player. On the basis of this, the court affirmed the sole fault of the spectator.

c. Skiing

202. Compared to general skiing, the safety precautions are increased when skiing is performed in a competition.[210] In order to protect the spectator, the focus lies especially on the separation of spectators and racers by means of appropriate fences. Thus, the finish area has to be secured so that ski racers who crash cannot tumble into the mass of spectators and cause injuries. Nevertheless, potential crash areas have to be closed off from spectators.

203. Even though injuries of spectators in the course of an alpine ski race are quite rare, people who help prepare the ski runs, track officials, coaches, track judges and others who are authorized to be on the race track are more in danger of damage and injury. The risk of injury to spectators is even lower in cross-country skiing. However, a respective decision has been taken in regard to *ski jumping*. The

207. OGH 20.3.1984 SZ 57/57 = EvBl 1984/81; cf. also OGH 21.6.2007 SpuRt 2008, 107 *(Resch)*.
208. OGH 23.4.2007 Zak 2007, 257.
209. *See* OGH 19.11.2019, 3 Ob 217/19m.
210. Cf. *Pichler*, Zur Verkehrssicherungspflicht bei internationalen Skirennstrecken, SpuRt 1999, 53 = ZVR 1994, 97; in reference to a private ski race OGH 11.11.1997 ZVR 1999/10.

injury of a spectator due to a ski which the jumper had lost in the course of a fall and which had rushed through the barrier fence into the spectator area led to the organizer's liability.[211]

d. Motorsport

204. Basically, a distinction has to be drawn between races on a *race circuit or a race track* and *road races*. While the risk for spectators has to be avoided to a maximum extent on permanent race tracks, the safety in road races is coming up against its definite limits as a complete safeguarding is not possible due to the respective length of the course. Furthermore, the behaviour of the spectators cannot always be observed and controlled even if all the provisions of the respective authority are followed and the executive forces are involved. Basically, any kinds of stands or spectator areas have to be secured.[212] If a spectator enters a marked prohibited area despite having been warned several times and if he is injured as a consequence by a skidding vehicle, the organizer is not liable.[213]

205. If a spectator is injured due to faulty behaviour of a competitor without any negligence in regard to safety obligations on behalf of the organizer, the organizer is still liable to the paying spectator in accordance with § 1313a ABGB. However, for events which do not require an entrance fee § 1315 ABGB is applied. In autocross-races, the driver is not at fault if a stone which has been swirled up causes an injury to a spectator.[214] In addition to that, crashes in motorbike races also do not justify a tort,[215] but the use of slick tyres despite starting rain does.[216] According to a new decision by the OGH,[217] the organizer of motor events is in no case affected by strict liability under the EKHG because he is not viewed as the owner of the vehicles which are participating in the race.

e. Horse Races

206. According to the OGH[218], the organizer of an event for horses and equestrians ought to ensure that the spectators walk the path in due distance temporally after and spatially behind the horses (e.g., through placing stewards). In doing so, the accident of the spectator, who was knocked down by a horse walking 10 to 20m behind her, could have been prevented.

211. OLG Innsbruck 19.12.1986 ZVR 1988/32.
212. In reference to a rally course OGH 7.12.1976 ZVR 1978/166.
213. In reference to a go-kart training OGH 22.9.1983 ZVR 1984/139; on motocross OGH 26.2.1992 ZVR 1992/101.
214. OGH 25.10.1988 ZVR 1989/137.
215. OGH 26.2.1992 ZVR 1992/101.
216. In reference to an accident during the Alpl mountain course race opposing OGH 10.4.1997 JBl 1997, 734 (crit *Apathy*).
217. OGH 25.10.1988 ZVR 1989/137; opposing also OGH 4.12.1957 JBl 1958, 126 = ZVR 1958/252.
218. *See* thereon OGH 26.6.2019 Zak 2019, 278.

2. Liability to Competitors

207. The organizer is also involved in a *contractual relationship* to the competitors which results in protective obligations and due diligence towards the competitors. Often the same safety measures serve to protect both the spectator as well as the sportsman. In this context, it has to be referred to the protective cage in discus and hammer throwing. In this regard a lot of comments already stated in §2.I can be applied to the protective measures in favour of the athletes.

208. However, one aspect results in a legally important difference: while spectators do not consent to any kind of danger to their physical integrity, *active sportsmen agree to the risk which is typically related to the respective sport*; thus, they act at their own risk. The organizer is only liable for damages due to atypical risks. Whether the risk is considered typical for the sport or already atypical has to be decided case-by-case and in respect to the specific sport. Thus, a ski racer consents to the risk of a crash, but not to an injury caused by a safety net which does not fulfil state-of-the-art standards.[219] In addition to that, the injury of a child who is playing football and is hurt by an insufficiently fixed small-size goal[220] or the injury in the course of a jump in an inappropriately prepared sandpit of a fitness course[221] are also no typical risks of the respective sport. If a bob which cannot brake anymore is not properly stopped due to insufficient equipment at the end of the bob run, the facility operators are subject to liability because the undamped collision of the bob with the end of the bob run is not entailed in the risk range of the respective sport.[222]

3. Exemption from Liability

209. Exemptions from liability play a role in the relationship organizer – spectator as well as in the contractual relationship organizer – competitor.

210. Whereas such an exemption from liability is regularly required in signed form from competitors (*see* below), the exemption from liability in relation to *spectators* is often announced via notice on posters or on the tickets. In the latter cases, it definitely has to be evaluated beforehand whether the exemption from liability is included in the contract with the spectator. This aspect has to be negated if the spectator has been informed about the exemption only after the contract has been concluded.[223] Furthermore, it has to be considered that the relationship between organizer and spectator is definitely defined as a consumer business. Therefore,

219. In reference to the case Brian Stemmle against the Kitzbüheler Ski Club in connection with the accident of the athlete in the safety net at the 'Steilhang' exit of the 'Streif' OGH 22.6.1993 JBl 1994, 338.
220. OGH 12.9.1989 JBl 1990, 113; however, cf. OGH 14.11.2000 SpuRt 2001, 193 = ZVR 2001/59 in reference to the accident of an adult using the small-size goal as a horizontal bar.
221. OGH 16.1.1980 JBl 1980, 590.
222. In reference to an accident in bob training OGH 25.6.1987 ZVR 1988/107.
223. OGH 9.10.1984 JBl 1986, 248.

according to § 6 Clause 1 Z 9 KSchG *declarations of liability exemptions* are *invalid* in relation to the primarily present *physical damage* in context.[224] In regard to *property damage*, the validity of the exemption is limited to *slightly negligent damages.*[225]

211. It definitely has to be questioned whether the relationship between organizer and *competitor* may be considered a consumer business in the general sense. If this is the case (e.g., participation of a hobby sportsman in a major marathon event), then the same contractual relationship as the relationship between organizer and spectator is present (*see* above). Nevertheless, in other cases, the contractual situation is hardly different: the renunciation of compensation claims may only be referred to damages and risks which are predictable and calculable.[226] Therefore, the athletes' trust in the fact that they are not threatened by atypical risks and dangers at the sports facilities should not be affected by exemptions from liability. The competitors assume that the responsible person ensures the safety measures within the dangerous areas and fulfils all the obligations to maintain safety. Declarations of liability exemptions ought to be understood only in this context for this given area. The clauses only clearly state that there is no liability for accidents which occur due to a typical risk which is connected to the respective sport. Only the typical risks of the sport are known to the athlete beforehand, and so they only want to sign declarations which relate to these risks. Therefore, these declarations of liability exemption do not cause a change in liability issues a priori because the typical risk in sport has to be carried by the athlete himself. In addition to that, the OGH has recently decided that declarations of liability exemptions included in the general conditions and relating to physical damage are considered as a gross disadvantage in the sense of § 879 Clause 3 ABGB and have been classified as void.[227] Nowadays, the exemption of liability in case of physical damage is generally assumed as *contra bonos mores* by jurisdiction and is therefore considered void.[228] In this context, the exemption from liability is only legal in regard to slightly negligent property damages.

4. Liability to Non-participating Third Parties

212. In terms of his obligation to maintain safety, the organizer is also liable to a certain extent to legal interests of non-participating third parties.[229] In regard to sports events, the extent of this obligation has definitely not been explored to its limits by judicature. The case in which – due to insufficient separation of race track and open ski run for general skiing – a ski racer collided with a normal skier who was

224. Cf. OGH 29.3.2000 ZVR 2000/94.
225. Cf. *Hinteregger* in *Hinteregger/Reissner*, Haftung 10.
226. Cf. OGH 3.12.1981 ZVR 1982/266; 19.1.1984 ZVR 1984/318; 22.6.1993 JBl 1994, 338 (case Brian Stemmle) as well as OGH 31.10.1996, 2 Ob 2298/96a for the accident on the way to the changing room and OGH 30.1.1997 ZVR 1997/105 for an accident during a mountain bike race.
227. In reference to a declaration of liability exemption for snow-rafting OGH 24.3.1998 JBl 1998, 151 = ZVR 1997/37.
228. In reference to a swimming accident OGH 22.2.2001 JBl 2001, 590.
229. OGH 27.11.2020, 2 Ob 8/20w.

using the generally accessible part of the ski run caused no problems in judgment. In this case, the liability of the organizer to the third party was legally confirmed.[230] Nevertheless, the often reported cases in which the legal interests of third parties are violated due to vandalism of so-called fans are more difficult to judge. So far the OGH only had to decide in one situation.[231] In this case, about 70,000 spectators had come to a major event – the landing of a Concorde at the airport in Linz – but the organizer had only estimated a maximum of 30,000 spectators. As a consequence, spectators entered areas and properties which had not been authorized in order to get a better view of the airplane, and climbed a shell and thereby caused considerable damage to the property. The OGH confirmed the liability of the organizer for these damages with the following justification:

> The concept of launching an event or activity in public space and thereby causing a risk to participants and/or third parties is nowadays not limited to the local-physical area in which respective safety precautions ought to be applied, but it entails safety measures for any kind of dangers. According to this principle, the organizers of sports events have to undertake the required safety measures for the protection of all the participants and spectators. If there is a chance that in the course of an event risks and dangers for others may arise, the organizer has to undertake measures against these risks within a reasonable scope. As the obligation to implement safety precautions requires provisions under consideration of all those whose legal interests may be damaged due to the risks and dangers, it also includes risks and dangers which might arise as a result of prohibited and intentional actions by third parties, provided that the possibility to impair legal interests of third parties may be objectively acknowledged. There is no doubt that each major event entails already a considerate amount of risk potential. It is also well-known that members of a mass follow specific psychological laws – in particular, they lose their inhibitions and tend to reckless behaviour. Even though the organizer had not expected such a large number of spectators, he for sure was aware of the fact that a couple of 10.000 people would come, especially as he had printed some 30.000 tickets. Based on these facts the organizer should have considered that the spectators might present a risk factor for the areas and properties bordering the event location.

213. These principles have not been applied to vandalism in the course of other sports events – especially in regard to the behaviour of football fans – but it may well be expected that jurisdiction in regard to the predictability of risks and dangers to legal interests of third parties located in close distance to the event will confirm the liability of the organizer if he does not meet the risk potential with appropriate measures.[232]

230. OGH 11.11.1997 ZVR 1998/10.
231. OGH 30.11.1987 JBl 1988, 318.
232. Cf. also *Hinteregger* in *Hinteregger/Reissner*, Haftung 23.

III. Liability of Maintainers of Ski Runs, Cross-Country Tracks and Cycling Tracks

214. The maintainer ('Halter') of an object is the person who uses the object at his own expenses and who has it at his disposal. Therefore, the maintainer of a ski run is the person who covers the costs for creating the ski run, maintaining, servicing and securing the ski run, who benefits from it, and who has the power to undertake the required measures. Nevertheless, the issue of maintenance in regard to ski runs is particularly complex because often a number of different legal entities participate in various ways in operating a ski run. If the property owner creates, maintains and prepares the ski run and makes it available to the skiers, he is the maintainer of the ski run and thereby carries the obligation of ski run safety. However, principally, the operators of mountain transport (cable cars, chair lifts, tow lifts) are the ones who create the ski runs, maintain the ski runs and make them available to their guests. Therefore, practically seen, only the operators of cable cars are possible candidates as the maintainer of the ski runs.[233]

215. Similar to ski runs, the maintainer of cross-country ski tracks and ski trails may be the proprietor, the tourist association or the community, a sports association or individuals such as restaurant operators or a retailer for sports equipment. Again, the maintainer is the person who covers the costs for creating the cross-country ski track, maintaining, servicing and securing it as well as who has the power to undertake the necessary measures.[234]

216. 'Wild ski runs' or 'wild cross-country ski tracks' (e.g., tracks of climbing up in ski touring) are not maintained by anyone, and therefore no one can be held liable for their condition.

A. Obligation to Secure Ski Runs

217. In practice, the circumstance that the obligation to secure ski runs results as a secondary obligation from the contract of transportation with the ski lift operations (cf. §4.III.A.1) is definitely more important. Apart from that, the liability of the maintainer of the road or track is relevant in the given context (cf. §4.III.A.2).

1. Contractual Liability

218. The fact that the obligation to secure the ski runs *results as a contractual secondary obligation from the contract for transportation* is based on the argument that the transportation of the skier by means of ski lifts is normally performed in order to enable the skier to use the ski runs and not just to make sure that he reaches the top. In fact, the main issue is a circular traffic in which the skier always returns

---

233. Cf. *Pichler/Holzer,* Skirecht 49.
234. Cf. *Pichler/Holzer*, Skirecht 56.

to his starting point – often even more than once – which is made possible by the ski lift operator who makes the respective ski runs available to the skier.

219. In this context, it has to be noted that if several cableways or lift companies join together to form a *tariff association* (in the present case: 'Ski Arlberg'), then the entrepreneur from whom the lift pass is purchased either contracts only in his own name or also acts as an agent for the other interconnected companies. In the latter situation, the relationship of representation has to be clearly disclosed. This then results in a split contractual relationship with several contracting parties and different sets of obligations. As a consequence, each member of the association is liable for his own cableways and lifts.[235]

220. The *spatial boundaries* between established ski runs and 'wild pistes' and the cleared ski area are not always easy to determine as not all these areas are marked in their borders. Areas which are prepared by means or machinery are definitely considered ski runs. Beyond that, up to a certain limit, the obligation to secure the ski runs extends to the edge of the ski run as well.[236] To this, jurisdiction also affirmed the liability of the maintainer of a ski run towards a skier who got injured by crashing into a facility of a snowmaking system in an area around 2m outside of the prepared slope. According to the court, the necessity of the protection does not solely depend on the distance of the object from the edge of the ski run but also on the design and orientation of the object and the runway course.[237] In contrast to that, the OGH[238] came in a recent decision to the opposite conclusion: In the present case, the accident occurred about 50m from the edge of the ski way in an unprepared terrain with only a few ski tracks in the deep snow. The plaintiff used this area of the piste as a shortcut to the lift car park, although the demarcation from the prepared ski run was clearly visible. The mere fact that many skiers act in this way does not justify an obligation to secure the path. In this sense, the court[239] also denied the liability of the maintainer of a ski run, who marked the edge of the slope with poles and boards. Moreover, the ski run was obviously unprepared.

221. *Ski routes* have to be distinguished from ski runs. A ski route is characterized by a centre line marking but is not prepared. In this regard, the maintainer's obligation to secure the ski route is basically limited to closing it due to risk of avalanches.[240]

222. The legal basis for the obligation to secure the ski runs within the contract for transportation results in the fact that the *burden of proof* in regard to the actual fault according to § 1298 ABGB is *shifted* in a way so that the ski lift operator has

235. *See* OGH 5.6.2020 EvBl 2020/132 (*Brenn/Reheis*).

236. *Pichler/Holzer*, Skirecht 28; on the extent of the obligation to secure the ski runs on behalf of the ski maintainer beyond the edge of the actual prepared ski run OGH 7.2.2007, 2 Ob 284/06p; 6.5.2008 Zak 2008, 277; 22.6.2012, 1 Ob 110/12a.

237. OGH 20.12.2018 ZfG 2019, 59.

238. OGH 28.1.2021 ZVR 2021, 418 (*Pechtl*).

239. Cf. in this context also OGH 25.4.2018 Zak 2018, 238.

240. *Pichler/Holzer*, Skirecht 33.

to prove that he as well as his employees, who are *helpers* in accordance with § 1313a ABGB, have completely fulfilled the secondary obligation of securing the ski runs which is included in the contract for transportation, with the result that the ski lift operator is not at fault for any damage which the passengers have suffered in the course of using the ski runs.

223. In regard to content, the obligation to secure the ski runs entails the protection of the ski run users from 'atypical dangers'.[241] Jurisdiction defines the obligation to secure the ski runs as follows: 'As the skier is obliged to control his skiing by means of closely observing the ski run and keeping to a speed limit in regard to the condition of the ski run, the maintainer's obligation to secure the ski runs has to lead to appropriate protective measures where the skier might run into risks which are contrary to the character of the ski run and where obstructions or dangers occur which are difficult to recognise or may not be recognised at all, thus making a respective warning essential. Besides, the skier accepts obstacles and risks which result from the character of the ski run and has to manage them on his own. The obligation to secure the ski runs may not be exaggerated in any case.'[242] According to a new decision by the OGH,[243] the ski lift operator is not liable for an accident caused by a frozen surface that has formed overnight on a professionally prepared ski run. Therefore, the court negated an atypical danger in the present case.[244] Furthermore, jurisdiction[245] also comes to the conclusion that the maintainer is not obliged to ensure the safety of a closed ski run.

224. In this sense, the maintainer of the ski run has to mark the ski run in a manner which enables the user to recognize difficulties and prevents the user from getting lost in the cleared ski area. Artificial obstacles such as ski lift pillars have to be secured. In addition to that, natural sources of risk may require security measures if they are unusual. This aspect refers to ice crevices or steep descents. Furthermore, ski runs have to be closed in case of avalanche risk, fog and mist, snow storms or complete icing.

225. Regarding the creation of artificial obstacles, the OGH[246] recently expressed the following: If the maintainer of a ski run has established a catch fence at the edge of a bend, this shows that he had recognized an atypical danger in advance. However, the steel anchors of the fence construction should have been secured in a more appropriate way. So catch fences ought to be installed down to ground level to prevent slipping through.

---

241. Cf. *Pichler/Holzer*, Skirecht 34.
242. OGH 31.1.1985, 7 Ob 509/85 ao. In reference to carelessness of a skier as a result of catching an edge, e.g., OGH 29.3.2007, 3 Ob 6/07i.
243. OGH 20.5.2021, 3 Ob 12/21t.
244. Cf. in this sense according to driving on a black runway OGH 19.4.2017, 6 Ob 30/17f.
245. OGH 24.5.2018 ZfG 2018, 123.
246. OGH 14.9.2022, 6 Ob 64/22p.

226. Apart from this, the OGH[247] also stated that the maintainer of a fun park assumes special safety obligations. In the present case, the skier got injured by a collision with another athlete while he wanted to enter the public ski run from the wave way. Such tracks are normally equipped with obstacles that induce a special course movement. Based on this, the maintainer is obliged to spatially demarcate this area from the normal ski run in order to provide an appropriate falling space and to keep away other skiers. Accordingly, the court assessed the distance around 10m to the edge of the fun park area as sufficient to ensure a controlled landing of the athletes. In addition to that, the maintainer asked the users to drive slowly with signs, and there were unobstructed viewing conditions. [248]

2. Liability of Road and Path Maintainer

227. The second system of liability which is relevant within the obligation to secure ski runs – even to a lesser practical extent – is the liability of road maintenance according to § 1319a.[249] Basically, it is completely indisputable that ski runs are '*paths*' in the sense of § 1319a ABGB, and therefore they are included in this liability regulation if they are inappropriately maintained and serviced.

228. § 1319a ABGB limits the *tortuous liability* of the road maintainer to the road user for those damages which result from *gross negligence or intention in maintaining the road properly* by *him or* his *helpers*. However, this privileged treatment of the road maintainer is replaced by contractual liability for fault if the use of the road is based on a contract. § 1319a ABGB contains a significance of its own for the obligation to secure the ski runs for those ski run users who use the ski run beyond a contractual relationship with the maintainer. However, as has been shown above, the usual case presents the constellation of a transportation relationship between the ski run user and the ski run maintainer, and therefore the obligation to secure the ski run is included as a secondary obligation. The case that ski runs are used without a contractual relationship is rather rare, for example, when skiers partly use a ski run for the descent in the course of a ski tour.

B. Obligation to Secure the Cross-Country Ski Tracks

229. It is rather uncommon that users of cross-country ski tracks have to pay a fee for the usage. In this case, the contractual partner of the cross-country skier has to fulfil his *contractual obligation* to ensure the flawless condition of the ski track. The situation that a cable car operator maintains ski tracks and makes them available to the public is even less common because normally cross-country ski tracks

---

247. OGH 23.2.2021 ZVR 2021/208.
248. *See* thereon also *Knibbe*, Funparks (Snowparks), ZVR 2017, 400 and *Stabentheiner*, Pistensicherung und verwandte Fragenkreise – 35 Jahre Seilbahnsymposium, ZVR 2016, 217 (258).
249. Cf. in detail *Stabentheiner*, Die Haftung des Pistenhalters und vergleichbarer Sportanlagenbetreiber, ZVR 2017, 452.

are basically located in the valley area. However, in glacier areas, some summer cross-country ski tracks are maintained. In these cases, the cable car operator is liable for securing the cross-country ski tracks due to his secondary obligation resulting from the contract for transportation. In both cases mentioned above, liability is based on contractual principles for any kind of fault, for helpers according to § 1313a ABGB and by means of applying the principle of burden of proof of § 1298 ABGB, as it has been presented in detail above in regard to contractual obligation to secure the ski runs (cf. §4.III.A). Nevertheless, a contractual relationship in regard to using the cross-country ski track does not result from paying tourist tax or purchasing a general map of the cross-country ski tracks.[250]

230. If the user of the cross-country ski track does not have to pay a fee – which is still common – the applicable system of liability is the *liability of the road maintainer*. The significant deviation from contractual obligation to secure the cross-country ski tracks results from the limitation of liability to the qualified type of fault due to gross negligence and intent. Whereas in the case of a contractual relationship the person who is responsible for the condition of the cross-country ski track is liable for any degree of fault, he is not liable for minor fault in accordance with § 1319a ABGB (cf. also §4.III.A.2).

231. In regard to the *helpers' liability*, which is typically relevant for the obligation to secure the cross-country ski tracks, § 1319a ABGB determines that the maintainer is also liable for damage caused by his helpers if the *inappropriate condition* of the cross-country ski track has resulted from their *gross negligence or intent* (*see* already §4.III.A.2).

232. § 1319a Clause 1 Sentence 2 ABGB orders a complete *exemption from liability* for the case of so-called *real action on one's own risk*. Basically, this regulation states:

> If the damage is caused in the course of prohibited use of the road, especially against its allocated purpose, and if the fact that the user is not permitted to use the road is obvious by means of the type of path, respective prohibiting signs, fences or other barriers, the aggrieved party may not invoke the deficient condition of the path.

This exemption from liability in case of action at one's own risk – as defined in § 1319a Clause 1 Sentence 2 ABGB – is relevant in regard to the obligation to secure the cross-country tracks in particular if a cross-country skier uses a track which has been closed by the maintainer due to inusability.

233. The *content of the obligation to secure the cross-country tracks* may be outlined as follows: tracks have to be marked. What is essential is the fact that the direction of the course has to be clearly defined in order to avoid collisions. It is recommended to indicate levels of difficulty. Furthermore, similar to ski runs, tracks

---

250. On an accident at a crossroad OGH 23.3.1983 ZVR 1984/176; cf. also *Pichler/Holzer*, Skirecht 56.

have to be secured and if necessary have to be closed due to alpine dangers and risks such as avalanches or falling rocks. In addition to that, if a track is completely iced up, the track might be closed if it entails difficult descents. However, the self-reliance of the cross-country skier plays a more important role than self-reliance of the alpine skier in the parallel situation of the completely icy ski run. The cross-country skier is able to notice the icy track right from the very beginning, without putting himself in danger, provided that the track does not start with a descent. Nevertheless, cross-country skiers should at least be warned if the tracks are completely iced up.

234. If possible, crossroads with ski runs, lift tracks and roads should be avoided when creating a cross-country track or a ski trail because they comprise alarming safety hazards as the cross-country skier has to stop at each crossroad, which might be difficult according to the respective landscape formations. If crossroads cannot be avoided, the tracks and ski trails should best be designed with chicanes in order to make it easier for the skier to stop. Furthermore, the crossroads should be clearly marked and designed so that they do not contain a dangerous stop.[251]

C. Obligation to Secure Cycling Tracks

1. Contractual Liability

235. Recently, the OGH[252] was faced with a decision concerning the securing of a race track in the highest national class. In the present case, the association paid the entry fee for its athlete. Therefore, it has to be questioned whether the organizer has fulfilled its *contractual obligation* to ensure the flawless condition of the track. The accident was caused by a collision between the athlete and a car turning left. The competent authority has issued a general driving ban with exception for residents and instructed the organizer to take further appropriate measures. Nevertheless, no safety guard or sign was placed at the junction in question. Based on these facts, the court judged that the 'Kurvenschneiden' (driving at high speed on a bend of a small street) is a typical practice while cycling races. Because of that, the organizer was obliged to ensure that there is no oncoming traffic in the main field of the track where a larger group collides.

236. However, these considerations do not apply if no cycling race of the highest national class takes place and the cyclist is not moving within the main field, but in a smaller group with a maximum of five vehicles.[253]

---

251. In reference to a crossroad OGH 23.3.1983 ZVR 1984/176; in reference to a junction with a road OLG Innsbruck 25.10.2000 ZVR 2001/101.
252. Cf. OGH 6.8.2020 Zak 2020, 339.
253. *See* OGH 27.4.2006 ZVR 2006, 496 (*Kathrein/Hauenschild*).

2. Liability of Road Maintainer

237. Based on the fact that cycling tracks are often used by hobby sportsman, who do not pay any fee, the applicable system of liability can also be the *liability of the road maintainer*. In this context, a decision concerns an accident during the passage of an electronic cattle barrier, which was intended to separate a bicycle path from a cattle pasture. In the present case, the OGH[254] also dealt with the demarcation of the liability in accordance with § 1319 ABGB and the liability of a path maintainer in the sense of § 1319a ABGB. Accordingly, the court stated that § 1319a ABGB displaces as a special norm the stricter liability for buildings if the path maintainer operates at the same time as the owner of an existing building in the course of the road. Only if there is a special interest in the building, § 1319 ABGB is applied. In this case, the cattle barrier was not intended to prevent the use of the bicycle path, but to enable it. Therefore, the building serves the cycling traffic. In the absence of the qualification as an atypical source of risk, the liability of the maintainer in the sense of § 1319a ABGB was finally negated. Apart from this, jurisdiction[255] assessed an accident on a mountain bike track, which occurred by driving through a barrier chain to the entrance of a museum as the result of an action on one's own risk according to § 1319a Clause 1 Sentence 2 ABGB. The barrier chain was visible from a distance of 15m and the no driving sign from around 90m. Based on this, the OGH affirmed the application of the exemption of liability.

238. In this context, the court also negated the liability of a path maintainer if the sign indicating the bulge is visible from a distance of 32m.[256]

IV. Liability for Sports Equipment

239. On the one hand, the general fault-based liability (*see* §4.IV.A) is one of the bases of liability.[257] Apart from that, product liability is relevant (cf. §4.IV.B).

A. Liability Based on Fault

240. The importance of fault-based liability for faulty sports equipment which causes damage has practically disappeared since the implementation of the strict product liability. Even though compensation for damages was facilitated by jurisprudence as well as by jurisdiction as the contract between retailer and producer is now presented as a contract which gives rise to the protection of the purchaser, thus supporting the damaged person by means of helpers' liability under § 1313a ABGB and sharing the burden of proof in accordance with § 1298 ABGB, the producer was

254. OGH 28.9.2017 Zak 2017, 418; cf. also OGH 25.8.2016 Zak 2016, 418.
255. OGH 23.3.2022, 1 Ob 19/22h.
256. Cf. OGH 26.5.2021 Zak 2021, 258.
257. Cf. thereon *Kissich*, Defektes Sportgerät – Wer haftet? in *Hinteregger/Reissner* (ed.), Sport und Haftung (2006) 24.

still able to exclude his liability to the purchaser in his contract with the retailer. Liability for a manufacturing error without fault ('Ausreißerschäden' – outlier damages) was not considered at all. Therefore, it is clear that aggrieved consumers first and foremost refer to product liability discussed in §4.IV.B.

241. However, there is one constellation in which the fault-based liability still contains a high level of practical importance. The issue is damage due to *inappropriately adjusted ski bindings*. Retailers sometimes offer skis and ski binding apart from each other and without mounting the binding on the ski. As a consequence, the purchaser gets the binding mounted and adjusted by the retailer. Even if both ski and ski binding are purchased as a set, the retailer will normally be asked to adjust the binding. Such an agreement in regard to mounting and adjustment of the ski binding is not considered to be an independent agreement, but is viewed as a legal secondary obligation resulting from the sales contract. Therefore, due to this agreement in regard to purchase as well as mounting and adjustment of the ski binding the sales person is obliged to explain and instruct. Thus, for example, he has to inform the purchaser that the ski binding does not function properly if combined with a ski boot which has been provided by the purchaser himself.

242. If skis are borrowed or – more often – are rented by the skier, the lender or renter is obliged to correctly and properly adjust the ski binding as a secondary obligation of contract. Deficient and improper adjustment of the binding is considered a breach of contractual secondary obligations on behalf of the sports equipment retailer or ski lender or ski renter, whereas he has to prove – according to § 1298 ABGB – that he and his helpers are not at fault in regard to the improper adjustment.

243. However, the aggrieved party has to prove that the retailer has adjusted the binding the way it has been adjusted at the time of the accident.[258]

B. Product Liability

244. If a person sustains a damage due to *defective sports equipment*, the *manufacturer*, in case of a production outside of the European Economic Area (EEA), the *importer*, is strictly liable for this damage. Defects which justify liability are construction defects, manufacturing defects including 'outliers' and instruction errors. Liability for personal injury is present to the full extent; in the case of property damage, a deductible has to be paid.[259]

245. Deficient sports equipment is mainly affected by manufacturing defects. For example, fencing weapons, high jump stands, horizontal bars, etc., may break. Construction and instruction defects and errors may be especially relevant in regard

258. Cf. *Pichler/Holzer*, Skirecht 120.

259. More details in *Posch/Terlitza* in *Schwimann/Kodek* (ed.), Praxiskommentar zum ABGB VII^4 (2016) § 1 PHG Rz 12 ff.

to liability in the case of fitness devices. Jurisdiction viewed the missing warning label, which should inform the user that the combination of a specific underwear with a specific dry diving suit is dangerous, as an instruction error.[260]

246. One especially significant decision by the Supreme Court in regard to the given context refers to the liability of the manufacturer for the break of an especially light aluminium handlebar of a mountain bike.[261] This light-weight handlebar was – as it had to be expected in bike sport – immediately mounted on the competitive race bikes of the racing elite. The Supreme Court stated that the essential issue for liability according to the PHG are the expectations of product-specific users in regard to safety. If the manufacturer can anticipate that the racing elite might use the product for competitive purposes, he has to assume that his sports device is used under extremely harsh conditions. If the manufacturer is unable to produce the device for these purposes without any defects, he is obliged to warn the consumer of the open area of risk. This obligation to warning is only exempt if the risks which are connected to the product are obvious to the skilled and competent user. Detailed information about the used material (e.g., results of performance tests for an alloy) are not necessarily part of the natural knowledge of a professional athlete.

247. Apart from this, the OGH[262] recently stated regarding to *construction defects* that it is precisely not the state of the art for a ski binding to open every time a fall occurs. In principle, an opening could only be assumed in the case of a forward fall (body in the direction of the ski tip) and a lateral twisting fall. Moreover, the loosening of the binding in the event of a purely backward fall, as suffered by the plaintiff in the present case, is currently not even technically possible. With that in mind, justified safety expectations were not disappointed. On the other hand, there might be an instruction error. Here, however, it is clear that a corresponding warning notice was attached to the bond. In summary, the OGH denied a product liability.

V. Employers' Liability and Co-employees' Liability in Sport

248. In this context, the employers' liability privilege (cf. §4.V.A) on the one hand as well as the co-employees' liability privilege of social insurance (cf. §4.V.B) on the other hand have to be considered.

A. *Employers' Liability Privilege*

249. Basically, according to general principles of tort law, an association as a legal entity is liable for any tort on behalf of its organs, those in power as well as

260. OGH 30.3.2001 ZVR 2001/71.
261. OGH 28.4.1998 ecolex 1998, 834.
262. OGH 16.9.2021 Zak 2021, 379.

the provisional helpers. Furthermore, beyond that, the association is also liable to its contractual partners, especially to its members, for its agents, namely especially, the complete coaching team. However, this liability is only legal to its full extent at the amateur level.[263] Nevertheless, the situation is different when a professional athlete in team sport suffers physical injury or is killed during sports exercise; thus, the incident is classified as an occupational accident.

250. In the field of employers' liability, the legal position on claims for damages partially interferes with an insurance solution. The employers' liability privilege of § 333 ASVG *exempts employers* and persons of equal position or power such as *authorized representatives* and *supervisors in the operation from any liability* if they cause an *occupational accident or* an *occupational disease by mere negligence.* They are only strictly liable to the aggrieved party in case of intentional damage. Nevertheless, the aggrieved party has to account for the deductions of the social security body by means of adjustment of profit under § 333 Clause 2 ASVG.[264] The liability privilege is granted to the employer due to the fact that he alone pays the contributions for the statutory accident insurance. The principles of civil law define who is the legal or authorized representative of the employer. The supervisor in an operation is defined by the fact that he has a certain authority to issue directives and – connected to that – a certain liability to the other employees in the situation in which damage is caused.[265] In this context, the Supreme Court[266] recently denied the liability of a therapy leader in a rehabilitation facility for an accident during a fitness boxing session. The therapy leader tried to demonstrate self-defence techniques on the plaintiff, whereby he left the usual therapy plan. According to the OGH, the accident insurance also applies to medical rehabilitation. In regard to this, an accident during therapy can be summarized under the terms of occupational accidents. Based on the fact that the defendant operated as the leader of the present exercise session and therefore as a supervisor, the court affirmed the application of § 333 ASVG and dismissed the claim of the casualty. In contrast to that, the OGH[267] stated in another decision in accordance with § 333 Abs 3 ASVG that the privilege is not applied if the occupational accident was caused *by means of transport*, which are subject to increased liability. This includes aircraft, such as hot-air balloons. However, the basic prerequisite thereby is the existence of a liability insurance sum.

251. In addition to the assessment of the employer, the OGH[268] recently referred to the classification of covered employees. Thereby, the court stated that § 333 ASVG is also applied if a person is incorporated into the operation like an employee. Based on this, a touring instructor in training, who got injured because

263. Cf. OGH 23.9.2004 SpuRt 2005, 106.
264. Thereon *Koziol*, Haftpflichtrecht I^{4} Rz 1/20 ff.; *Krejci/Böhler* in *Tomandl* (ed.), System des österreichischen Sozialversicherungsrechts (loose-leaf, 37th supplement) 3.3.; *Auer-Mayer/Pfeil*, Österreichisches Sozialrecht^{13} (2021) 89 ff; *Tomandl*, Grundriss des österreichischen Sozialrechts^{7} (2019) 208 ff.
265. *Krejci* in *Tomandl*, System 3.3.2.2.3 (loose-leaf, 35th supplement).
266. OGH 14.12.2021 ARD 6791/8/2022 with further references.
267. OGH 17.12.2018 ZVR 2019, 253 (*Huber*).
268. Cf. OGH 29.6.2020 ARD 6751/11/2021.

of the disregard of the safety instructions during a client's fall, is covered by the provision. In summary, the employer liability privilege of a professional tour guide towards his companion in training is applied. After all, according to mere negligence liability was denied.

252. However, in case of *intention* or *gross negligence*, the *employer and the persons representing him* have to *bear* the *refund of the costs* which have to be supplied by the *social insurance body* for the given insurance case in accordance with § 334. This is not a claim which is derived from the compensation claim of the aggrieved party but a specific claim of the social security institution. However, the social security institution may partially or completely renounce the compensation according to § 334 Clause 5 ASVG if it is justified by the financial and economic situation of the person who is liable to pay compensation.

253. Concerning sport, this legal situation is gaining importance in professional team sports as the active athletes are employees covered by compulsory insurance in the statutory accident insurance, and therefore accidents in the course of training and competition are qualified as occupational accidents. If an employed athlete has such an accident, and if the association, thus, its organ is at fault, because the condition of the sports facility is deficient or because an advertisement band has been improperly set up, the association is only liable to the athlete in case of intentional damage.[269] If the association cannot be accused of gross negligence – in this case, it would be obliged to refund the costs of the accident insurance – the association is not liable at all. This aspect is not only valid for cases where the statutory organs of the association are at fault but also for cases in which coaches and assistant coaches are at fault because they are included in the liability privilege as supervisors in the operation.[270] They are also exempt from any liability if they, for example, overstrain the athlete, thereby acting in slight negligence, and are responsible for an injury which the athlete suffers in the course of the training session as a result of this overstrain.

B. Co-employees' Liability Privilege

254. The social insurance institution which is under obligation to pay in case of a sports accident may seek recourse on behalf of an injuring party. This procedure is an option to seek recourse from an injuring party beyond the employers' liability by means of *legal cession* under § 332 ASVG. Basically, the legal cession *transfers* the *casualty's rights to compensation from the injuring party to the social security institution* if the injuring party is under obligation to pay.[271]

269. In reference to an advertising band OGH 26.8.2004, 6 Ob 11/04 t.
270. Cf. *Neumayr/Huber* in *Schwimann/Kodek* (ed.), Praxiskommentar zum ABGB VII^4 (2016) § 333 ASVG Rz 62 ff.
271. Cf. *Krejci/Böhler* in *Tomandl*, System 3.2 (loose-leaf, 35th supplement).

255. However, limitations to recourse are imposed on the social insurance body as the legal cessionary. The most important case in this given context is the *co-employees' exclusion of recourse*. This exclusion is structured in a way that there is *no legal claim to recourse against a co-worker* who is employed in the same operation and who has merely acted *slightly negligent* under § 332 Clause 5 ASVG.[272] This issue results in the fact that the injuring party, the co-worker who has merely acted out of slight negligence, is not liable for an injury of his co-worker as the compensation payments are supplied by the social insurance body. However, there is no payment supplied by the social insurance body which may equate with *compensation for pain and suffering* in accordance with § 1325 ABGB; therefore, the co-worker is *still liable* to the casualty in this aspect.

256. The legal situation is applied in sports – especially in professional team sports – when a player culpably causes damage to a teammate by merely acting under slight negligence – no matter whether this incident occurs during a game or during a training session.

VI. Doping and Tort

257. In connection with doping, two constellations are relevant in regard to tort law: on the one hand, athletes may be doped without their consent by responsible persons in the association; on the other hand, they may be doped in agreement between athlete and association.

258. If an athlete is *doped by responsible persons in the association without his consent*, this issue – when leading to respective health damage or even death – may even result in the offence of physical assault or homicide under criminal law (cf. Part IV, §3.I). In regard to the offence of physical damage under civil law, the respective tort consequences under § 1325 ABGB are applied, basically liability for medical expenses, if necessary loss of earnings and compensation for pain and suffering. The fact that in this given case the employer or a person who is connected to him has caused the physical damage may be disregarded – on the one hand, because they may often be accused of dolus eventualis, and on the other hand, because health impairments due to doping cannot really be summarized under the terms of occupational accidents or occupational diseases. Basically, the employers' liability privilege of § 333 ASVG does not apply in case of intentional assault and is only relevant for occupational accidents and occupational diseases which are caused by the employer.

---

272. OGH 3.4.1973 ZAS 1977, 21; *Koziol*, Haftpflichtrecht II^3 216 ff; *Krejci/Böhler* in *Tomandl*, System 3.2.2.6 (loose-leaf, 37th supplement); *Barta/Eccher*, Einige Fragen der Arbeitskollegenhaftung, ZAS 1977, 8; *Grillberger*, Die Haftung bei Arbeitsunfällen unter Arbeitskollegen, DRdA 1974, 256.

259. It has to be questioned whether the *consent of the doped athlete* to the doping procedure may justify the act on behalf of the responsible person in the association. The consent of an aggrieved party to an assault (but not to homicide) only excludes the illegal nature of the infringement in accordance with § 90 Clause 1 StGB when the infringement is not *contra bonos mores*.[273] Both the objectionable and the dangerous nature of doping are normally obvious. Therefore, the consent of the doped athlete cannot be used as a justification. Nevertheless, the consent might be viewed as contributory negligence as provided for in § 1304 ABGB.[274]Apart from this, it has to be questioned whether the doped athlete can also be liable. In this context, the OGH comes now to the conclusion that self-doping constitutes a fraud according to §§ 146 f StGB by the doped athlete (cf. in detail Part IV, §3.II). This justifies the illegality. Thereby, a damage in terms of sponsorship money, paid accommodation costs and expenses for skiing equipment can be assumed on behalf of the organizer.[275] In contrast to that, literature basically denies the occurrence of a damage regarding the payment of a victory bonus. The donor would have paid out the bonus anyway, albeit to a different athlete.[276]

VII. Strict Liability in Sport

260. In connection with alpine ski sport, liability of cable cars (*see* §4.VII.A) is particularly important in practical terms. In addition to that, the relevance of regulations on strict liability for the areas of motorsport and air sport will be discussed (cf. §4.VII.B).

A. *Liability of Ski Lift Operators*

261. Here, it has to be differentiated between large systems (cf. §4.VII.A.1), tow lifts (§4.VII.A.2), and slope maintenance vehicles (§4.VII.A.3).

1. Cable Cars and Chairlifts

262. Cable cars and chairlifts are *railways*. Thus, liability for accidents during the operation of these ropeways is regulated in the *EKHG*.[277] Therefore, the operator of a cable car is subject to strict liability. Basically, the operator of a cable car

---

273. Cf. *Markowetz*, Haftungsrechtliche Ansprüche im Zusammenhang mit Doping, ÖJZ 2004, 407.
274. *Holzer/Fritzweiler*, Auswirkungen von Dopingverstößen auf Arbeits-, Lizenz- und Sponsorenverträge, in *Fritzweiler* (ed.), Doping – Sanktionen, Beweise, Ansprüche (2000) 59; cf. also *Hajszan*, Arbeitsverträge, Sponsoring und Doping: Strafbarer Betrug?, JBl 2022, 273.
275. OGH 23.12.2020 ZWF 2021, 259 (*Boyer*).
276. Cf. *Pirnat*, Zum Sportbetrug, JSt 2010, 165 (166 f); *Markowetz*, Strafrechtliche Probleme des Dopings, JBl 2004, 409 (418 ff).
277. Cf. thereon *Pirker*, Schi- und Snowboardunfälle – Haftung von Wintersportzentren und Sportlern, in *Hinteregger/Reissner* (ed.), Sport und Haftung (2006) 114.

is also liable for damages resulting from operating accidents when neither he nor his operating helpers are at fault. The cases which contain the highest risk factors are cases in which persons enter or exit the lift facilities. The OGH, which generally defines accidents which happen during entrance or exit of a train as accidents during the operation of a train, also views respective cases for cable cars in the very same context.[278] However, the operator of the cable car is *exempt from liability* if the accident exclusively results from the faulty or clumsy behaviour of the transported skier – this case is normally viewed under the circumstance of an *unavoidable incident* in the sense of § 9 Clause 2 EKHG.[279] According to this, jurisdiction recently negated the liability of a chairlift operator. In the following case, the OGH[280] was faced with a crash out of a chairlift seat at the entry point. Due to a child going with, the lift had to stop gently in the station area, when the safety bars were still opened. The court assumed an *unavoidable incident* and therefore affirmed the exemption from liability. Contrary to that, the Supreme Court[281] denied the application of § 9 Clause 2 EKHG because of non-compliance with the utmost care possible under the circumstances of the individual case. In the present case, the defendant lift operator had invited a special school class to his skiing area. Out of inexplicable reasons, a mentally disabled pupil remained seated on the chairlift. While trying to pull her out of the lift, the teacher got injured. Thereby, the OGH stated that the operator had been obliged to slow down the lift to fulfil higher due diligence standards because of inviting a special school class.

263. Nevertheless, if the accident is based on *extraordinary operating risk*, the exemption from liability due to an unavoidable incident under § 9 Clause 2 last Subset EKHG is severely limited. For example, if the user of a chairlift starts swinging with the chair and thus causes the rope to jump the rails, and subsequently other passengers are injured, the chairlift operator is liable to these passengers due to exceptional operating risk caused by a non-operating third party.[282] Apart from this, the OGH[283] acknowledges the liability when the plaintiff gets directly pulled out of the double chairlift travelling through the station at undiminished speed because of the negligence of a fallen fellow user. In this given case, the court assumed an *extraordinary operating risk* caused by another lift user.

264. It may be difficult to evaluate case constellations in which the precipitating incident for exceptional operating dangers (e.g., ruptured cable or rope, jumping cable or rope, broken pillar, crash of a cable car) might occur by vis major such as lightning, strong and sudden wind, mudslide or avalanche. In these cases, the liability of the operator has to be questioned as § 9 Clause 2 EKHG explicitly states liability due to exceptional operating dangers only if the damage is caused by the

---

278. OGH 30.9.1982 ZVR 1983/128; 16.12.1982 JBl 1993, 660; 25.8.1987 ZVR 1988/112; 29.12.1993 ZVR 1995/30; 18.1.2007 Zak 2007, 118; 24.4.2020 Zak 2020, 278.
279. Cf. OGH 14.10.1980 ZVR 1981/172; 30.9.1982, 8 Ob 170/82.
280. OGH 24.4.2020 Zak 2020, 278.
281. *See* OGH 23.2.2017 Zak 2017, 99; cf. with reference to the fall of a skier at the entry conveyor of a cable car OGH 25.5.2016 Zak 2016, 239.
282. *Pichler/Holzer*, Skirecht 80.
283. OGH 18.1.2007 Zak 2007, 118.

aggrieved party, an animal or a third party not participating in the operation. *Klug*[284] has negated the question of liability on the grounds of the draft law. Contrary to that, *Koziol*[285] is of the opinion that the damage still ought to be ascribed to the maintainer and not the aggrieved party if the accident was caused by an incident beyond the maintainer's influence but was accompanied by exceptional operating risk. This principle has been acknowledged by judicature as well.[286] The only exception which may be made is related to the fact that the aggrieved party itself has caused the exceptional operating risk due to its behaviour. In this given case, the aggrieved party has to cover the damage itself, and the maintainer is not liable. Therefore, in the presented cases, liability of the operator is assumed. However, the preliminary aspect of the exceptional operating risk being caused by vis major – and subsequently causing damage – is essential.[287] Liability for a direct damage by vis major is in no case included.[288]

265. Carelessness on behalf of the aggrieved party has to be considered as a diminishing aspect within the field of strict liability as well (§ 7 Clause 1 EKHG in connection with § 1304 ABGB). Within strict liability the issue is actually slightly more difficult because the carelessness of the injured party has to be put in relation to the operating risk of the ski lift operation. However, negligence on behalf of the injured is not relevant if the behaviour of the aggrieved party is considered an inevitable event. Thus, in the following case, the court decided in favour of exemption from liability on behalf of the lift operator: a passenger had fallen off the chair when the double chairlift stopped because he had opened the safety bar beforehand. The preliminary opening of the safety bar by the passenger was assessed as an inevitable event for the operator which excludes the operator's obligation to compensation in accordance with § 9 Clause 2 EKHG.[289] In another case, the OGH[290] decided that a passenger, who was stuck on a defective chairlift, who finally jumped off the chair and subsequently was injured, is not subject to the issue of carelessness – on the contrary, the operator is liable to damage because operating staff had not effectively informed the passengers of the ongoing rescue operation and had not warned passengers about the dangers of jumping off the lift.

266. However, if the prerequisites for inevitable events are absent jurisdiction and jurisprudence normally assume a ratio of 1:1 between usual operation risk and slight negligence on behalf of the aggrieved party.

---

284. Die Haftungsbefreiungsgründe des § 9 EKHG, ÖJZ 1965, 229 (230).
285. Haftpflichtrecht III: Gefährdungs-, Produkt- und Eingriffshaftung[3] (2014) 105 f; in accordance *Pichler/Holzer*, Skirecht 81; *Schauer* in *Schwimann/Kodek* (ed.), Praxiskommentar zum ABGB VII[4] (2016) § 9 EKHG Rz 41 ff.
286. OGH 30.3.1978 SZ 51/36; 20.4.1982 ZVR 1983/318.
287. Cf. especially also *Pichler*, Zur Haftung bei Schleppliftunfällen, DRdA 1978, 21; OGH 12.5.1977, 2 Ob 88/77; 12.10.1995, 2 Ob 1142/95.
288. *Pichler/Holzer*, Skirecht 81; *Schauer* in *Schwimann/Kodek* VII[4] § 9 EKHG Rz 8.
289. OGH 14.10.1980 ZVR 1981/172.
290. OGH 1.7.1965 SZ 88/112.

2. Tow Lifts

267. Due to a special regulation of the 1970s in which the tow lifts were included in the *EKHG liability*, they are now almost completely equal to the other ski lift facilities. Therefore, the comments in §4.VII.A.1 may well be applied without restriction to the liability issue of tow lift operators. However, within the liability in accordance with EKHG, a specific aspect arises, namely the fact that liability is *not* referred to the *condition of the lift track*; thus, here the issue of fault-based liability remains present (§ 9a EKHG). Within the scope of *fault-based liability* of the tow lift operator, the peculiarities of transportation by means of tow lifts have to be considered. The tow lift contract is basically a specific contract for transportation. Successful transportation does not only rely on the proper service of the operating staff and the proper operation of the transportation facility; therefore, it does not only depend on the services of the lift operator but is also – to an important extent – dependent on the cooperation and sportive skills of the skier who is transported.[291] Nevertheless, the passenger on the lift is by no means 'active in the operation' in the sense of § 3 Z 3 EKHG; thus, provisions in terms of exemption from strict liability are inapplicable.[292]

268. According to § 9 Clause 2 EKHG, an *incident or event* is considered to be *inevitable* and the *obligation to compensation is excluded* when the incident is caused by the behaviour of an animal or by a third party which is not active in the operation. An incident is also viewed as inevitable if it is related to the behaviour of the aggrieved party. In the case of tow lifts, such a behaviour of the aggrieved party may be a fall if the fall results neither from defective condition of the lift facility nor failure in the operation of the lift facility. The most common causes for falls on the tow lift are lack of skills and lack of concentration on behalf of the skiers, thus assigning serious practical significance to these reasons for liability exemption.[293] In this context, the Supreme Court[294] recently denied the existence of an inevitable event because of an *extraordinary operating risk* in the exit area of a tow lift. In the given case, the skier got caught in the lift with his jacket – therefore he was not able to leave the lift. The lift attendant noticed this at the halfway of the exit area. So, the skier was pulled along for about 10m and when the tow lift stopped, the ski hanger loosened and the skier fell into the embankment. As already stated in another decision[295] with reference to a wooden construction at the end of the exit area, the OGH affirmed the liability of the tow lift operator due to the lack of undertaking protective measures in order to fulfil the utmost care possible under the circumstances of the individual case. This is especially based on the fact that the exit area is only 10m long. Consequently, the attendant would have to become aware of the issue immediately in order to prevent the accident.

---

291. *Pichler/Holzer*, Skirecht 92.
292. *Pichler/Holzer*, Skirecht 101; *Schauer* in *Schwimann/Kodek* VII^4 § 3 EKHG Rz 16; *Apathy*, EKHG § 3 Rz 12; differentiating *Koziol*, Haftpflichtrecht III^3 53 ff.
293. *Pichler/Holzer*, Skirecht 105.
294. OGH 22.3.2018 Zak 2018, 178.
295. *See also* OGH 14.2.2008 ZVR 2008, 423 (*Kathrein*).

269. If the accident is directly related to exceptional operating risk due to the behaviour of a third party not actively participating in the operation or to the behaviour of an animal, the facility operator is liable to damage regardless of the incident being inevitable or not. The fact that exceptional operating dangers may also be caused by vis major has already been discussed in §4.VII.A.1. It is of the highest practical significance that the fall of a passenger, his lying in the track or even sliding down the track has to be qualified as an exceptional operating risk, due to the fact that the lift track basically has to be free of obstacles in order to provide normal transportation and enable the skiers to glide on the track. Due to the specific means of transportation, the passengers are to a large extent bound to the track, can only avoid a collision to a limited extent, cannot shut down the lift by themselves, and normally cannot get off the lift on the track without putting themselves at risk.[296]

270. In regard to self-reliance of the tow lift passenger, basically the comments on cable cars and chairlifts may be taken into account. However, it has to be considered that the cooperation of the passenger is even more important for tow lift transportation than in regard to other lift facilities. Therefore, the issue of *carelessness* has to be raised more often.[297]

3. Slope Maintenance Vehicles

271. Slope maintenance vehicles present a specific safety hazard for skiers and other users of ski runs. They are dangerous obstacles on overcrowded ski runs. Severe accidents between skiers and tracked vehicles on ski runs have already happened several times. How should these accidents be legally evaluated? Starting point for an assessment is the fact that slope maintenance vehicles are *no motor vehicles* in the sense of the KFG. Basically, according to § 1 Clause 1 KFG, a vehicle is defined by its allocated use on the road or by its actual use on the road, by the fact that it is operated by means of technically generated power and that it is not connected to rails. Consequently, the relation of a motor vehicle to a road as the respective traffic surface is essential for the application of the KFG. As such a relation between slope and cross-country track maintenance vehicles on the one hand and the road on the other hand is absent, these vehicles are not subject to the general regulations of this law. Nevertheless, the EKHG can only be applied to accidents in the course of operating the motor vehicle. Due to the fact that slope maintenance vehicles are not considered motor vehicles in the sense of KFG, the liability provisions of the EKHG also do not apply immediately.[298]

296. OGH 12.5.1987 RZ 1987/65; *Pichler/Holzer*, Skirecht 107; *Schauer* in *Schwimann/Kodek* VII[4] § 9a EKHG Rz 1 ff.
297. Cf., for example, OGH 6.10.1983 ZVR 1984/320.
298. *Pichler/Holzer*, Skirecht 63.

272. According to both jurisprudence and jurisdiction, *strict liability for damages resulting from dangerous operations* is assumed *in analogy to liability provisions.*[299] The extended liability of the operator which has been specifically stated for individual cases by legislature in regard to particular operating dangers basically has to be applied to any dangerous operating body. The reason for extended liability on behalf of the operator presents in the fact that in these operations the operator is entitled to take actions which ought to be prohibited if the legal system were to observe only the compromised interests of third parties. Therefore, the analogous application of strict liability for motor vehicles on ski runs is still widely accepted in jurisprudence,[300] but after a number of indecisive statements,[301] it has been rejected in a recent decision.[302]

273. So, jurisdiction applies the concept of *fault-based liability* according to accidents caused by slop maintenance vehicles. Basically, such vehicles may only be used in exceptional cases during slope operation. Then, according to the OGH,[303] the maintainer is obliged to warn approaching skiers, for example, by placing a piste post or a short-term barrier.

B. Motor and Air Sports

274. In regard to *air sports*, strict liability according to Austrian Aviation Act (LFG) is applied in favour of persons and objects which are not being transported. This aspect is especially relevant for damages which are inflicted on spectators at aviation events. They are definitely entitled to compensation for damages by the maintainer of the aircraft without consideration of the pilot's fault – however, liability is limited to a maximum amount of damage as in any kind of strict liability regulation.

275. In *motorsport,* strict liability is widely applied according to the EKHG. According to this law, the maintainer of a vehicle is liable without fault to damages which he causes by 'operating' the vehicle. The *vehicle holder* is the person who *operates the vehicle at his own costs and at his own risk.* The circumstance that the organizer of a race event is not the owner or keeper of the vehicles which are participating in the event has been discussed before. Motor vehicles in the sense of the EKHG are – according to a reference to the KFG – vehicles which are allocated to

---

299. *Koziol*, Haftpflichtrecht I^4 218 und III^3 371 ff; *the same*, Umfassende Gefährdungshaftung durch Analogie?, in FS Wilburg (1975) 173; *Posch*, Zum Stand der Reform der Gefährdungshaftung, in Assistenten-FS Wilburg (1975) 165; OGH 28.3.1973 JBl 1974, 199 ao.

300. *Pichler/Holzer*, Skirecht 64; *Rabofsky*, Rechtsfragen aus der Verwendung von Motorfahrzeugen im Skigelände, Mitteilungsblatt des ÖISS 1971, H 3, 61; *Reindl*, Die zivilrechtliche Haftung bei Unfällen mit Pistengeräten, ZVR 1999/195; *Schauer* in *Schwimann/Kodek* VII^4 § 2 EKHG Rz 15 f; *Pirker* in *Hinteregger/Reissner*, Haftung 118.

301. OGH 25.6.1986, 1 Ob 582/86; 17.12.1996 ZVR 1997/65; OLG Innsbruck 2.7.1984 ZVR 1985/157.

302. OGH 15.9.2004 ARD 5574/12/2005.

303. *See* thereon OGH 17.12.2018 Zak 2019, 78 with further references.

be used on roads or are used on roads, which are operated by technically generated power and are not connected to rails. Thus, the *EKHG* doubtlessly ought to be applied to *motorbikes* or *cars* which are used in *road races*.

276. However, the question remains whether it should be applied to those racing vehicles which are a priori not supposed to be used on roads but are exclusively used and operated on *specific race tracks*, such as go-karts, monoposto bolides, etc. Basically, to a great extent jurisdiction *affirms* this view,[304] also for the case that the motor vehicle is not authorized to use the roads at all.[305]

277. Main beneficiaries of this strict liability – which is again subject to limitation of maximum amounts for damage – are primarily the spectators of race events.[306] Nevertheless, liability is excluded in the case of so-called inevitable events. Such an event would especially concern incidents which result from the aggrieved party's behaviour, if under the given circumstances respective considerable and essential measures in regard to diligence and care have been undertaken in the operation of the motor vehicle (§ 9 Clause 2 EKHG). Such an incident may be assumed if, for example, a spectator of a rally event leaves the safety area, enters the race track and is run over. Persons who are involved in the operation of the motor vehicle are not protected by strict liability (§ 3 Z 3 EKHG). This aspect may be particularly relevant for co-pilots of car rallies because a co-pilot may not be equated with any other passenger at all. The control over the operating risk of rally cars is significantly influenced by its directive. If a co-pilot is injured due to his own mistake, strict liability is normally not applicable to him.[307]

278. The EKHG is not applied to *motor boats*. The Supreme Court has rejected an analogous application for this case.[308]

304. In reference to a killed track marshal OGH 16.4.1985 SZ 58/55 = ZVR 1986/6.
305. In reference to an accident at motocross OGH 26.2.1992 ZVR 1992/101; 18.12.2020, 2 Ob 181/20m.
306. In reference to the Alpl mountain course race OGH 10.4.1997 JBl 1997, 734 (*Apathy*).
307. Cf. thereon especially *Schauer* in *Schwimann/Kodek* VII^4 § 3 EKHG Rz 14 ff.
308. OGH 19.6.1985 ZVR 1986/59.

Chapter 2. Private Regulation

§1. Legal Basis for the Use of Private Land for Sports Exercise

I. Introduction

279. Due to the ever increasing significance of mass sport, more and more areas are required for sport. In Austria, the legal problems involved are mainly discussed in reference to the example of skiing (alpine skiing, cross-country skiing) – in the following, the focus will lie on skiing – however, the results may well be applied to other types of sport (e.g., mountain biking, golf, football). It does not have to be emphasized explicitly that each property owner is naturally free to use his property for the purpose of exercising sport. Thus, the following chapter will focus on the legal aspects which allow the utilization of someone else's property for sports.

II. Existence of Servitude

280. Such a servitude can be granted by means of contract (cf. §5.II.A) or may be means of acquisitive prescription (cf. §5.II.B).

A. Granted by Contract

281. In the case of ski slopes and cross-country skiing trails, servitudes may be regular as well as irregular.

282. A *regular servitude* may be relevant if a cable car company owns a respective neighbouring property, and the servitude of the ski slope may be registered for its own benefit.

283. An *irregular servitude* may be granted in favour of certain entities (ski lift companies, tourist offices or communities).

284. Servitudes may not be *extended by one party* and may not be expanded beyond the limit which has been drawn by the legal title. Viewed in this light, the acquisition of snow cannons or additional preparation of cross-country trails for skaters might be an illegal expansion of servitude.[309] In regard to this, the OGH[310] also stated that a cycle path servitude granted by contract does not cover the use of mountain carts.

309. Cf. *Vogl*, Rechtsprobleme des Kunstschnees (Teil II) Privatrechtliche Gesichtspunkte der technischen Beschneiung, RdU 2019, 17.
310. *See* OGH 13.1.2018 Zak 2018, 92.

B. Acquisitive Prescription

285. Property rights cannot only be acquired by means of normal and appropriate contract and registration in the land register but also by means of acquisitive prescription.

286. In the early times of skiing, most of the farmers and foresters did not oppose to skiing on their property as there was no measurable adverse effect whatsoever on the use of their land. Thus, each village had its own ski and sledding hills. Subsequently, communities as well as ski lift operations instrumented this fact and claimed that the servitude of these properties was acquired by means of *acquisitive prescription* in favour of the general public, thus trying to assert the *utilization* of the property for skiing *without compensation*. This approach was successful in a number of cases due to the rather generous attitude of the Supreme Court.[311] However, later on the criticism of jurisprudence[312] in this regard was taken into account and jurisdiction which had favoured acquisitive prescription was revised.[313] Now, it is certain that the development towards mass sport also has to be viewed as an expansion of servitude, just as much as the transition to mechanical slope preparation. However, hiking trails may still be used by an alpine association by means of acquisitive prescription. Thereby, it is essential that alpine association clearly demonstrate their will to possess, for example, by maintaining and marking the hiking trails.[314] Such entitled utilization of an alpine association can besides this also be considered in regard to ascending and descending mountains with touring skis in favour of the general public.[315] Apart from this, the OGH[316] repeatedly states that communities may also acquire such servitudes by means of acquisitive prescription. The court[317] followed up on this opinion in another, more recent decision regarding a hiking trail. Moreover, it has been supplemented in the present case that a chain stretched across the trail does not trigger a freedom acquisitive prescription according to § 1488 ABGB if it can be easily climbed over or passed sideways by the hikers.

III. Precarium ('Bittleihe')

287. One possibility of making one's own property for skiing available to interested third parties is the so-called Bittleihe or precarium. Nevertheless, this concept is only relevant in practice in connection with the use of private roads and paths for

311. OGH 19.4.1961 JBl 1962, 148; 12.11.1968 JBl 1969, 606.
312. Cf. *Mayer-Maly*, Die Skiabfahrt als Rechtsproblem, Stb 1970/9.
313. Cf. OGH 25.4.1978 JBl 1979, 429.
314. OGH 4.5.2004 RZ 2004, 228; 29.4.2015 Zak 2015, 213.
315. *See* in detail to the prerequisites regarding the acquisitive prescription of alpine association *Wagner/ Ecker*, Tourengehen auf Skipisten – Eine rechtliche Analyse zur Entgelterhebung für Naturkonsum, RdU 2018, 225; *see also Ringhof*, Wegerecht und Bergsport (2015) 131.
316. Regarding a lake promenade OGH 17.10.2018 EvBl-LS 2019/53 (*Weixelbraun-Mohr*) with further references.
317. Cf. OGH 21.10.2021 Zak 2022, 34.

cross-country skiing purposes. Actually, in regard to alpine skiing, the interests of the property owner are affected to such a great extent that the proprietor will only rarely agree to a precarium. In addition to that, especially cable car operations are normally not served well with a *precarium* of property as the proprietor still has the right of *revocation at any time*, and the cable car operating body has to make substantial investments in the long run (ski lifts, cable cars, etc.).

288. If property is made available by means of precarium or 'Bittleihe', this cannot lead to acquisition by prescription (§ 1464 ABGB).

IV. 'Bestandvertrag': Lease Contract

289. The cession of property against payment may also be realized by means of rental and lease contracts. As the property is normally let merely for usage and not for the agricultural use of the land, the type of agreement is a *property rent* and not a lease contract.

290. The essential issue for the parties concerned is the question of whether such a property rent is subject to the *protection for tenants against cancellation under the MRG.* According to § 1 Clause 1 MRG, this law has to be applied to 'business spaces of any kind' (e.g., premises, warehouses or depots, working areas) including building spaces and areas which have been rented as part of the business space (e.g., gardens, storage space, parking and loading spaces). Consequently, a property rent – the so-called *rent for area* – is only protected if the property has been 'co-rented' with a business space. The *mere rent for area* is therefore *not* covered by the *MRG.*

291. It has to be considered that besides the MRG, the *Sports Facilities Protection Act 1990* ('lex Flugplatz Trausdorf') can offer special protection from termination for sports facilities which are not regarded as 'business spaces'.[318] This law is applied to rental contracts for areas which have been let by regional authorities before the year 1986 to charitable persons for the general purpose of sports exercise; rental property which serves alpine skiing or cross-country skiing is exempt.[319] Besides football fields and the like, this law might also include, for example, areas which are used for air sport, golf sport, motorsport, or trotting sport. However, it has to be examined for each case whether the exercise of the respective sport is actually in the interest of the general public. Based on this, the OGH[320] assessed a sport facility for clay pigeon shooting as covered by the scope of application if the membership of the association is not closed and the practice of the shooting sport is possible for everyone.[321]

---

318. Cf. *Grassl-Palten*, Das neue Sportstättenschutzgesetz, WoBl 1990, 113; *Madl*, Einige Anmerkungen zum Sportstättenschutzgesetz, ecolex 1990, 538; OGH 7.5.1992 WoBl 1992, 185 (*Würth*).
319. Cf. *Kulhanek* in GeKo Wohnrecht I § 1 SpSchG (Stand 1.10.2017, rdb.at).
320. OGH 27.4.2005 ecolex 2005, 842.
321. Opposing this in regard to a golf course OGH 15.2.2000 WoBl 2001/14.

V. 'Wegefreiheit': The Right of Way

292. The question if and to which extent a person is allowed to move about in the open landscape without restrictions contains three different facets from the legal point of view. The right of way is naturally relevant for public roads (cf. §5.V.A), to a certain extent it is also important for forests in accordance with the ForstG (cf. §5.V.B), and finally, it may also be applied to non-productive, barren mountain areas on the basis of various state laws (cf. §5.V.C). Furthermore, recently it has been discussed in detail whether and to which extent air sports (cf. §5.V.D) and water sports (cf. §5.V.E) can be practised at the individual's liberty.

A. *Public Roads and Trails*

293. In general, this category entails roads and paths or trails which are *in parts* – namely the surface of the road, the bike path, but not the ditch or the side of the road – *used by the general public*. In regard to this aspect, the ownership structures are secondary, a property which is owned by a private person may also be a public road.[322] Public roads (public paths or trails) are *contrary* to the *private road* (*private path or trail*). Private roads are respective areas which are not used by the public.

294. Public roads may be *used* by *anybody* as allocated and in accordance with the stipulation of police regulations regarding roads and vehicles (*see* below). There may be roads and paths or trails which might be allocated to, for example, cycling; others might be closed to cyclists. Depending on these guidelines, mountain biking, for example, may be permitted or not.

295. According to § 64 Clause 1 StVO *sports events on roads* have to be approved of by the respective authority.[323] The authorization may only be issued if the event does not considerably affect safety or the easy and effective flow of traffic, and if no harmful effects on the public or the environment may be expected due to noise, smell or pollutants. Conditions may be linked to the authorization if required in order to protect the public and environment or ensure safety and effective and easy flow of traffic. In particular, it may be prescribed that the organizer of the event as well as the individual participants have to take out a legal liability insurance for damage to persons and property with an Austrian insurance company – the authority will determine the appropriate amount of the sums insured. As already discussed (cf. §4.II.B.1), the organizer may be obliged to take further appropriate measures to fulfil his contractual safety obligations. However, during a cycling race, the organizer cannot count on compliance with the StVO by the participants.[324] If it is required by traffic safety and if traffic situation allows it, a road may be completely

322. Basically *Merli*, Öffentliche Nutzungsrechte und Gemeingebrauch (1995) 188 ff.
323. *See* in general *Nußbaumer*, Zur Genehmigung von sportlichen Veranstaltungen auf Straßen, ZVR 2015, 153.
324. Thereon recently with regard to a cycling race OGH 6.8.2020 Zak 2020, 339.

or partially closed to traffic by the respective authority for the duration of a sports event. In such a case, the authority may permit exceptions to driving rules if no concerns regarding traffic safety are present.

296. According to § 87 Clause 1 StVO, the *exercise of winter sports* on roads within the area of a city, town or village, on federal highways, regional roads as well as priority roads is prohibited. However, in the sense of this regulation, walking with the skis on your feet or pulling a toboggan is not considered an exercise of winter sports. This concept is also applied to crossing a public road with the skis on your feet. A person with skis on his feet who is walking is mainly considered a *pedestrian*, who has to follow the rules of the pedestrian traffic (§ 76 StVO) and has to yield to other road users and make way in the sense of § 87 Clause 3 StVO. In addition to that, in general skiers have to show consideration for other road users and make way (§ 87 Abs 3 StVO) as well as obey the significant traffic rules if they are using public roads where skiing is not prohibited.

297. *Cycling* is generally permitted on public roads if the bicycle is properly equipped according to regulations of the road traffic law (e.g., bell, lights, reflectors). § 66 Clause 2 StVO in connection with § 4 Fahrradverordnung presents an exemption for *racing bicycles*, which are only used during daylight and on days with good visibility.[325] Furthermore, athletes with racing bicycles may ride side-by-side during training sessions in accordance with § 68 Abs 2 StVO.

298. According to § 79 StVO *horseback riding* is permitted on public roads under the following conditions: horseback riders have to be physically suitable and able to ride; in addition, they have to be 16 years old. Persons of younger age may only ride if accompanied by an adult; however, this regulation does not account for riding in the course of farming activities if the rider is 12 years of age. Riders may only use the roadway, and on roads with bridle paths, they must use the very same. If they use the road, they have to obey the rules of traffic. In case of twilight, darkness, heavy fog or other unfavourable weather conditions, riders have to carry a bright and luminous lamp on the left side if they use the road and there is insufficient street lighting.

299. According to § 88a StVO, *roller skating* is permitted on pavements, footpaths and pedestrian crossings.[326] Skating on the road is prohibited unless the skater intends to cross the road. Regarding this aspect, the OGH[327] has recently stated that the provision is also applied to residential roads with low traffic volume. Exceptions to this prohibition are:

---

325. *Kaltenegger*, Der Radrennfahrer in der StVO, ZVR 2002, 67; *Reissner*, Mountainbiking, in *Hinteregger* (ed.), Trendsportarten und Wegefreiheit (2005) 136 ff.
326. On this subject cf. *Grundtner*, 20. StVO-Novelle: Rollschuhfahren, ZVR 2000, 74; *Michalek*, Rollschuhfahren auf Fahrbahnen, ZVR 2001, 408; *Cizek/Schnider*, Inline-Skater in Österreich: Rechtlicher Slalom zwischen Fußgängern und Radfahrern, SpuRt 2003, 14.
327. *See* OGH 6.8.2020, 2 Ob 169/19w.

(1) cycling facilities, however not the separate bicycle lanes outside the area of a city, town or village;
(2) residential roads and pedestrian zones;
(3) roads which have been exempt from the prohibition of playing on the roads according to § 88 Clause 1 StVO; and
(4) roads which have been opened to roller skating due to regulations which have been issued by the competent authority.

300. If roller skaters use cycling facilities, the skaters have to obey the respective rules of conduct. They may not endanger or interfere with other road users; in particular, they have to adapt their speed to the speed of other road users – especially pedestrians – on pavements, footpaths, pedestrian crossings, in pedestrian zones as well as on residential roads. Children under 12 years of age are only allowed to roller skate on roads with public traffic if they are supervised and accompanied by a person of 16 years of age, unless they have acquired the bicycle badge (a permit which entitles children between 10–12 years of age to riding their bicycle on public roads without being accompanied by an adult). The same considerations also apply to riding nowadays popular *Micro-Scooter* (cf. § 88b StVO).[328]

B. Right of Way in the Forest

301. Up to thirty years ago, anyone was – by means of custom and more or less implicitly tolerated – allowed to access the forests, linger there, look for mushrooms and berries as well as ski there as long as the property owner did not object – anyway, he was entitled to object without giving reasons. However, when the ForstG was issued in 1975 the formerly use of the forest due to custom was largely legalized, and a public and subjective legal claim was nominated which benefits each and every natural person. A so-called *legal servitude* was created.[329]

302. The ForstG is a federal law. However, the right of way often collides with interests which are protected by state law, for example, the hunting law and nature conservation law. In regard to this aspect, the mutual *consideration imperative* for federal and state legislature gains specific constitutional relevance.[330]

328. Cf. *Pröstl/Riccabona-Zecha*, Weg frei für den Micro-Scooter! Mit dem Micro-Scooter legal und sicher in die Schule, ZVR 2017, 66.
329. Thus, basically *Zeinhofer*, Bergsport und Forstgesetz (2008).
330. In reference to it *Malaniuk*, Bergsportrecht^2 50 mwN.

303. § 33 Clause 1 ForstG determines that basically every individual may access the forest for recreational reasons and may linger there.[331] In this context, jurisdiction[332] defines recreational aspects in the sense that commercial events are not covered by the provision. Based on this *canyoning tours* against payment are not permitted.

304. Some areas are *exempt* from this right to access and stay – these are forest areas for which the authority has issued a trespassing ban on legal grounds, such as forest areas with specific forestry facilities as well as re-afforestation areas and areas where forests are being replanted, as long as vegetation has not reached a height of 3m (cf. § 33 Clause 2 ForstG). Basically, this trespassing ban also applies to snow-covered young forests.

305. According to § 33 Clause 3 ForstG, any use of the forest which *exceeds the use mentioned above* – for example, camping in the dark, setting up a tent, entering the forest in a vehicle or on a horse – requires the consent of the proprietor. The same regulation applies to forest roads – here the consent of the person who is responsible for the maintenance of the respective forest road is required. *Skiing down* through the forests is only permitted on marked slopes or ski routes *within the range of climb assists* (ski lifts, cable cars). *Cross-country skiing* in the open landscape (without cross-country ski trails) is permitted if necessary precautions are taken; any use of the forest which exceeds the aspects mentioned above, such as the preparation and use of a new cross-country ski trail, requires the consent of the proprietor.

306. Therefore, the legal servitude is applicable to different kinds of alpine sports, such as *hiking, mountain climbing, and rock climbing,*[333] as well as *ascending mountains with touring skis. Wagner/Ecker*[334] are in this context of the opinion that the ascent on mechanically prepared slopes or ski routes, even if they lead through the forest, may trigger payment obligations. Concerning the *descent with touring skis*, what has to be considered first is the prohibition of skiing in the forests within the range of climb assists (*see* above). According to the historical legislator,[335] the ascent and following descent through the forest, even in the area of climb assists, with touring skis once per day should not be prohibited. Only athletes who repeatedly go up the mountain and sometimes drive through the forest within the range of climb assists should be covered by the prohibition. If there are no climb assists in considerable proximity, the primary question comes to the fore whether a decent on skis should be considered 'entering the forest' or 'entering the forest on a vehicle'. Jurisprudence holds the view that the legislator intended to have skiing

---

331. *See* with reference to the genesis of the right of way in the forest *Pepelnik*, Zur historischen Entwicklung der Wegefreiheit im ForstG – Unter besonderer Berücksichtigung des Befahrens des Waldes mit Fahrrädern, ZVR 2016, 514.
332. OGH 29.11.2017 Zak 2018, 35.
333. Fundamental on the range of servitude in regard to securing climbing routes *Hinteregger*, Felsklettern und Grundeigentum, ZVR 2000, 121 f; cf. also OGH 29.3.2006, 7 Ob 63/06z.
334. Cf. regarding touring skiers *Wagner/Ecker*, RdU 2018, 225 (226).
335. Explanatory notes on 285 BlgNR 17. GP 4.

included in the notion of entering.[336] In contrast to that, *toboggan* and *ski bob* are self-contained devices which do not allow any movement respective to walking. Therefore, using these devices ought to be comparable to entering the forest on a vehicle, thus being prohibited. The same aspect may well be applied to *snowboards*. Thus, the organization of *orienteering events* also exceeds the aspect of 'entering the forest' due to the fact that the various destinations of the course have to be marked and a large number of participants are present.[337]

307. Cycling or *motocross* in the forest is, even if it serves recreational purposes, definitely considered as entering on a vehicle, and therefore it requires the consent of the proprietor or the person who maintains the road. Apart from this, pushing the bicycle along the forest road remains permitted.[338] Infringements against the ForstG are viewed as criminal administrative offences.[339] Especially the compliance with regulations of § 33 Clause 3 ForstG may be controlled by bodies of public safety and order.

1. Excursus: Permission to Self-Defence

308. Recently, the issue of taking the law into one's own hands has occurred more and more often, especially in regard to mountain biking. The questions has been raised whether a property owner is entitled to take the law in his hands and confiscate the sports equipment in order to identify the sportsman so that an action of trespass can be filed. In jurisdiction, it has been decided some time ago that the person who has been disturbed is entitled to take away the object of disturbance such as a ball from the disturber (e.g., playing football on somebody else's field).[340] Furthermore, towing of vehicles which are parked on foreign property is in general not considered permissible according to recent jurisdiction.[341] Thus, it is obviously permitted to carry out (only) *securing measures* to secure evidence (taking away the ball, taking away the sports equipment) in order to maintain the rights of property. Interventions which affect the physical integrity or threats with firearms (e.g., hunter) are definitely inadmissible. The (tragic) case of a Tyrolean farmer was reported in which he set up a trap in order to protect his chicken by means of erecting a rampart with a trench behind on one side of his farm's passage. This construction caused the death of one mountain biker and severe injuries of another. The fact

336. Cf. *Pichler*, Ist das Befahren des Waldes mit Skiern erlaubt? Stb 1986/1, 7.
337. In this sense also *Malaniuk*, Bergsportrecht^2 64 f.
338. *See* OGH 18.10.2017 Zak 2017, 434.
339. *See* thereon with reference to mountain biking LVwG of Upper Austria 28.5.2018 ZVG-Slg 2018, 319 (*Hübsch*); cf. also *Ermacora*, Öffnung der Forststraßen für das Mountainbiken – Juristische und politische Aspekte der Freigabe von Forststraßen aus Sicht des Alpenvereins, ZVR 2016, 528.
340. OGH 11.9.1923 SZ 5/206.
341. Cf. OGH 20.12.2017 ZVR 2018, 490 (*Stichlberger*); *see* thereon *Messner*, Probleme der Selbsthilfe am Beispiel des Abschleppens unzulässig abgestellter Kraftfahrzeuge, JBl 2020, 209 and *Pittl/Moritz*, 'Beiseiteräumen' oder 'Abschleppen' als zulässige Selbsthilfe?, wobl 2018, 385; *see* to another opinion *Legerer*, Zur Zulässigkeit des Abschleppens besitzstörend abgestellter Fahrzeuge von Privatgrundstücken, ÖJZ 1998, 607.

that the farmer had taken the law in his own hands was viewed as completely inappropriate, and furthermore this incident led to his conviction due to involuntary homicide, to physical injury resulting from negligence (§§ 80 ff StGB) and to compensation payments in reference to civil law (§§ 1295 ff, 1325 ff ABGB). Another procedure – also reported from Tyrol – which is similarly illegal and basically presents analogous consequences, is the incident of a property owner who fixed an almost invisible wire (without warning) approximately 50 cm above the ground over the forest road which was leading to his pasture in order to stop mountain bikers. Biking was prohibited on the forest road – nevertheless, bikers kept using the road.[342] Even if the security measures are appropriate, assistance from the competent authority has to be requested.[343]

C. Right of Way in Mountain Areas

309. Various state regulations[344] guarantee a rather unrestricted right of way in wasteland which may serve as the legal basis for mountain climbing, rock climbing and hiking.[345] In addition to that, the laws concerning the right of way have central significance for winter sports such as ski touring, deep-snow skiing and off-piste skiing.[346]

310. However, the preparation of cross-country ski trails and ski slopes is not covered, but the appropriate and admissible use of this wasteland by skiers might lead to the development of a 'natural slope'.

D. Freedom of Airspace

311. Paragliding[347] does in no stage cause trespass according to the LG St. Pölten[348] as there is no unlawful interference. The walking and running movements when jumping off do not have any different effect on property than those of hikers or skiers. Concerning the period of time for flying over the property, the freedom of airspace is valid according to § 2 LFG unless the paraglider drops below the acceptable minimum height. Paragliders are aircraft by means of § 11 LFG. This also

342. *See* OGH 19.5.1994 ZVR 1995/61.
343. In general *Reissner* in *Hinteregger*, Trendsportarten 154 f with further references.
344. *Carinthia*: K-WBG KLGBl 2013/85; *Salzburg*: Gesetz über die Wegfreiheit im Bergland 1970 SLGBl 2005/58; *Styria*: Wegfreiheit im Bergland StLGBl 2013/87.
345. In general *Hinteregger*, ZVR 2000, 116; *Hinteregger*, Wandern, Klettern, Alpinbergsteigen, in *Hinteregger* (ed.), Trendsportarten und Wegefreiheit (2005) 42 ff with further references.
346. Cf. thereon *Neumayr*, Wintersport und Wegfreiheit im Bergland, in *Pilgermair* (ed.), Skisport und Recht (2021) 373.
347. In general *Kleewein*, Hängegleiten, Paragleiten, Segelfliegen und Ballonfahren, in *Hinteregger* (ed.), Trendsportarten und Wegefreiheit (2005) 205 ff.
348. LG St Pölten 29.4.1992 ZVR 1992/160.

applies to *parachutes*. In this context, jurisdiction[349] also considered a *base-jumping-rig* (this sport concerns jumping from fixed objects) as comprised by the respective provision. Therefore, the regulations regarding parachute jumps are directly applicable.

312. The use of airspace is free to aircraft and aviation equipment in flight. The quoted paragraph standardizes an ownership restriction. Owners of land are obliged to accept the use of airspace above their property by means of public interest. According to the LFG, principally only airports may be used for take-off and landing.[350] However, out-landings of gliders, paragliders as well as hot-air balloons are exempt from this 'airport constraint'. This also applies to parachutes outside densely populated areas.[351] The basic requirement for this privilege under § 10 Clause 1 lit c is the fact that the aircraft is not motor driven. For out-landings of gliders, § 10 LFG determines that owners have to grant toleration and only concede claims for damages. This provision also applies to the paraglider.[352]

E. Public Use at the Waterside

313. If water sports are not practised in facilities which are specifically designed for them, the issue is raised whether and to what extent they may be practised in rivers or lakes without the proprietor's consent.[353]

314. *Swimming* is – according to § 8 Clause 1 WRG – considered to be subject to so-called general public use, which allows swimming in *public waters* without a given consent by the owner and free of charge. Nevertheless, setting up campfires on the lakeshore is in any case not covered by public use.[354] However, one has to mind that public use of the water is only possible if the water is entered via authorized access. The right to enter the water is definitely not guaranteed by means of public use.[355] This circumstance gains special significance for swimming events with a mass start, such as a triathlon, where a relatively large area of access to the water is required.

315. Apart from this, jurisdiction[356] holds the view that *commercial canyoning tours* go beyond the general public use.

---

349. Cf. LVwG of Tyrol 5.4.2016 ZVG-Slg 2016, 459 (*Warner*).
350. VwGH 2.9.2019 RdU-LSK 2020/56.
351. *See* LVwG of Tyrol 5.4.2016 ZVG-Slg 2016, 459 (*Warner*).
352. In this context also *Malaniuk*, Bergsportrecht[2] 65.
353. Cf. *Hattenberger*, Nutzung der Natur zur Ausübung von Extrem- und Risikosportarten, in *Büchele/ Ganner/ Khakzadeh-Leiler/Mayr/Reissner/Schopper* (ed.) Aktuelle Rechtsfragen des Risiko- und Extremsports (2018) 13; *Hattenberger*, Canyoning, Paddeln, Rafting und Floßfahren, in *Hinteregger* (ed.), Trendsportarten und Wegefreiheit (2005) 175.
354. *See* OGH 22.6.2021 immolex 2021, 346 (*Holly/Palma*).
355. *Hattenberger* in *Hinteregger*, Trendsportarten 192.
356. OGH 29.11.2017 Zak 2018, 35; 10.2.2004 EvBl 2004/146.

316. As far as *boat sports* are concerned, public use of *public waters* is regulated in the SchifffahrtsG.[357] According to § 4 Clause 1 of this act, shipping on public waters is permitted to everybody under consideration of legal provisions. However, the SchifffahrtsG itself contains a number of authorizations to issue ordinances which restrict the common use. These authorizations are especially designed to restrict rafting and other types of white-water sports.[358]

317. Practising water sports in *private waters* naturally always requires the consent of the owner.

§2. Sport and Neighbour Rights

318. The owner of a property may prohibit his neighbour from causing problems related to sewage, smoke, gases, heat, smell, noise, vibration, and similar insofar as these problems exceed the usual level of the local circumstances and substantially affect the local use of the property. Direct and immediate immissions are by all means strictly prohibited without specific legal title (§ 364 Clause 2 ABGB).

319. Occasionally, sports facilities may cause impairments for neighbouring properties. Thus, golf balls, tennis balls, and footballs may fly to the neighbouring property.[359] Furthermore, noise pollution is a source of increasing potential for conflict,[360] especial the noise of a shooting ground,[361] engine noise, etc. Balls which have flown over are also considered a strictly prohibited direct immission.

320. Apart from that it is essential whether the sports facility has been *approved by the competent authority*. Particularly the regional development and building regulations of the various states define to what extent sports facilities ought to be approved by the competent authorities. In such an approval procedure, residents are treated as a party in these proceedings and their interests need to be preserved.

321. If an approval procedure by a competent authority has not been conducted, the neighbour may be entitled to ask for an *injunctive relief* under civil law according to § 364 Clause 2 ABGB due to immissions which affect the well-being and

357. BGBl I 1997/62.
358. In detail *see Hattenberger* in *Hinteregger*, Trendsportarten 200.
359. Cf. OGH 30.6.1977 SZ 50/99; 29.10.1992 ecolex 1993, 451. The last decision was issued not only on tennis balls but also on the sand of the tennis courts being blown over; 3.10.2006 ecolex 2007,420; 17.2.2014 wobl 2014,170.
360. Cf. OGH 28.3.1979 SZ 52/53 in reference to a sports ground; OGH 3.11.1982 Miet 34.033 in reference to a soccer stadium; OGH 29.10.1992 ecolex 1993, 451 and 19.3.2013 Zak 2013, 174 in reference to noise by tennis players; OGH 26.11.1997 RdW 1998, 260 in reference to a skating rink; furthermore, cf. *Fitzal*, Rechtsprechungsübersicht Lärmimmissionen im Zivilrecht, ecolex 1999, 872.
361. OGH 18.2.1975 SZ 48/15.

exceed the level of local conditions.[362] In this context, the OGH[363] has recently stated that the owner of a property which includes a water access covered by public use according to § 8 WRG is not obliged to constantly control the authorized usage by swimmers.

322. If the immission is produced by a sports facility which has been approved by a competent authority, no injunctive relief can be enforced. However, the neighbour is entitled to a compensation claim provided that the immissions exceed the level of local conditions (§ 364a ABGB).[364] In a new decision, the OGH[365] affirmed the application of the quoted paragraph concerning the grant of a building permit for a cable car according to the SeilbG. Thereby, the court stated with reference to the jurisdiction on the EisbG that the neighbours may not claim noise immissions within their legal standing in the respective proceedings. Apart from this, the Supreme Court has pointed out that injunctive reliefs are, even in the absence of a legal standing, also regarding unusual and significant immissions not possible because cable cars serve as facilities of common interest.

323. If the concerned resident does not object to noise pollution for more than three years, the 'local standard' has to be evaluated under consideration of the newly added noise. An injunctive relief of the caused immission may not be enforceable anymore.[366]

---

362. OGH 26.9.1972 SZ 45/98 in reference to noise of a bowling alley.
363. Regarding campfires on the lakeshore OGH 22.6.2021 immolex 2021, 346 (*Holly/Palma*).
364. Cf. OGH 11.6.1981 JBl 1982, 595 (*Jabornegg*), who granted a compensation claim for the injury of a bull which had been scared and balked because of the noise of a motocross event. Furthermore, e.g., OGH 10.11.1982 SZ 55/172 on emission of cooling agent in an artificial ice rink.
365. OGH 24.9.2019 Zak 2019, 437.
366. OGH 26.4.2000, 3 Ob 201/99a in reference to an asphalt curling course; cf. also regarding a tennis court OGH 8.4.2003 SZ 2003/36; *see also* in reference to a part of the immissions OGH 24.9.2019 Zak 2019, 437.

Part III. Sport and Employment

Chapter 1. Public Regulation

§1. The Legal Position of the Sportsman

I. Introduction

324. In the following chapter, two issues will be addressed: on the one hand, the legal position of the association sportsman (in the narrower sense) (cf. §1.II) and on the other hand, the legal position of the professional sportsman (cf. §1.III). Finally, the legal position of an injured leisure sportsman towards a possible employer or his social insurance will be discussed (cf. §1.IV).

II. Association Sportsman

325. The rights and obligations of the 'mere' association sportsman, that is a sportsman who is active as a non-professional in a sports club or sports association, are based on the *association statute*. The association statute is an obligatory guideline *for a sportsman, who joins the club or association as a member*. According to civil law, membership results from joining the association based on a membership contract between association and applicant for membership. Further legal relations, in particular additional special contracts between sportsman and association, are basically not included here.

326. Within the framework of the respective association in the broad sense (single association, federation), an 'association criminal law' may also exist. The sportsman is subject to the association criminal law as a result of his membership to the association or by statements of submission – in particular in the case of a superior 'federation criminal law'. The most severe sanction in the criminal law of a single association would be the exclusion from the association; this decision can be reviewed by ordinary courts – much like all the other decisions of association organs.[367] However, an exclusion from association may only occur due to important

367. Cf., e.g., OGH 20.1.1993 EvBl 1993/117; *see also* in reference to the dogmatic foundation and the prerequisites of the proceeding *Weber/Cach*, Ausschluss von Vereinsmitgliedern aus wichtigem

reasons. Such a reason may also be a defamatory enunciation.[368] Regarding the competence to pronounce an exclusion from the association, the OGH[369] holds the view that the mere competence of the president to impose lighter sanctions in accordance with the statute does not include the right to waive the exclusion.

327. In this context, it also has to be noted that the double jeopardy prohibition according to Art 4 Protocol 7 ECHR is not applied regarding the exclusion from the association. Therefore, the failure of nomination for the team in the upcoming golf season on the one hand and the exclusion from association on the other hand are allowed.[370]

III. Professional Athlete

328. Professional athletes are paid for sports exercise pursuant to a contract.[371,372] *The employment contract* is predominant (cf. §1.III.A).

329. *A contract for work* is generally not possible because no sportsman can or wants to commit himself to a certain success. As an exception, contracts for services would be possible in show arrangements, for example, in the figure skating sport.

330. *Free contracts of service* might be conceivable as well in similar marginal areas. This form of contract contains continuous obligations without personal dependence of the contractor (in reference to these legal terms also cf. §1.III.A). To

---

Grund – Dogmatische Grundlage und ausgewählte verfahrensrechtliche Fragen, GesRZ 2018, 224; *Sprung/König*, Überprüfung und inhaltliche Voraussetzungen eines Vereinsausschlusses, RdW 1984, 226.

368. Regarding the accusation of protocol falsification through a member of a golf association OGH 17.1.2018 RdW 2018, 226; in general also *Weber/Cach*, GesRZ 2018, 224 (227).
369. *See* thereon OGH 23.1.2019 RdW 2019, 386.
370. OGH 17.1.2018 RdW 2018, 226.
371. In general *Firlei*, Zur Arbeitnehmereigenschaft von Sportlern unter besonderer Berücksichtigung der Grauzone des Amateursports (1988); *Reissner* (ed.), Sport als Arbeit (2008); in reference to professional soccer sport *Holzer*, Das Dienstrecht der Lizenzfußballer im ÖFB, DRdA 1972, 63; *Tomandl/Schrammel*, Die Rechtsstellung von Vertrags- und Lizenzfußballern, JBl 1972, 234, 289; *Thaurer*, Ausgewählte arbeitsrechtliche Probleme beim Berufsfußballer in Österreich (1998); *Schrammel*, Die arbeits- und sozialrechtliche Stellung der Berufsfußballspieler, in *Karollus/Grundai/Prammer* (ed.), Aktuelle Fragen des Fußballsports (2003) 87; *see also* regarding more types of professional sports *the same*, Das Verhältnis des Berufssportlers insbesondere auch des Einzelsportlers zum Verband unter besonderer Berücksichtigung der sozialrechtlichen Stellung, in *Grundei/Karollus* (ed.), Berufssportrecht IX (2020) 1; cf. *Holzer*, Arbeitsrecht und Sport, ZAS 2015, 148; in reference to the members of the ski pool of the Austrian Ski Federation *Eisenberger*, Berufssport und Recht. Die Rechtsbeziehungen zwischen Sportverbänden, Sportlern und Sponsoren am Beispiel des Skirennsports (1998).
372. In detail *Reissner*, Hobbysportler, Arbeitnehmer oder freier Dienstnehmer – Rechtsbeziehungen von Sportlern aus arbeitsrechtlicher Sicht, in *Reissner* (ed.), Sport als Arbeit (2008) 3 ff; *see also* regarding cycling *Resch*, Radsport als Beruf – arbeits- und sozialrechtliche Fragen, in *Büchele/Ganner/Khakzadeh-Leiler/Mayr/Reissner/Schopper* (ed.), Aktuelle Rechtsfragen im Radsport (2017) 117.

a large extent, the contractor is free of restrictions in terms of personal behaviour. There are no or only insignificant commitments to working hours, to workplaces and working sequences, etc. If the 'Teaching Pro' can independently organize and arrange his lessons at the golf course, he could be bound by free contracts of employment to the golf club and at the same time give private lessons to individuals.[373]

331. In certain sports, *contracts of association* (in general, civil law associations according to §§ 1175 ff ABGB) are common between sportsmen and organizers as well as sportsmen and coaches or trainers, for example, in boxing, tennis, or golf.

332. Labour law (cf. §1.III.A, §1.III.D) can generally *not* be applied to such contracts. Due to the fact that particularly some freelancer in sport will be a so-called *quasi-subordinate contractee,* consequently the *ASGG* (concerning the conduct of a case; in addition also §1.III.D) as well as the *DHG* (in order to facilitate liability to pay damages) are applied if necessary. Quasi-subordinate contractees are legally independent but economically dependent (cf. § 51 Clause 3 Z 2 ASGG), that is, economically dependent on one or few powerful entrepreneurs or contracting partners. Recently, 'small' *freelancers* within the meaning of *§ 4 Clause 4 ASVG* have been included in labour law under consideration of selective issues, thus *in the BMSVG* (cf. § 1 Clause 1a leg cit) and *in the IESG* (cf. § 2a leg cit). Apart from that, *only those norms* of labour law which cannot be reduced to the *protective principle* as the basis of this field of law can be applied by analogy to the free contract of service. Hence, the rules of ABGB on the termination of the employment contract are applied, but not the norms of holiday law, severance pay, the continuation of wage payment in the event of illness and so forth.

A. Employment Contract

333. In *team sports,* the employment contract (employer-employee relationship) presents more or less the only option for the employment relationship between association and professional athlete.[374]

334. If a contract is defined as an employment contract *labour law* is applied even if the parties concerned might prefer excluding this issue. The labour law is a law of protection, and in many areas, it breaches private autonomy in favour of the

373. In reference to contractual relationships of coaches and trainers in general *Reissner*, Lern- und Übungsbuch Arbeitsrecht[6] (2020) 16 f with further references.
374. Thus *Schrammel*, Sport und Arbeitsrecht, in: Studiengesellschaft für Wirtschaft und Recht (ed.), Sport und Recht (2006) 37 f; furthermore, e.g., *Naderhirn*, Arbeitnehmereigenschaft von Sportlern unter besonderer Berücksichtigung der Diskussion um den Entwurf eines Berufssportgesetzes, in *Resch/Trost* (ed.), Arbeits- und sozialrechtliche Fragen des Profisports (2005) 17 ff with further references as well as *Rebhahn* in *Neumayr/Reissner* (ed.), Zeller Kommentar zum Arbeitsrecht[3] (2018) § 1151 ABGB Rz 142. In reference to professional soccer sport, *Holzer*, DRdA 1972, 64 ff.; *Tomandl/Schrammel*, JBl 1972, 235 ff.

typically economically inferior employee. The question has to be raised which aspects actually constitute the employment contract.[375]

335. The employment relationship is a *continuing obligation* which involves the provision of work performance. Continuing obligations do not terminate automatically after performance, but they actually require a specific act of completion (e.g., termination; limitation).

336. An employment relationship is characterized by *personal dependence* of the employee. The employee is integrated into business organization: he is bound to working hours, to workplace and work sequence, and he is inferior to the decisional authority of the employer. The employee is subject to the control of the employer and is accountable in terms of discipline. The employee is generally covenant to do his work in person; hence, he cannot be represented. The employee owes his labour, but not a certain successful work result. The result of the work belongs to the employer; normally, he provides the means of labour. The employee is bound to 'fiduciary obligations' (e.g., restraint of competition; obligation of confidentiality), the employer is bound to his 'obligation of care' and thus has to protect important legal interests (e.g., life, health, property) of the employee. The registration for social security and the deduction of income tax present evidence for employee status.

337. If the typical elements in favour of employment relationship outweigh the aspects against employment relationship (in quality) labour law is applied. The definition of the contract is only relevant in case of doubt.

338. Regardless of the fact that many people consider sport a hobby and game, it is an occupation for the 'pro'. Starting point of the legal assessment is the question *concerning the personal dependence of the sportsman*: if the sportsman is integrated into the sports operations (in particular training obligation; 'quartering'; dietary regulations; obligation to inform oneself about sport-strategic or tactical concepts) in connection with, for example, representative functions and obligations for the benefit of the association or his sponsor, the evidence for employee status is in principle present. Furthermore, it has to be considered that a team sportsman will not be able to send a representative. Whether the association internally qualifies the sportsman as an 'amateur', 'licence player', 'cadre member' is irrelevant as the registration for social security is mere evidence of his status.

339. Today there are no more discussions about the fact that contract players of the top divisions in (men's) football[376] or ice hockey[377] are employees of their clubs

375. In general, e.g., *Reissner*, Arbeitsrecht[6] 2 ff.
376. Cf., e.g., OGH 1993 DRdA 1994, 320 *(Binder)*; 16.7.2004 DRdA 2005, 288 *(Wolfsgruber)*.
377. Cf., e.g., OGH 18.10.1977 DRdA 1978, 346 (*Holzer/Posch*) = ZAS 1979, 54 (*Schuhmacher*); 29.11.2001 DRdA 2002, 245 = ARD 5302/3/2002.

or associations. Especially in team sports with professional management, it is obvious that the work is largely directed by others, as the parties concerned have developed a practice based on solid experience which sets up strict organizational and disciplinary guidelines in reference to training and lifestyle in order to achieve a high quality in sport; anyway, cohesion of and harmony within the team are essential requirements for success in sport. Furthermore, the employment contract is the basis of the legal relationship of those sportsmen who commit themselves to the provision of performance in a single sport, especially if the presented general criteria of personal dependence (above all, integration in the sports operations being expressed by detailed personal instructions) are strongly pronounced.[378] Thus, the Supreme Court,[379] for example, has qualified a boxer as an employee of his manager. It is remarkable that judicature also resorts to the aspect of payment for the performance in sports in order to assess the employee's status: the Supreme Court, for example, has qualified a football player of the Carinthian Regional Division, who earns a bonus of ATS 800 for each scored point in the championship plus an expense allowance (which is not excessive), as a leisure sportsman and not as an employee of the club. However, the football trainer, who signed a 'contract for work' with the association in order to mislead the tax office and social security agencies and tried to gain a higher monthly income than the income from his occupation as a secondary school teacher, was classified as an employee.[380] In these decisions, the Supreme Court has apparently connected the levels of remuneration to the – basically substantial – heteronomy. However, personal dependence – particularly in terms of integration in different structures in relation to working hours, workplace and working sequence – must be considered a central aspect for classification. If a football player did not participate in the training or did not go to an away game and these actions were to have legal consequences such as the termination of contract, this would prove a distinctive work obligation and consequently an employment relationship. The Supreme Court allows a pragmatic approach for the assessment of individual cases: relatively high payments to a sportsman are evidence for the fact that his legal relationship will show strong personal commitment (in terms of personal dependence). Viewed in this light, sportsmen in lower divisions may also act under personal dependence. However, if the (team) sport has not yet been appropriately professionalized – one example would be women's football in Austria but not necessarily women's handball – even participating in the games of the highest division may be considered a hobby and not an occupation.

B. Are Sportsmen Blue- or White-Collar Workers?

340. The Austrian labour law distinguishes between *blue-* and *white-collar workers*.[381] Starting point are the special regulations on employment contracts *in the*

378. Thus relevant *Rebhahn* in ZellKomm[3] § 1151 ABGB Rz 142.
379. OGH 29.5.1979 DRdA 1981, 232 *(Schrammel)* = SZ 52/87.
380. OGH 12.2.1998 ARD 4945/9/98.
381. In general *Reissner*, Arbeitsrecht[6] 23 ff.

AngG 1921 which still secure a privileged position for white-collar workers in certain areas (e.g., with regard to the due date of the salary and aliquoting of special payments).[382] According to the right of termination, it has to be noted that the notice periods and terms of notice for blue-collar worker were adjusted to those for white-collar workers by October 2021.[383] However, according to § 1159 Clause 2 Sentence 3 ABGB, an exemption for sectors, in which seasonal operations predominate (e.g., construction industry), has remained. Therefore a collective agreement for blue-collar workers may still stipulate shorter notice periods in such industries.[384] 339 White-collar workers are mainly obliged to perform commercial services, higher non-commercial services or office work (cf. §§ 1 ff AngG).

341. There are considerable doubts whether professional sportsmen are white- or blue-collar workers. They certainly perform neither commercial services nor office work. If they wanted to be 'white-collar worker', they would have to rely on the legal passus '*higher non-commercial services*'.

342. According to consistent case law,[385] 'higher services' are present when 'work' has to be performed:

> which, indeed, requires no specific course of studies but which demands previous knowledge and training courses in the professional field at hand, which involves trust and a certain skilled performance in the task. This task may not be carried out as a simple mechanic exercise and cannot be performed by any random replacement.

In addition, based on these wordings, judicature pays strict attention to the fact that the respective work which is performed is rather 'headwork' than physical work. In the case of professional athletes (ski instructors, professional football players), mostly blue-collar worker status is assumed, based on the very fact that not

382. *See* thereon the compilation in *Figl*, Die weiterhin bestehenden Unterschiede zwischen Arbeitern und Angestellten, ecolex 2021, 612.
383. BGBl I 2021/121; cf. *Reissner*, Arbeitsrecht[6] 39 f.
384. See regarding the gastronomy and hotel sector OGH 24.3.2022 ARD 6801/6/2022 *(Lindmayr)* = ecolex 2022, 477 *(Mazal)*.
385. Cf. esp. the compilation of *Löschnigg/Reiff* in *Löschnigg/Melzer* (ed.), Angestelltengesetz I[11] (2021) §1 Rz 112.

enough intellectual work is performed.[386] This has to be criticized as being a one-dimensional view.[387] However, (professional) coaches in team sports are definitely to be qualified as white-collar workers.[388]

C. *'Betriebsverfassungsrecht': Industrial Relations Law*

343. The industrial relations law is regulated in part II of the ArbVG (§§ 33 ff leg cit).[389] If the organizational form is that of an operation entity, staff is entitled to elect a works council, which may exercise rights of co-determination and thus, influence the management in social, economic and personal affairs.

344. The question of whether a professional football association, for example, presents an 'operation entity with obligatory works council' under the ArbVG has to be distinctly affirmed. The definition of the *operation entity* is outlined in § 34 ArbVG.

345. All characteristics which define an operation entity according to this regulation are listed: presence of work equipment, of personnel, of an organizational body as well as the permanent pursuit of a purpose. An *'obligation to elect a works council'* is given if the statutory minimum number of five members of personnel is reached (§ 40 ArbVG). Thus, this requirement is met as not only professional sportsmen (football player, coaching staff) but also management and administrative staff belong to the personnel of this company.

346. Participation rights of the personnel are cancelled extensively in so-called *tendency operations*. These operations directly serve political, confessional, scientific, educational, or charitable purposes (cf. § 132 ArbVG). Nevertheless, sports associations and sports organizations are no tendency operations, and therefore participation rights may be applied extensively.[390]

---

386. In reference to a ski instructor OGH 14.7.1955 Arb 6247; in reference to a professional football player OGH 2004 DRdA 2005, 268 (critically *Wolfsgruber*) = Tracing in 2004, 253 (krit *Crisp*); 26.8.2004 Tracing in 2005, 67 (critically *Crisp*); *see also Holzer*, ZAS 2015, 148 (150 f); cf. regarding cycling athletes *Resch* in *Büchele* et al. Radsport 119-124.
387. criticized in *Holzer*, DRdA 1972, 66 f; *Firlei*, Versetzung eines Profifußballers zu den Amateuren, DRdA 2003, 184 f; *Strasser*, Profifußballer: Arbeiter oder Angestellte?, in *Resch/Trost* (ed.), Arbeits- und sozialrechtliche Fragen des Profisports (2005) 102 ff with further references; *Reissner* in *Reissner*, Arbeit 15 ff. However, on classification first *Schrammel* in: Studiengesellschaft für Wirtschaft und Recht, Sport 39 f; cf. already *Tomandl/Schrammel*, JBl 1972, 237 f.
388. *Holzer* Die Rechtsstellung von Trainern aus arbeitsrechtlicher Sicht nach österreichischer und deutscher Rechtslage, in *Dury* (ed.), Der Trainer und das Recht (1997) 37 f.
389. *Friedrich*, Ausgewählte Rechtsfragen des kollektiven Arbeitsrechts im Berufssport, in *Reissner* (ed.), Sport als Arbeit (2008) 52 ff.
390. On German law BAG 23.3.1999 SpuRt 1999, 249; cf. also *Holzer* in *Dury*, Trainer 39; *Friedrich* in *Reissner*, Arbeit 53.

D. Consequences of Applicability of Labour Law

347. For sports operations, the applicability of labour law particularly involves the following practical ramifications – regardless of whether they are considered appropriate in terms of legal policy (sports policy, social policy):[391]

348. The application of *working time legislation* implies among other things the forty-hour week and the regulation that basically twenty hours overtime are allowed per week (cf. §§ 3, 7 AZG). Furthermore, a *weekend rest or weekly rest* has to be granted (cf. §§ 3 ff ARG).

349. The applicability of *holiday law* based on the UrlG implies a minimum of five-week paid holiday per year (§ 2 UrlG) which is used for recovery and may not be compensated in money during valid employment relationship (principle of payment in kind; § 7 UrlG).

350. Concerning *continued payment of wages in case of illness* and particularly *in case of injuries,* the EFZG for blue-collar workers and § 8 AngG for white-collar workers have to be applied. Any further regulations in the contract, such as regulations relating to the duration of continued payment of wages, which are in favour of the employee, are legitimate in terms of general principles of labour law (so-called favourability principle).

351. During vacation or sick leave, the remuneration has to be continued according to the loss-of-pay principle. Hence, incentives and similar performance-related allowances have to be calculated, projected for the appropriate periods of time and included in the amount beforehand.[392]

352. An obligation to *continued payment of wages* is also effective when the work performance ceases *due to circumstances on the part of the employer* even though the employee is ready to work (§ 1155 ABGB).

353. In this context is a debatable point as to what extent the *suspensions of the sportsman* on behalf of the association or federation may initiate this continued payment of wages. If a player is, for example, doped by a person in charge of the association without being aware of it and is subsequently suspended because of doping, a circumstance on the part of the employer – the resulting incapacity of the sportsman to work – arises which obliges the employer to continued payment of wages according to § 1155 ABGB. Even if the suspension was issued as, for example, the consequence of a tactical foul, which had been ordered by the association, this legal situation is to be applied. If a sportsman has been willingly doped or is responsible

391. In detail *Reissner* in *Reissner*, Arbeit 18 ff; *see also Holzer*, ZAS 2015, 148 (151).
392. On German law BAG 24.11.1992 AR-Blattei IT – sport No. 21; 6.12.1995 AR-Blattei IT – sport No. 23.

for a suspension and is suspended by the federation, § 1155 ABGB does not necessarily imply an obligation to continued payment of wages as there are no exclusive circumstances on the part of the employer which have led to the incapacity to work. On the contrary, the player has not only contributed to his incapacity but is also responsible for it. However, in this constellation, jurisprudence opposes the claim for continued payment of wages according to § 1155 ABGB.

354. Nevertheless, differentiating aspects may be considered, leading in two different directions: on the one hand, it has to be considered that § 1155 ABGB is an optional law. Therefore, the problem of inability to work due to suspension can be regulated in the contract in any direction. Thus, it may also be regulated in order to make the obligation to continued payment of wages possible.

355. On the other hand, the concept of incapacity is disputable in the given context. In the case of short-term suspensions, the aspect of incapacity cannot necessarily be applied as the player keeps taking part in the complete sports activities of his association, apart from competitions.[393]

356. *Release restrictions* are regulations which control the transfer of a professional athlete from one employer to another employer by means of special restrictions and limitations. In practice, release restrictions are (or were; in reference to that *see* below) generally provided in the statutes of the association. Typically, the professional athlete or his new employer has (or had) to present a declaration of the former association (employer) to the federation stating that the respective athlete is released. If such a certification can or could not be presented, sanctions according to association law, in particular suspensions, result (or resulted) from this. Apart from that, it may also occur that release restrictions are incorporated in individual employment contracts – this phenomenon is more common in general work life than in the labour law of sportsmen. Thereby, the sportsman is prohibited from working for specific other associations or – in general – sports operations after his contract has been terminated. The question of how such release restrictions correspond with labour law has to be discussed.

357. From the point of view of *European law*, this problem has already been addressed by means of the 'Bosman' decision. Despite the fact that its field of application is limited to transnational issues, European law has critically contributed to forcing back the release restrictions established in the statutes of associations.

358. *According to national law*, relevant statutes of associations referring to restrictions for the employee in terms of earning a living are void insofar as the employee would not be allowed to exploit or use his knowledge and skills after the employment relationship has been terminated.[394] Possibly, an offence *contra bonos*

393. *Holzer/Fritzweiler*, Auswirkungen von Dopingverstößen auf Arbeits-, Lizenz- und Sponsorenverträge, in *Fritzweiler* (ed.), Doping – Sanktionen, Beweise, Ansprüche (2000) 61 and 64.
394. Thus already *Holzer*, DRdA 1972, 63 ff.; *Tomandl/Schrammel*, JBl 1972, 289 ff.

mores is present (§ 879 ABGB).[395] If release restrictions are included in employment contracts, they are normally – in the point of view of labour law – competition clauses. Such clauses are regulated in §§ 36 f AngG or in § 2c AVRAG (for non-white-collar workers). Basically, competition clauses are acceptable, but they are strictly regulated by the statutes mentioned above. In particular, these clauses must not unreasonably impede the employee in his professional advancement after consideration of the mutual interests.

359. Due to the special circumstances in the field of sports (e.g., championships with few potential employers; limited time for the sportsman during which he can exercise sport at the highest level), contractual release restrictions can normally not be sustained, neither in labour court nor in social court[396] – from the point of view of the employee these clauses are occupational sanctions or even employment bans.

360. It has just been demonstrated that claims to *transfer fees* which are derived from release restrictions are legally hardly tenable. Thus, transfer fees may only be justified under consideration of two aspects:

(1) If a *player who is bound by contract* wants to transfer to another association, he has to terminate his current contract by mutual agreement which is only possible with the consent of the employer, obviously the current association. The association is allowed to demand the payment of a transfer fee in return for the consent to the mutually agreed contract termination. A transfer fee may certainly not be achieved after the expiration of fixed-term or temporary contracts or after termination of unlimited contracts due to cancellation. Thus, a player 'without a transfer fee' is typically a player who is not bound by contract anymore because his employment contract has expired.
(2) However, transfer fees could also be interpreted as a reimbursement for educational and training costs. However, in terms of labour law, only training costs under § 2d AVRAG may be concerned. These include de facto expenses of the employer provided for a successfully completed training or education which offers special knowledge, skills and training for the employee. For the employee, knowledge and skills must also be applicable to other employers. The acquisition of skills or athletic performances due to training is certainly not such a vocational training; therefore, these expenses cannot be transferred to the next employer in regard to labour law. If such clauses are included in contracts with minors, for example, children who attend a 'football academy' and the like *inter alia* the consent of the legal representative and.[397] Thereby,

395. In reference to an ice hockey player OGH 27.3.1996 ARD 4820/34/97; thus *Holzer*, Freigabe eines Eishockeyprofis durch einstweilige Verfügung des Arbeits- und Sozialgerichts, DRdA 1996, 528 ff. Cf. furthermore on the 'Goldberger Case' LG Ried im Innkreis 19.11.1997 SpuRt 1998, 69; on the 'Elfi Eder Case' OLG Linz 22.12.1997 SpuRt 1998, 72.

396. In reference to a competition clause for a professional football player which was declared to be void OGH 25.6.1998 DRdA 1999, 139 *(Mayr)* = SpuRt 1999, 62 *(Reissner)*.

397. In reference to a ski racer OGH 13.7.1998 SpuRt 1999, 24; in reference to the Austrian Tennis Federation's (ÖTV) pool team OGH 28.2.1990, 3 Ob 623/89; *see König/Fischer*, Ausbildungskosten – Rückersatz eines Leistungssportlers bei Vereinswechsel, in FS Dittrich (2000) 465.

further issues refer to the question of whether an additional approval of the curatorship court is required: In contrast to his previous jurisdiction, the OGH[398] recently held that the legislator intended to refrain from the requirement of such an approval by revising the prerequisites in § 2d AVRAG. Nowadays, the consent of the legal representative is sufficient.

361. The German Federal Court[399] has also rejected an action for payment of training compensation for *amateur sportsmen*. These amateur players were transferred to an association in a higher division and became contract amateurs. The Supreme Court viewed these regulations on compensation which were integrated into the statutes of the Niedersachsen Football Association as a restriction of freedom to engage in work which is established in the constitution.[400]

362. The implementation of operational *disciplinary law* is bound to precise conditions according to labour law. Applied to sport, disciplinary law comprises two aspects:

(1) Punishment for violation of discipline and fairness in sports.
(2) Punishment for breach of obligation defined in the employment contract. Normally this is an infringement of labour law as such penalties are only possible if they are provided in a collective agreement (i.e., in a contract between employers' association and labour union which – according to §§ 2 ff ArbVG – contains a norm effect, an effect like a law in fact) or an appropriate works agreement (i.e., a contract between the proprietor and workforce which has according to §§ 29 ff ArbVG similar effects to the collective agreement) and if the works council agrees to such penalties in individual cases (cf. §§ 96 Clause 1 Z 1, 102 ArbVG). Nowadays, all these requirements are almost nowhere in sport present. Nevertheless, the ability to collective agreements has already been granted to the national football league some time ago,[401] and a corresponding collective agreement in coordinance with the labour union has become effective with the season 2008/2009. This collective agreement contains disciplinary rules.

363. Further issues refer to *questions of termination*, dealing with aspects which are concerned with the dissolution of employment contracts in the field of sport.[402]

(1) In professional team sports, contracts for a year and multiannual contracts – that is *fixed-term employments* – are the general rule. Whereas in Austria only the succession of fixed-term employment contracts ('Kettenarbeitsvertrag')

398. OGH 2.9.2021 wbl 2022, 105 (*Grillberger*).
399. BGH 27.9.1999 SpuRt 1999, 236; cf. *Resch*, Europarechtliche Fragen zur Ausbildungsentschädigung, Transfersystem und dem Recht des Spielers auf Freigabe, DRdA 2004, 87.
400. Analogously for Austria *Reissner in Reissner*, Arbeit 24 ff.
401. VwGH 28.7. 1995 DRdA 1996, 215 *(Klein)*.
402. Cf. *Trost*, 'Verkauft', 'Zurückgetreten', 'kostenlos frei', 'sich selbst gehörend' – Fragen der Beendigung des Sportler-Arbeitsverhältnisses, in *Reissner* (ed.), Sport als Arbeit (2008) 97 ff.

requires an objective justification,[403] such a presentation is in Germany[404] already then necessary if the contract is concluded for the first time. In this context, the OGH[405] affirmed the admissibility of such a succession regarding a professional football player because of the preservation of flexibility, the performance of the athlete or the interest of the audience. In this sense, the German Federal Labour Court[406] also confirmed more recently the legality of a fixed-term contract with a professional football player, which included an extension option if 23 national league matches are played. In the legal assessment the court referred to the specific nature of employment relationships within the professional sports area (e.g., limited professional time of players, ensuring flexibility in the playing squad, etc.).[407] However, the customary practice of fixed-term contracts in the football sector alone is not sufficient as an objective justification.

(2) In this context, also *option agreements* gain special significance in the football sector. Thereby, mostly only the employer is entitled to unilaterally extend the contract with the player. After all, the possibility to exercise the option then generally leads to the above-mentioned succession of fixed-term contracts.

First and foremost, it is a debatable point if such clauses are eligible to be viewed in the light of the equal right of termination (§ 20 Clause 4 AngG, § 1159c ABGB in the old version and § 1159 Clause 4 ABGB in the new version).[408] Furthermore, the question is raised whether such unilateral clauses can be contra *bonos mores*.

In jurisprudence, the problem is discussed controversially: *Brodil*[409] is of the opinion that the equal right of termination is not applied directly in these constellations.[410] So, such option agreements could be eligible, especially taking into account the uncertain development of young professional football players. In this sense, according to *Holzer*,[411] unilateral extensions are particularly questionable if the market value of the player has risen in the meantime. Moreover, also *Kietaibl*[412] states that an appropriate solution can be found in an examination of the clauses for their compliance with *bonos mores*. *Friedrich*[413] also deals with these doctrines and argues in favour of an examination due to compliance with *bonos mores*.

403. *See* §§ 19 Abs 1 AngG, 1158 Abs 1 ABGB; *Reissner*, Arbeitsrecht[6] 134 f.
404. Cf. § 14 German Part-time Employment Act; unless the contract is only concluded for two years.
405. *See* OGH 10.2.1999 ZAS 2000, 149 (critically *Reissner*).
406. Cf. BAG 16.1.2018 CaS 2019, 247.
407. Cf. § 14 Abs 1 Z 4 German Part-time Employment Act.
408. So affirmative *F. Müller*, Vertragsverlängerung durch einseitige Erklärung – Dargestellt anhand der Praxis im österreichischen Berufsfußball ZAS 2007, 213 (216 f) and *Reisinger*, Mustervertrag für FußballspielerInnen in der Österreichischen Fußball-Bundesliga, DRdA 2011, 112.
409. *See Brodil*, Brodil, Bedingte Vertragsbestandteile im Profi-Fußballsport – Ein Beitrag zur Bedingungslehre im Arbeitsrecht, in GS Rehbahn (2019) 22 and *Brodil/Dullinger*, ecolex 2016, 511.
410. In the same sense regarding the comparable situation in German law: ArbG Ulm 14.11.2008, NZA-RR 2009, 246.
411. *Holzer*, ZAS 2015, 148 (157).
412. *See* in detail *Kietaibl*, Optionsverträge für Fußballer, in *Berger/Hattenberger* (ed.), Recht SPORTlich 3 – Aktuelle Rechtsfragen des Sports (2017) 47.
413. *Friedrich*, Einseitige Optionsrechte – Die Causa Onisiwo, in *Grundei/Karollus* (ed.), Berufssportrecht VIII – Aktuelle Rechtsfrage des Berufssports (2017) 73 (98) with further references.

This issue has already been addressed in jurisdiction. Thus, the OGH[414] avoided answering the questions of the general admissibility of such unilateral option agreements or the regulatory power of the collective agreement. In the present case, the admissibility of such clauses only has been denied due to the fact that provisions of the applicable collective agreement have not been observed. Contrary to § 6 Z 4 of the collective agreement for players in the national football league, there is no equivalence between the unilateral right of extension of the association and a player's entitlement due to the absence of a specific tariff or conversion table. The association did not present any concrete facts, e.g., on the age of the player, his skills and prognosis. Besides this, the court referred parenthetically to the fact that the clause enables an extension for another two years. However, the fixed-term contract was initially only concluded for one year.[415] This legal judgment has been assessed critically.[416]

Besides this, the German Federal Labour Court[417] recently held the view that two-sided extension options would in any case not violate the principle of equality of termination. However, the court referred regarding unilateral option clauses to the opinion of *Rein*.[418] He assumes an illegal circumvention of the right to equal termination in this context. Then, in contrast to the legal assessment of the German Labour Court,[419] the consequence would be the invalidity of the clause and not its reinterpretation as a bilateral extension right. In contrast to that, in another decision, the German Federal Labour Court[420] affirmed the contractual commitment of a football player because he has voluntarily entered into a four-year contract (unilaterally extendable to five years). However, thereby the court has not ruled expressly on the inadmissibility of unilateral option agreements.

364. A fixed-term employment can only be *cancelled prematurely* during its term *on important grounds*; a termination is not possible.

(1) An appropriate and relevant reason for termination of contract which is specific to sport is to be viewed *in doping*. A player who dopes himself without his employer's knowledge or without his employer's intent or order violates his employment contract. The obligation to refrain from the use of drugs does not require explicit specification. It is immanent in the sportsman's obligation to work which includes the delivery of proper performance in sport. Thus, the

---

414. OGH 28.10.2016 ARD 6527/9/2016; in contrast, the lower courts clearly denied the admissibility of such option agreements viewed in the light of *the equal right of termination* (ASG of Vienna 11.11.2015, 17 Cga 40/15y and OLG of Vienna 26.4.2016, 8 Ra 18/16z).
415. However, these considerations point to an examination of the compliance with *bonos mores* in view of the above-mentioned jurisprudence (especially the opinion of *Kietaibl*).
416. Cf. *Friedrich* in *Grundei/Karollus*, Einseitige Optionsrechte 87 ff with further references.
417. *See* BAG 16.1.2018 CaS 2019, 247; cf. regarding the equal right of termination § 622 Clause 6 German Civil Code.
418. Cf. thereon in detail *Rein*, Kontrolle einseitiger Verlängerungsoptionen in einem Spielervertrag – Besprechung von ArbG Ulm, NZA-RR 2009, 246.
419. ArbG Ulm 14.11.2008, NZA-RR 2009, 246.
420. In BAG 25.4.2013 SpuRt 2014, 32 the question did not arise more accurate due to the conclusion of a settlement and the payment of the transfer fee by the young player; *see* thereon also *Brodil/ Dullinger*, Optionsverträge im Berufsfußballsport, ecolex 2016, 511 (512).

sportsman has to answer for a possible doping suspension and is in no case entitled to a continued payment of wages (*see also* above). In fact, the employer is entitled to dismiss the player prematurely due to breach of contract on important grounds.[421]

(2) In a professional team sport, more and more frequently, the question has been raised whether the employee is provided with significant arguments for a legitimate and premature termination of the employment. Such an argument for preliminary termination can be of enormous interest for the employee if he had the chance to accept an offer on behalf of another association which might be profitable in terms of sport and money. According to § 26 Z 2 Case 1 AngG, a reason for resignation is, for example, present when the employer improperly reduces the remuneration or withholds it from the white-collar worker. An analogous situation for blue-collar workers results from § 82a lit d case 1 and lit e GewO 1859. 'Cutting the payment' describes the unilateral and illegal reduction of remuneration – for example, by means of violation of the employment contract – to which the employee is entitled. 'Withholding the payment' is present if the actual claim and its extent are not denied but, nevertheless, the remuneration is not fully paid or is not paid on time; the same applies if the employer states in a pre-announced explanation that he is not going to pay. However, the reasons for cutting the payment or withholding the payment are irrelevant; it makes no difference whether it is due to inability or unwillingness, sloppiness or intentional discrimination.[422] In general, the employee can immediately cancel the contract if the aspects of improper reduction or withholding of remuneration are present. He is only required to set an additional respite if he has agreed to an extension (express or implied) by accepting, for example, arrears of payment or instalments.[423] However, if the employer has already become bankrupt, the employee is only entitled to termination by means of § 25 IO but not according to general regulations of labour law in § 26 Z 2 case 1 AngG, § 82a lit d case 1 and lit e GewO 1859.[424]

(3) If a head coach resigns because he gets bullied by members of the football association by which he is employed – for example, the president of the association maltreats the coach because of lack of success in recent games, defames the coach with the press referring to his professional competence or incompetence, attacks him with racial slur, etc. – this can be defined as a legitimate premature resignation due to violation of 'obligation of care' or due to considerable libel (§ 26 Z 3 or 4 AngG) if these issues, especially the issue of racial slur, are properly sustainable:[425]

---

421. Cf. *Holzer/Fritzweiler* in *Fritzweiler*, Doping 69.
422. Cf., e.g., OGH 25.6.1985 Arb 10.471; 13. 2 1997 RdW 1997, 687 = ASoK 1997, 287.
423. Cf., e.g., OGH 17.2.1987 DRdA 1990, 131 (*Eypeltauer*).
424. OGH 25.4.1996 wbl 1996, 325; 27.2.2020, 8 ObS 13/19y.
425. OGH 22.2.2006 SpuRt 2006, 111 *(Reissner/Herzeg)* – Ivica *Osim versus Sturm Graz*; *Reissner*, Austritt eines Fußballtrainers auf Grund von Mobbing, DRdA 2005, 277.

365. In many cases, it is regulated that the player's contract is automatically terminated if the association he is working for is relegated. Such *withdrawal conditions* are legally recognized if the point of time to which the condition is met – here the end of season – is certain (reduces uncertain condition; dies incertus in certus quando).[426]

366. If an employment contract exists for more than three years, the employee is entitled to *a severance pay* in case the employment is terminated ('old system of severance payments'; § 23 AngG, § 2 ArbAbfG), unless the sportsman has given notice himself.

Severance payment is not affected if the player issues a *declaration of non-extension* before his fixed-term contract expires in order to prevent an automatic contract extension. In such a case, which is theoretically controversial in terms of whether the fixed term of the contract has expired or whether the contract has been terminated – the latter may eliminate severance pay – the severance pay is adjudged by the Supreme Court.[427] This concept can definitely be justified as at least the parties concerned do not view the *declaration of non-extension* as a notice of termination, which can be interpreted as more favourable to the employee and therefore may be considered an acceptable regulation in terms of rights on severance pay.

367. For any kind of employment contract issued 1 January 2003 a *staff provision scheme* ('new system of severance pay') according to BMSVG is required.

This is a change from the performance-oriented 'old system of severance pay' (*see* above) to a defined contribution system in which the employers have to pay social security contributions as well as at the same time contributions to a staff provision scheme. In case of termination of the employment, regardless of the specific kind of termination, the employee may claim the amount, which has been paid continuously during the time of employment, including investment return. The employee may dispose of severance pay in different aspects (cf. § 17 BMSVG). These new conditions are definitely more favourable for professional sportsmen than the old system; on the one hand, employees are also entitled to severance pay in case of short-term employment – such as less than three years of permanent employment; on the other hand, this rigid system is less 'susceptible to avoidance', as long as the social security regulations are regarded (cf. section §1.III.E).

368. Does a professional athlete have *a right to actual employment*? The 'right to employment' is a catchword which poses the question of whether the employee really has the right to be employed by the employer. In case of non-employment on behalf of the employer, a mere claim to continued payment of wages according to § 1155 ABGB (*see* above) is assumed.

---

426. Cf. OGH 9.11.1982 ZAS 1984, 227 (*Schrammel*); 25.9.1991 ZAS 1992, 160 = DRdA 1992, 286. In reference to conditional award of a bonus cf. OGH 10.4.2008 ZAS-Judikatur 2008/120; cf. also *Brodil*, GS Rehbahn 21.

427. OGH 10.2.1999 DRdA 2000, 41 (approvingly *Holzer*) = ZAS 2000, 149 (critically *Reissner*); *see also Jabornegg*, Befristete Verträge von Profisportlern mit Verlängerungsklauseln, in *Resch/Trost* (ed.), Arbeits- und sozialrechtliche Fragen des Profisports (2005) 130 ff.; *see* relevant discussion *Reissner* in *Reissner*, Arbeit 27 ff with further references.

In Austrian labour law, judicature is traditionally opposed to a 'right to employment'. *Inter alia* a right to employment cannot generally be assumed in Austria *de lege lata* (this accounts for any kind of employment relationship). However, for specific employees, it is justifiable and is based on two significant legal approaches, namely in § 18 TAG and in §§ 9, 18 BAG, which are both open to generous legal analogy. The reason why the 'right to employment' was laid down for the professional group of actors is related to their audience-oriented activity; the reason for a right to employment for apprentices and employees in the period of their 'Behaltezeit' (period of time for which the employer is legally obliged to employ the apprentice or member of staff after the end of training) is related to the 'interest for education' on behalf of the respective employer. However, not only actors have a 'public interest' – an interest to present their professional skills to the general public and to keep in touch with the like – and in a similar manner not only apprentices and fully trained employees are interested in education and advanced training.

369. The professional athlete has a right to appropriate employment for both reasons,[428] and the Supreme Court[429] has explicitly decided in the case *Markus Schopp against Red Bull Salzburg* (in reference to 'appropriateness' or relativity of this right, *see* below). On the one hand, professional athletes are certainly to a similar extent dependent on the public and on the media reporting and coverage as actors, thus making a public appearance enormously important. Their potential earnings are very much determined by their 'current value'. On the other hand, the parallels to professions with high demands in educational training and upgrading measures cannot be ignored as professional athletes would immediately and permanently lose their qualities in the game if they were not to participate in training sessions. However, based on this decision, a professional ice hockey player recently claimed a financial loss resulting from the reduction of his market value. Thereby, the OGH[430] has pointed out that the 'current value' of an athlete summarizes his abilities (e.g., talent, experience, prominence and popularity), but does not constitute a financial loss. Thus, the relevant property loss can be seen in the resulting reduction of the source of income and not in value. In the absence of any specification to this effect, a claim is inconclusive.

370. The right to employment is relative: an employee with the right to employment must be used 'appropriately', whereas attention must be paid to 'contents of contract' (the contents listing the obligation to work), to 'qualities and skills' of the employee, as well as to the 'type of operational management'. Given the example of a professional football player, these issues prove that an employee of that kind definitely has the right to participate in training. However, the fully established cadre player will only owe the employer the training in the premiere team according to his contractual obligations to work; hence, normally, he cannot be validly

---

428. Thus already *Holzer*, DRdA 1972, 79.
429. OGH 1.2.2007 DRdA 2007, 477 *(Brodil)* = ZAS 2008, 86 *(Thomas)*. In OGH 2004, 8 ObA 38/04b ('case Sturm Graz against Ferdinand Feldhofer'), the core issue was avoided by means of formal reasons; cf. in addition also *see* the case study *of Firlei*, DRdA 2003, 186 ff. on the (German) case Bernd Schuster ArbG Solingen in 1995 AuR 1996, 198.
430. OGH 25.3.2021 ARD 6751/9/2021.

transferred to youth training – this procedure is handled differently under specific circumstances such as after injuries. The professional football player may not generally assume the right to participation in the game; it should be clear to every professional football player that his participation in the game depends not only on his football performances but also on considerations of the association management (choice of tactics as well as talents and skills of the team).

371. It has to be criticized that the Supreme Court in its decision on the case of 'Markus Schopp' underestimates the athlete's interest in public presentation. The right to employment is granted especially in the area where sports performance and qualification ought to be protected. The employee is not entitled to participate 'in all the other representative events of the association or of the players for the purpose of public relations by the employer'. However, it is viewed that the proper presentation of the athlete on team photos, at publicity events, etc., is a legitimate concern to the sportsman. Otherwise, he is threatened with the serious fate of disappearing from public perception which might be problematic for his future development and professional advancement. Therefore, these minor side issues concerning the right to employment deserve consideration in the case of professional athletes.[431]

372. According to AuslBG, *foreigners* (non-EU citizens or EEA-citizens) require a work permit issued by the AMS.[432] The employer is liable to prosecution if he employs a foreigner without work permit, and the contract is void. However, the employer has to pay for rendered service as if the contract were still valid.

373. After naturalization, neo-residents can only be appointed to the national team according to the association statute, and there are restrictions, which are legally questionable (cf. Part II, §2.III).

374. Besides, usually only a limited number of foreigners may be employed according to the association or federation statutes. However, in relation to European law, this regulation only applies to citizens from states which are neither a member of the EU, the EEA, nor which have concluded a so-called association agreement with the EU:

- It has been tried regularly to withhold disputes about player contracts from national jurisdiction in order to discuss them in arbitral court. §§ 577 ff ZPO provide such an option if, among other things, an explicit and written arbitration agreement is signed in due form. However, § 9 Clause 2 ASGG encloses a restriction referring to disputes in labour law to the effect that arbitral courts can only be established for disputes which have already arisen, but not for potential future disputes.
- In contrast, *arbitration and conciliation clauses* regulate the implementation of conciliation procedures prior to court appeals. These clauses are not touched by

431. Following this argument also *see Brodil*, DRdA 2007, 483.
432. Thereon recently with reference to football player VwGH 21.4.2020 ARD 6726/11/2020.

§ 9 Clause 2 ASGG and are basically to be considered acceptable. If legal proceedings are initiated despite a previous arbitration, the claim of relief is to be dismissed due to lack of current enforceability.[433]

E. Sport and Social Security

375. In the following section, issues of compulsory insurance (cf. §1.III.E.1), the contribution system (cf. §1.III.E.2) as well as the provisions on the right to benefits in Austrian social security law will be discussed (cf. §1.III.E.3).[434]

376. Among other aspects, the difference between *social insurance* and *private insurance* is defined by the fact that social insurance is regulated by law (compulsory insurance), whereas private insurance is a voluntary contract between an insurance company and a person. For example, many associations often take out a private accident insurance for their active athletes. If the sportsman is also covered by statutory accident insurance, then statutory compulsory insurance and voluntary private insurance exist side-by-side.

377. The social insurance institutions are self-governing bodies under the supervision of the Ministry for Social Affairs. Important social insurance institutions are, for example, the General Accident Insurance Institution (AUVA), the Regional Health Insurance Funds ('Gebietskrankenkassen') and the Pension Insurance Institutes for Employees.

1. Compulsory Insurance

378. The social insurance law includes an order in which the compulsory insurance is to be controlled and reviewed.

a. Employment Relation

379. If the athlete's employment relation has to be determined, this results in *compulsory insurance according to the ASVG.* The compulsory insurance according to ASVG contains *accident insurance, health insurance and pension insurance*. Furthermore, if the athlete is covered by health insurance, he is also covered by *unemployment insurance* according to the unemployment insurance law. In addition to that, the *insurance against non-payment in case of insolvency* is combined with the unemployment insurance according to the IESG. In case of a *minor employment*

433. OGH 5.9.2001 Arb 12.128; 9.4.2008, 2 Ob 84/08d; *Neumayr* in *Neumayr/Reissner* (ed.), Zeller Kommentar zum Arbeitsrecht^3 (2018) § 9 ASGG Rz 14, *see also Reith*, Rechtsschutz im Berufssport, Zak 2015, 246.

434. *Tomandl*, Sozialrechtliche Probleme des Berufssportrechts – dargestellt am Beispiel Fußball, ZAS 2002, 66; *the same*, Die sozialversicherungsrechtliche Beurteilung von Sportler-Ausrüsterverträgen, in FS Krejci II (2001) 1735; *see also Strohmayer*, Die sozialversicherungsrechtliche Stellung von Sportlern, in *Grundei/Karollus* (ed.), Berufssportrecht IX (2020) 23.

(employment with a limited number of hours worked), the sportsman only has to have a compulsory insurance in terms of accident insurance (§ 5 Clause 1 Z 2 in connection with Clause 2 ASVG); the limiting amount of payment is adjusted annually and, for example, for the year 2022 the amount is EUR 485,85 monthly.

380. Employees are – according to § 4 Clause 2 Sentence 1 ASVG – persons who are occupied in a relation of personal and economic dependence against remuneration. This concept for employee essentially corresponds with that of labour law, and especially the term 'economic dependence' has to be understood as a partial aspect of the personal dependence of the employee. It must be pointed out that in regard to social insurance, this legal term requires remuneration, and the mere integration without valid contract (i.e., illegally employed foreigners) is sufficient for the existence of employee status. According to § 4 Clause 2 Sentence 2 ASVG, a person who is subject to income tax in regard to § 47 Clause 1 in connection with Clause 2 EStG is also considered an employee.

381. Under consideration of these aspects, jurisdiction[435] has recently qualified a lead jumper at the Ski Flying World Championships in Kulm as an employee. In the present case, the jumper was already part of the squad and had the task to test the conditions of the ski jump. However, the athlete does not have the possibility to refuse his activity (which includes, e.g., the preparation phase) as a lead jumper in general, but only a dangerous jump in particular situations. Based on this, the VwGH affirmed the involvement in the operation.

b. Free Contract of Service

382. Even though § 4 Clause 4 ASVG is subsidiary to the regulations mentioned before, it equates certain persons with employees who are obliged to certain employers by means of *free contracts of service* – if they receive remuneration for this occupation, *essentially provide the services in person*, and have *no considerable resources of their own* – unless they are otherwise insured (§ 2 Clause 1 Z 1 to 4GSVG, § 2 Clause 1 and 2 FSVG).

383. According to these regulations, despite of § 4 Clause 2 ASVG and basically in accordance with employer status defined by labour law, the very 'small', 'quasi-subordinate' contractees with independent contracts (but not, e.g., contractees for work) are included in the social insurance scheme of the salaried workers; thus, they are included in the ASVG. For the employer, this aspect comprises the analogue civil obligations similar to those for an employee, in particular registration requirements and contribution obligations. Under consideration of the limit for financial subsistence payments, the compulsory insurance is relevant in all branches of insurance according to ASVG, thus also unemployment insurance or insurance against non-payment in case of insolvency.

435. VwGH 3.4.2019 ARD 6657/10/2019.

384. In this context, jurisdiction[436] opposes a free contract of service and an employment relation if members of an association with non-profit status give individually agreed private flight lessons to other members. Irrespective of the fact that the instructors receive a small compensation of expenses from the association. In the present case, the court was of the opinion that there was neither a duty to perform work in person nor any duty to take action at all.

385. Apart from this, the following considerations are dedicated to analyse relevant case law regarding the demarcation between free service contracts and employment relations or non-employment relations.

386. Thereby, it has to be noted that the VwGH[437] recently held the view that a *sponsoring contract* with a motorcycling athlete generally does not constitute a free contract of service. In the present case, a young sportsman had an accident and has been paraplegic ever since. Before, the athlete entered into a verbal agreement to participate in 14 matches to present the motorcycles of the manufacturer. In doing so, the athlete usually provides 'advertising' in order to enhance the positive image of the sponsored party. In addition to the provision of equipment (e.g., motorcycle), he received a remuneration in the amount of approximately 500 euros per race. Due to the lack of a personal dependency, the court denied the qualification as an employment relation. Thereby, the following aspects have been considered: The participation in certain events and a training camp does not automatically justify an involvement in the operation on race days. The same counts for the submission to a code of conduct. The specification of race days and times was also seen as a neutral criterion. Besides this, the VwGH stated that due to the absence of an exchange ratio, there will typically also be no provision of services. Accordingly, a free service contract has to be denied. Nevertheless, taking into consideration the true economic content of the activity (cf. § 539a ASVG), the application of § 4 Clause 4 ASVG could also be affirmed. Viewed in this light, it is essential that the athlete not only appears for advertising purposes but also provides other services to assume an operational integration. To that, it can be referred to the above-mentioned decision regarding the lead jumper in Kulm.[438] Besides the presentation of various sponsors on his jersey, the athlete was in addition obliged to test the conditions of the ski jump.

387. Under these considerations, a decision of a lower court[439] is to be emphasized. In the present case, the BVwG affirmed the personal dependency because of an operational integration of a 15-year-old synchronized swimmer, who was sent to the European Games by the ÖOC after completing a selection process. Among other things, according to a written agreement on the occasion of the nomination,[440] the

---

436. VwGH 27.4.2020, Ra 2020/08/0036.
437. VwGH 29.1.2020 DRdA 2021, 35 (critically *Födermayr*).
438. *See* VwGH 3.4.2019 ARD 6657/10/2019.
439. BVwG 10.3.2017 ASoK 2017, 464 (critically *Friedrich*).
440. Cf. to the normative treaty in general *Schneider*, Soziale Sicherheit im Sport und ein paar Grundbegriffe aus dem Sportrecht, in *Brameshuber/Aschauer* (ed.), Sozialversicherungsrecht Jahrbuch 2020, 91 (102).

pupil was obliged to participate at official events wearing equipment with logos of the ÖOC. As a result of a traffic accident on the way to the training, the plaintiff suffered an irreversible paraplegia. Due to the fact that the athlete had no influence on the arrival, return journey, training, competition times and competition country or press appointments, the court acknowledged the qualification as an employment contract in accordance with § 4 Clause 2 ASVG. Thereby, the subjugation to regulations (e.g., code of conduct) and so the possibility to set disciplinary measures had also been considered. With reference to the total value of no cash-benefits up to EUR 2,200 (e.g., clothes and sport nourishment), the court also affirmed the legally required remuneration.

388. Taking into account the above-mentioned decision of the highest court, it has to be noted that the case law of the courts regarding the qualification of employment relationships in the professional sports sector is contradictory. Unlike the BVwG,[441] the VwGH[442] held that the submission to a code of conduct and the binding to given times and days of competition do not automatically justify a personal dependency. In contrast to the contract with the motorcycling athlete, a remuneration was not expressly agreed concerning the 15-year-old pupil, and merely consisted in no cash-benefits. However, regarding the second case, it is not possible to determine from the facts established whether the case is based on an association relationship or a sponsoring contract. Apart from this, it should also be taken into account that the accident of the motorcycling athlete occurred during the race, while the one of the swimmer happened on the way to the training. In any case, these legal assessments do not create legal certainty for sponsorship agreements with professional athletes.

c. Other Freelancers

389. Freelancers who carry out a paid activity by means of a business licence are covered by social insurance *of the commercial freelancer* according to GSVG.

390. Furthermore, the so-called *new freelancers* are included in the GSVG, regardless of the forms of contract (contract for work or free contract of service), a trade licence and the consequent membership to the chamber of economics – the latter two having been an essential obstacle in conventional conception. § 2 Clause 1 Z 4 GSVG defines these persons as:

> freelancers who generate income from work activities in terms of §§ 22 Z 1 to 3 and 5 and (or) 23 EStG if they are not yet covered by another compulsory insurance in the respective insurance ranges on grounds of this activity.

391. The compulsory insurance depends on the *amount of income*: If the freelance activity is the only source of income, compulsory insurance arises with an

441. BVwG 10.3.2017 ASoK 2017, 464 (critically *Friedrich*).
442. VwGH 29.1.2020 DRdA 2021, 35 (critically *Födermayr*).

annual income of EUR 5,830.20 (§ 4 Clause 1 Z 5 GSVG). This dynamic amount corresponds to twelve times the monthly limit for minor employment.

392. Those freelancers and contractees of services who are included by the GSVG are covered by compulsory insurance in terms of accident, health, and pension insurance, but not by unemployment insurance. They have to register with the respective social insurance institution, the Commercial Social Insurance Institute, and they also have to pay the complete contributions themselves. However, compulsory insurance only arises with those new freelancers (who hold no trade licence) if the amount of income mentioned above is exceeded.

d. Compulsory Insurance for Sportsmen

393. Normally, the usual form of contract in *team sports* is a contract of service (cf. comments on employment contract: section §1.III.A).

394. In *individual sports*, an organizational integration of the sportsman is not given to the same extent as in team sport. Different forms of contract such as free contracts of service or contracts for work can be present, which may also lead to compulsory social insurance according to the regulations mentioned above.

395. *A free contract of service* which justifies *the compulsory insurance according to § 4 Clause 4 ASVG,* including registration requirements and contribution obligations on behalf of the employer, is present if:

- basically no replacement is possible;
- the athlete does not have any significant resources of his own;
- the athlete or coach may organize places for competitions, games and training sessions, organize game, competition or training sequences as well as schedule the times for games, competitions and training sessions, more or less being entitled to changing the very same.

396. A free contract of service which justifies the compulsory insurance as a freelancer according to GSVG is present[443] if:

- the possibility of a replacement is given;
- the athlete provides significant resources of his own;
- place, time and sequence of training can be determined by the athlete himself.

397. A contract for work is present if:

- the two parties have agreed upon a remuneration based on success irrespective of the duration of the activity (e.g., score-related bonus);
- no permanent integration in sports operations is given.

---

443. Cf. *Schellner*, Neue Selbständige gemäß § 2 Abs 1 Z 4 GSVG bei Einzelsportarten, ASoK 2000, 210.

398. Anyway, according to § 49 Clause 3 Z 28 ASVG *compensations for travel expenses,* which are granted to athletes by the sport association and do not exceed the amount of EUR 60,00 per day of use of the sportsman, are thus no remuneration and are consequently non-contributory if the monthly amount is in addition not more than EUR 540,00.[444] This social insurance privilege is recognized to apply to athletes, coaches, referees or members of adjudication boards who are registered with the social insurance institutions as either employees (§ 4 Clause 2 ASVG) or freelancers (§ 4 Clause 4 ASVG). The activity must be exercised within a sports association or a sports federation. However, these persons must not perform their activities full-time by regular occupation. Moreover, the activities may not constitute the main source of income, and these persons have to be entitled to tax exemption according to § 3 Clause 1 Z 16c Sentence 2 EStG.

2. Contribution System

399. According to ASVG, the association must state the income of the athlete and *pay the respective social security contributions* (employer's and employee's contributions), in fact up to the maximum contribution basis, that is a monthly income of EUR 5,670 (2022; the amount is adjusted annually).[445] Incomes which exceed this maximum contribution basis are exempt from social security contributions. The contributions are collected by the regional health insurance funds and are forwarded to the other insurance institutions, for example, the AUVA.

400. If an employer causes *a procedure for supplementary subsequent insurance* because he has failed to register the athlete with social security or he has stated the athlete's income incorrectly or insufficiently or too low, he might also have to pay the employee's contribution that is he might lose his right to deduct.

401. According to § 67 Clause 10 ASVG, *association organs* which represent the association to external institutions and organization *are liable* for the contribution payments as guarantor for default risk, provided that contributions are not paid due to their negligence.[446] If they do not pay contributions which they have retained from the employee, they are committing an offence according to § 112 Clause 2 ASVG.

---

444. ; *see* according to new regulations Koordinierter Leitfaden des Bundesministeriums für Finanzen und der Sozialversicherung zur SportlerInnenbegünstigung (2019); cf. *Schrank*, Beitragsfreie Bezugsbestandteile, in *Schrank* (ed.), Arbeitsrecht und Sozialversicherungsrecht (loose-leaf, 89th supplement) Rz 51; *see also Toifl/Hosp*, Schwarzarbeit im Sport oder doch pauschale Reiseaufwandsentschädigung?, SWK 2021, 877 with further references.
445. *Resch*, Die beitragsrechtliche Erfassung des Profisportlers, in *Reissner* (ed.), Sport als Arbeit (2008) 153.
446. Cf., e.g., VwGH 12.12.2000 ASoK 2001, 127; *see also Dollenz/Zollner*, Haftungsfallen für Sportfunktionäre, in *Berger/Hattenberger* (ed.), Recht SPORTlich 3 – Aktuelle Rechtsfragen des Sports (2017) 81 (95).

3. Services of Social Insurance

402. Different services are provided in the various branches of insurance.

a. Accident Insurance

403. The accident insurance covers two insured events, namely the occupational accident and the occupational disease.

404. In sport, the *occupational accident* is of particular practical relevance. The term 'occupational accident' results from § 175 ASVG. The quoted paragraph also comprises accidents occurred on the way to work or back home (cf. § 175 Clause 2 ASVG).[447] Apart from this, accidents regulated in § 176 ASVG are equated to occupational accidents. This applies, for example, to accidents during professional training and continuing education courses. In this context, the OGH[448] denied an insurance protection if a professional ice hockey player is contractually obliged to prepare on his own for the coming season. As stated by the court, an official training on the part of the association has not taken place. However, the mere preparation for the commencement of professional activity is not protected.

405. *An accident* is defined as a sudden and unexpected incident. The notion reaches its limits, for example, in the case of frostbites resulting from an emergency bivouac during climbing.

406. An *occupational accident* must be directly associated with the occupation in terms of time, place and cause. Accidents on the way to and from work are also considered occupational accidents. The relation between occupation and accident needs to be questioned in cases such as so-called *facility damages.*[449] Indeed, here the damage has arisen at work; however, it could also have happened on any other occasion.

407. The OGH has already commented on the *problematic issue of sport in operation entities* and the legal point of view on accident insurance: if the authorized foreman initiates a football game against the employees of another employer without informing his own employer about the game, the planning and the cost coverage, the players are not covered by accident insurance, even though the game may take place during working hours and the time for playing is paid.[450] Thus, a strict judicature is continued in order to classify the respective sports activities in the operation entity, basically stating that sports activities which are *organized by the employer and are generally accessible are protected* as they offer *compensation* for (mainly) one-sided *professional stress and strain*. However, competitive sports and

447. BVwG 10.3.2017 ASoK 2017, 464 (critically *Friedrich*).
448. OGH 13.9.2019 ZfG 2019, 134.
449. In reference to a ruptured Achilles tendon during warm-up cf. OLG Wien 19.4.1972 ZAS 1973, 195.
450. Cf. OGH 7.5.1996 SSV-NF 10/49 = ARD 4779/30/96.

other *serious sports activities are not covered* by the respective legal accident insurance (unless they are included in obligations of the employment contract) as they are not in the operation entity's interest.[451] Thus, company outings such as common ski excursions[452] and the skiing holiday of a department,[453] which include staff meetings, are covered by insurance, but insurance coverage is not applied to company ski championships,[454] company football tournaments,[455] company tennis tournaments[456] or rafting trips at company outings of office workers.[457] In this context, the OGH[458] recently opposed a claim because of an occupational accident. In the following case, the plaintiff works as a managing director of a company operating an online platform, where Austrian organizers can offer different sporting activities. The plaintiff got injured during a climbing tour with his friend, who was already employed by the company as a contractor for work in the past. The two intended to talk about business during the activity. Based on the fact that the private interest predominated in the present case, an occupational accident was denied. While a focus on competitive sports is considered to be detrimental in the latter cases mentioned above, the joint events of an operation entity might not be characterized as such in different settings or the sports activities might not be properly linked to the activities covered by insurance. Examples of these cases are present in: participation in a skiing weekend, organized by the recreational club of the company and financially supported by the management of an insurance company without obligation to a joint programme;[459] supervision of a ski tournament which is organized as a leisure activity for the participants of a congress and takes place in the break of the congress,[460]

451. Cf. also *Dörner/Holzer*, Ein Betriebsschitag, DRdA 1990, 372; *Gitter*, Sport und gesetzliche Unfallversicherung, DRdA 1991, 17; *see Mosing*, Betriebssport als Arbeitsunfall, RdW 2016, 272. Thus, negative OGH 30.11.1999 infas 2000 S 31 on the European Championship of the prison officers; in addition OLG Wien 10.3.1981 ZAS 1983, 73 (*Holzer*) on Justizsport; thereon criticizing *Friedrich*, Arbeits- und sozialrechtliche Aspekte des Betriebsskifahrens, in FS Marhold (2020) 55.
452. OGH 13.10.1992 SSV-NF 6/117; OGH 22.12.2005 ARD 5675/7/2006.
453. OGH 22.12.2005 ARD 5675/7/2006.
454. OGH 30.6.1992 DRdA 1993, 49 (*Novak*) = SSV-NF 6/79; 21.12.1993 SSV-NF 7/128; 6.3.2001 ARD 5264/9/2001. An accident on obligation according to § 90 B-KUVG has been asserted in OGH 30.4.2002 ZASB 2002, 36 in case of participation in European Ski Championship of Police Forces due to official order.
455. OGH 29.8.1989 SSV-NF 3/90; 23.11.1994, 10 ObS 188/94. However, assertive in OGH 27.8.2002 ASoK 2003, 203 in the case of an indoor football media tournament; negative in OGH 1.9.1998 SSV-NF 12/115 on a football game *politicians v. journalists*; negating on a football game organized by the police sports association OGH 1.9.2020 ARD 6723/13/2020.
456. OGH 9.5.1995 SSV-NF 9/45; also negative OGH 20.10.1998 ZAS 1999, 152 (*Jöst*) on a business tennis tournament; in the same sense according a police tennis tournament OGH 19.1.2021 ARD 6739/12/2021.
457. OGH 13.10.1992 SSV-NF 6/115. However, on a canyoning accident during a company outing OGH 27.11.2007 infas 2008 S 14 = ASoK 2008, 239.
458. OGH 16.4.2020 ARD 6712/12/2020.
459. OGH 12.2.1991 SSV-NF 5/11.
460. OGH 15.6.1993 SSV-NF 7/59; cf. also OGH 4.10.1994 DRdA 1995, 390 (*Müller*) and OGH 8.6.1995, 10 ObS 96/95.

horseback riding as part of a company seminar[461] as well as participation in a golf taster course which is presented as the winning prize of an employee competition and is paid by the employer.[462]

408. Therefore, based on analogous considerations, a grammar school pupil who has an accident during a dance meeting in preparation for the school prom (held by a professional dance instructor who is employed by a private entity with the consent of the headmaster) is not covered by school accident insurance.[463] According to § 8 Clause 1 Z 3 lit h ASVG, *pupils* are partially insured in the accident insurance (a respective regulation for *students* is included in § 8 Clause 1 Z 3 lit i leg cit – therefore, the principles which are presented in the following also generally apply to this group). The pupil accident insurance is non-contributory (cf. § 74 Clause 5 ASVG). The *protected area of life* results from § 175 Clause 4 and 5 as well as from § 176 Clause 1 Z 11 ASVG.[464] According to § 175 Clause 4 Sentence 1 ASVG, occupational accidents are accidents which occur in local, temporal and causal context with school education covered by insurance. This general regulation for the definition of the pupil's accident is an imitation of § 175 Clause 1 ASVG and has to be interpreted likewise the general regulation of an occupational accident. Furthermore, 'organization theory' (which tries to protect only those activities which take place by means of using school facilities) is not the main issue but 'role theory', which reflects on the role of the insured individual as a pupil and thus entails activities of learning or acting in internal context with private (pursuing economic aims of his own) areas of life.[465] In § 175 Clause 4 Sentence 2 ASVG, it is stated that the general rules and regulations of the pupil accident insurance are to be applied respectively in cases of commuting accidents of pupils. Thus, accidents on the way to and from school are also protected. According to § 175 Clause 5 ASVG, accidents are covered by pupil accident insurance if they are occupational accidents which occur during participation *in school events and school-related activities* in the sense of the Austrian School Education Act, as well as accidents during activities which are compulsory or commonly practised in regard to the school curriculum. According to Austrian School Events Regulation, these school events and activities include, for example, hiking days and other sports days, sports weeks, school skiing holiday and school ski days[466] as well as school excursions.

---

461. OGH 4.10.1994 DRdA 1995, 390 (*Müller*).
462. OGH 8.6.1995, 10 ObS 96/95.
463. OGH 20.8.1996 SSV-NF 10/81 = infas 1997 S 2.
464. In general *Tomandl* in *Tomandl* (ed.), System des österreichischen Sozialversicherungsrechts (loose-leaf, 37th supplement) 2.3.2.3.3. with further references.
465. In reference to an accident during the afternoon care in a daycare centre OGH 23.11.1993 SSV-NF 7/118; in reference to an accident during unobserved recreation period in a closed boarding school 27.1.1998 SSV-NF 12/16; on a fall during sleep from the bunk bed on ski week OGH 12.2.1991 ZAS 1992, 55 (*Winkler*) = SSV-NF 5/13.
466. OGH 10.12.2002 DRdA 2004, 41 (*Reissner*). However, it would be different if, e.g., a pupil, who leaves the school event without permission and for private reasons, consequently has an accident; cf. OGH 25.10.1994 infas 1995 S 30 = SSV-NF 8/108.

409. The Supreme Court[467] also managed to specify those requirements under which *a hobby sportsman who is taking part in competitions* is *in exceptional cases* covered by *legal accident insurance*: an athlete who is employed in the mountain bike store of his wife and is successfully taking part in competitions might substantially contribute to the economic success of the mountain bike store; however, if the success of the store mainly results from his offers and contacts to the mountain bike racing scene, and if he is injured in the 'free practice' during the Austrian Mountain Bike Championships, this accident is directly connected to his employment and consequently has to be qualified as an occupational accident.

410. Within the field of *accidents of the same (legal) standard* in the sense of § 176 ASVG, in particular accidents during educational courses, practice or rescue operations of *voluntary rescue organizations* according to § 176 Clause 1 Z 7 leg cit (e.g., Austrian Alpine Rescue Service, Austrian Water Rescue Service) have to be mentioned. However, if a member of the Alpine Rescue Service instals a climbing wall for an event, this activity is not part of the protected area of life.[468] The latter case presents a mere voluntary work for the association. Besides this, accidents during community events of these operations are also comprised of the scope of the accident insurance. However, the basic prerequisite is the assumption of a certain function during the event on behalf of the organization. The mere participation as a guest is not enough.[469] Eventually, occupational accidents are accidents *which occur during rescue activities* or within the scope of the adequate *voluntary support of official acts of security forces*[470] (§ 176 Clause 1 Z 2 leg cit).

411. An occupational illness – in contrast to occupational accidents, occupational illnesses assume a permanent damaging effect – is only approved of in regard to the register of occupational illnesses and diseases in attachment 1 to the ASVG (abstract occupational illness; § 177 Clause 1 leg cit) or on a case-by-case basis among others if harmful substances or radiation are involved (concrete occupational illness; Clause 2 leg cit).

412. This insurance case is rather insignificant to sport, particularly as no officially recognized occupational illness is linked to sports exercise.

413. Among others, medical care and treatment, rehabilitation, various payments as well as – most importantly – the invalidity pension are provided as *benefits from the accident insurance.*

---

467. OGH 4.11.1997 ARD 4911/3/98.
468. OGH 10.11.1992 SSV-NF 6/123 = ZASB 1993, 15.
469. Cf. thereon opposing regarding an event of the volunteer firefighters OGH 1.9.2020 ARD 6723/12/2020; on the contrary affirming an insurance protection OGH 20.2.2018 ARD 6595/9/2018.
470. In reference to a fatal avalanche accident following accident investigations of the Alpine Gendarmerie in high mountain regions *see* OGH 8.7.1997 SpuRt 1998, 113 (*Reissner*).

b. Health Insurance

414. The insured events of the health insurance contain illness, inability to work as a result of illness, threats to health and maternity.

415. Benefits from the health insurance include medical care, hospital care, remedies, and substitutes (non-cash benefits in case of illness), sickness benefit of up to seventy-eight weeks after the continued remuneration on behalf of the employer (due to the insured event of inability to work as a result of illness), preventive medical check-up (due to the insured event of health threat[471]) as well as maternity benefit, childbirth benefit and medical aid (due to the insured event of maternity).

c. Pension or Retirement Insurance

416. The field of pension insurance covers the insured event of *ageing* which entails benefits such as *retirement pension* and *early old-age pension*. Pensionable age is different according to sex – for men it is 65 years, for women 60 years. *The qualifying period* for the *normal prospective entitlement* (§ 236 Clause 1 Z 2 lit a ASVG) amounts to 180 contribution months within the last 360 calendar months before the effective date (§ 223 Clause 1 ASVG). For the so-called *perpetual entitlement to a pension* (§ 236 Clause 4 Z 1 lit b ASVG), the applicant needs – regardless of any time frame – overall at least 300 contribution months or other insurance months (regulation since 1 January 1956) up to the effective date (§ 223 Clause 1 ASVG).

417. Furthermore, the insured event of the *impaired ability to work* is of enormous practical relevance as it may lead to *occupational disability pension* for white-collar workers and *invalidity pension* for blue-collar workers.

418. The ability to work in his occupation or in a reference occupation must have decreased to a limit of less than 50% of a healthy insurance holder. The *reference occupations* are different according to education: the worse the education, the more reference possibilities.

419. Thus, *professional athletes* can be *referred to the coaching profession*. However, the Supreme Court[472] does not grant any *occupational protection*[473] to *professional football players*, for example. In regard to pension or retirement insurance, they are treated as unskilled and unqualified workers. An unskilled and unqualified worker is only considered invalid when he is not able to carry out a professional activity – which is valuable on the market and can be expected from him in regard to his profession – due to his physically or mentally impaired condition, and when he is not able to earn at least half of the remuneration which a physically

471. Cf. regarding the qualification of health threats as an insured event *Ivansits*, Das Recht der Prävention und Gesundheitsförderung in der österreichischen Sozialversicherung, DRdA 2015, 500.

472. OGH 10.11.1998 DRdA 1999, 382 (*Karl*) = ZAS 1999, 186 (*Holzer*). Furthermore, *see Pfeil*, Sport und Sozialversicherungsrecht, in: Studiengesellschaft für Wirtschaft und Recht (ed.), Sport und Recht (2006) 64 ff.

473. Cf. also OGH 24.1.2006 ZAS 2006, 191 *(Resch)* in reference to a professional ice hockey player.

and mentally healthy insurance holder can normally earn (§ 255 Clause 3 ASVG). Hence, professional football players have to accept to be referred to the complete employment market, and therefore they will (primarily) hardly get an invalidity pension. After severe injuries they will still be able to work as a porter or as a ticket sales person. Any kind of occupation which is an opportunity on the job market may be a possible reference occupation. It suffices if there are about ninety appropriate jobs all over Austria, no matter whether these are vacant or filled.

420. The most important *benefits* from the unemployment insurance are unemployment benefit and emergency assistance.

421. Important *eligibility requirements* – besides being entitled to a claim – are unemployment, ability to work and willingness to work. The unemployed person must be ready to accept a reasonable employment.

d. Insurance Against Non-payment in Case of Insolvency

422. This social insurance protects employees and freelancers in the sense of § 4 Clause 4 ASVG from the risk that their employer (contractee) becomes insolvent. This insurance also *compensates* – if necessary – *remaining claims in regard to labour law* up to a certain extent, which has already proven its significance for professional sportsmen several times.

423. According to § 1 Clause 1 IESG, particularly *employees* and *freelancers* are entitled to claim for insolvency payments if they fulfil the conditions for claim laid down by law, even if the contractual relationship has ceased. The primary starting point is the *initiation of bankruptcy proceedings on the domestic assets of the current or former employer* (contractee). The initiation of bankruptcy proceedings *is equivalent* to a number of phenomena listed in § 1 Clause 1 Z 1 to 6 IESG (e.g., commencement of composition proceedings, rejection of a petition in bankruptcy due to lack of sufficient assets in order to cover procedural costs). The benefit is granted on *request* by an 'Insolvency-Payment-Fund-Service Ltd' (cf. § 6 IESG), which takes action by order of the BMWA. The *insolvency payment* replaces remaining claims in regard to labour law, in particular remunerations; however, these remunerations are *restricted* to certain *time periods* (e.g., remunerations for maximum six months prior to the initiation of the insolvency proceedings; cf. §§ 3a ff IESG) and *maximum limits* (cf. § 1 Clause 3 Z 4 in connection with Clause 4 and 4a IESG). Claims which exceed these restrictions and are not secured must be asserted in the insolvency proceedings. In return, the employee will receive only proportionate satisfaction (in accordance with the achieved settlement and insolvency pro rata contribution).

IV. Claims of Insured Non-professional Athletes in Regard to Employment Law and Social Law

424. The following section refers back to the legal bases in labour law as well as in social insurance presented in section §1.III. Apart from tort law, non-professional athletes who have had an accident may naturally also file claims with private insurance.

A. *Employer's Obligation to Continued Payment of Wages in Case of Leisure Sport Accidents*

425. The *continued payment of wages* within the legal framework (according to § 8 Clause 1 and 2 AngG, § 2 EFZG, etc.) is *only blocked* if the sportsman has *deliberately or as a result of serious negligence* evoked an accident. His actions are considered deliberate if he is aware of the illegality if he foresees the injurious and harmful result and accepts this incident. Somebody who is injured due to serious negligence disregards the necessary diligence, so damage is probable.

426. During the examination of a sports accident due to serious negligence, it has to be considered whether the casualty's act has differed strongly from the 'rules of the art' in the given case (e.g., a skier on a ski tour who enters alpine terrain where he is definitely exposed to avalanches, nevertheless putting his life in danger with his eyes wide open). Exercising sport under the influence of alcohol – for example, skiing – is generally considered a serious negligence.[474]

B. *Benefits of Social Insurance in Leisure Sports Accident*

427. Treatment and payments are covered by social *health insurance*. However, payments are 'refused' or 'forfeited' in case of deliberate self-harm and self-destructive behaviour, invocation of an insured event by means of an intentional criminal act (leading to a prison sentence of more than one year), alcohol or substance abuse or participation in a brawl with a final sentence in accordance with § 91 StGB (cf. §§ 88, 142 ASVG). Nevertheless, the social insurance law takes precautions to protect the relatives: if the insured person has lost his claim to sickness benefit because of drunkenness or substance and drug abuse, additional insured relatives, who rely on financial support and maintenance payment from the insured person, receive at least a so-called standard benefit in accordance with § 142 Clause 2 ASVG. This standard benefit consists of 50% of the amount of the refused sickness benefit. However, it is assumed that – among others – relatives who are claiming maintenance have not been culpably involved in the act which caused the forfeit.

474. Cf. with reference to company skiing days *Friedrich*, in FS Marhold 59 f.

428. Sometimes the *accident insurance* has an obligation to services, for example, in case of an accident at a company sport event. Sports activities which have been 'ordered' by the company and which are mainly characterized by their overriding community nature are covered by accident insurance.

§2. Characteristics of Athlete's Taxation

429. In this context, a number of different constellations have to be discussed:

I. Taxation of Domestic Athletes with Primarily Foreign Assignments

430. Based on a decree by the BMF,[475] freelance athletes are subject to a *general calculation of income tax on a flat-rate basis*. This calculation may only be applied if the athlete is liable for taxes without any restrictions and if he mainly participates in sports events abroad during the respective calendar year. The general calculation ought to contain the incomes from sports activities including the athlete's advertising activities. The proportion of the income which is liable to taxation due to the Austrian systems and which includes advertising activities amounts to 33% of the income earned in the respective calendar year by means of sports activities and advertising activities.

431. If the tax liability is identified by such a general calculation, foreign taxes which may have been paid for these incomes are not taken into account. Foreign income resulting from an assignment as an athlete, including advertising activities, has to be considered when establishing the tax for the remaining income. Whereas – in regard to *determination of the common tax base* – the *income* of the athlete is *only* allocated *by a third*, the *tax rate* is determined *under consideration of 100% of the complete income.*

II. Influx Privilege for Athletes Based on Residency

432. According to § 103 Clause 1 in connection with Clause 3 EStG, in regard to athletes whose immigration from abroad lies in the interest of the general public, the BMF is entitled to limit taxation to their domestic income and even compound it. This influx privilege, which is presented in detail in the Influx Privilege Regulation,[476] may be issued to foreigners, Austrian citizens as well as citizens with dual nationality. Persons who have already had their centre of life and interest in Austria before are subject to an additional prerequisite for application – between their moving away and their moving back, a minimum time period of ten years must have passed. This influx privilege was used by the race-car driver Ralf Schumacher, for example, when he changed his place of residence and moved to Salzburg.

---

475. BGBl II 2000/418.
476. BGBl II 2016/261.

III. Tax Deduction for Limited Tax Liability

433. Persons who have *neither a domicile nor a habitual residence* are subject to limited taxation. This situation is definitely rather common among athletes who are Austrian citizens but have chosen their domicile in a tax haven.

434. Income tax of a person who is subject to limited taxation is levied by *tax deduction.* This aspect covers incomes resulting from domestic activities or utilized freelance activities as writers, lecturers, artists, architects, athletes, artists or performers in an entertainment show. In regard to sport, the main issues are especially starting fees and prize or trophy money, which are distributed in the course of sports events such as tennis tournaments, athletics meetings, cycle races, boxing events, etc. Furthermore, incomes from advertising activities such as, for example, poster advertising and television advertising[477] as well as wearing emblems of operating bodies or ski goggles against payment,[478] are also subject to tax deduction. However, it is not relevant whether the athlete is a professional or an amateur. In addition to that, remunerations which athletes with limited taxation privilege living abroad receive from a domestic manufacturer of sports equipment for catalogue advertising may also be subject to tax deduction.[479]

435. Withholding tax is generally *20%.* A rate of *25%* is considered when expenses which are directly connected to the income may be deducted (§ 99 Clause 2 Z 2 EStG). The party which is liable for the withholding tax is the recipient of the income, thus the athlete. The liable party for these incomes, normally the organizer of the sports event or the sponsor, is liable for deduction and payment of the taxes. The complete amount of the remuneration is subject to the tax deducted. As a further privilege, the withholding tax which has been assumed by the liable party is also subject to tax deduction.

436. The person liable to withholding tax has to keep records of the tax deduction at source in a way so that these records may be presented to the tax authority within a reasonable period of time. Furthermore, the person liable to tax deduction has to communicate the amount of financial contributions liable to tax deduction at source as well as the amount of deducted tax to the authorized tax office.

437. If the home country and the residential state of the athlete have a *double taxation treaty,* this treaty has to be considered as in some cases the withholding tax may be cancelled (e.g., according to the double taxation treaty with the USA for income up to USD 20,000). If the tax deduction at source is omitted due to such a treaty, it may be useful to supply and keep a certification of residency of the recipient of the income. If tax relief is merely based on a double taxation treaty, the amount which is subject to the tax deduction and the reduced withholding tax has to be stated.

---

477. Rechtsansichten des BMF, ecolex 1994, 430.
478. BMF, SWI 1991, 209 or SWI 1994, 74.
479. Thereon BMF, SWI 1996, 317 as well as SWI 1998, 104.

438. Even though it is not necessary for the recipient of the income to state the income it might still be useful to do so if the withholding tax is an advance for tax assessment or if the recipient of the income may apply for a refund of withholding tax due to an applicable double taxation treaty.

IV. Tax-Free Income According to the Association Regulations 2001

439. According to Rz 772 of the Association Regulations of 2001 *incomes* of athletes, coaches and referees are *irrelevant up to an amount of EUR 75,* as it may be assumed that operating expenses and advertising costs up to this amount may incur. In case of higher income the monthly amount of EUR 75, is deductible as *operating expenses* or *advertising costs* without any proof. Rz 774 of the Association Regulations 2001 provides that *no income* of the person mentioned above is present in regard to *travel expenses* if the mentioned limits for subsistence costs, costs for mass transportation plus compensation for travel expenses are not exceeded. Moreover, in regard to RZ 774b of the Association Regulations 2001, it has to be noted that this only applies to persons who do not receive a *compensation for travel expenses* on a flat-rate basis according to § 3 Clause 1 Z 16c EStG. Therefore, elected officials are, for example, comprised. Besides this, the quoted legal provision is applied to athletes, coaches or referees, so that their travel expenses are to be qualified as income.[480] Apart from this, this privilege is not valid for association without non-profit status. Outsourced professional teams are, for example, not entitled to privileges (*see* Part II, §3.III). Moreover, the tax-free income privilege of § 3 Clause 1 Z 16c EStG remains possible regarding amateur and junior players, even if they are used in the professional team on a case-by-case basis. As the VwGH[481] stated in a recent decision, this also applies to foreign athletes in the amateur sector.

§3. The Deductibility of Expenditures of the Sponsors

440. Voluntary contributions are not deductible even if they are initiated by considerations within the operation. Payments by sponsors of an operation are viewed as *operating expenses* if they are almost exclusively based on economics and if they may be considered an appropriate service in return to the obligations to advertising activities which have been assumed by the sponsored party. Sponsoring ought to imply a broad and public advertising effect.[482]

441. First of all, one of the conditions consists of the fact that athletes and associations *confirm advertising services*, which may also be legally enforced by the sponsor if necessary. The sponsored athlete has to be *suitable as an advertising*

480. *See also* answering questions in this context *BMF*, Vereine und Steuern – Ein Service für Vereine und ihre Mitglieder (2016) 8.
481. VwGH 12.6.2019 SWK 2019, 1358 (*Wolf/Hack*).
482. Einkommensteuerrichtlinien Abschnitt 5 Nr 1643.

medium, and *advertising expenditures* as well as *suitability* have to be in an *appropriate relation*. The advertisement agreed upon has to be obvious, for example, by means of labels and inscriptions on the sports equipment or on sports clothes, bearing the sponsor's name in the association's name, etc. The advertising function may also be recognized by means of being present in the mass media. The service of the sponsor must not lie beyond any reasonable relation to the advertising activity. If the association is only known to a small number of persons, there is no typical advertising effectiveness.[483]

442. The demand for advertising effectiveness is disregarded in terms of contributions to disabled sport[484] (§ 4a Clause 4 lit d EStG). Nevertheless, the deductibility is limited to 10% of the taxable income.

483. VwGH 25.1.1989, 88/13/0073 in reference to sweat suits for a tennis club; VwGH 1.9.2015 ecolex 2016, 430.

484. § 4 Abs 4 Z 6 was abolished by BGBl I 26/2009.

Part IV. Doping and Sport

§1. General Issues

443. The general criminal law is fully in force in the field of sports. Under the given context, two issues ought to be raised: on the one hand, the question should be discussed whether and to what extent sport may lead to the realization of offences against health and life (cf. 2.). On the other hand, the controversial problem of criminal penalties on doping are discussed (cf. 3.).

§2. Damage to Health and Life Due to Sports

444. Offences/torts of *physical injuries resulting from negligence* (§ 88 StGB) and of *homicide* through negligence (§ 80 StGB) are especially relevant. Both can be realized in a specific form.

445. Concerning the criminal liability of the sportsman in terms of physical injuries and manslaughter, a distinction – similar to civil liability – between *contact sports* and *sports* which are practised *side-by-side* (so-called parallel sports or individual sports) is made. 'Side-by-side sports' are sports which are practised in the same sports facility as part of a competition (e.g., track events) or as a training session (e.g., individual training). There is no physical contact with other sportsmen if the sport is practised according to regulations.

I. Contact Sports

446. In contact sports, physical injuries resulting from negligence and homicide through negligence are not liable to prosecution if they occur despite compliance with the rules of the game or if they are based on minor violations of the rules typical for this kind of sport. In case of serious rule violations which may substantially increase the risk for health and life of others, the criminality of the offender basically has to be affirmed.

447. According to the prevailing view, this legal calculation is not gained based on § 90 Clause 1 StGB because of the fact that the justification of consent which is therein anchored only refers to the success, therefore the physical injury itself. However, compliance according to § 90 Clause 1 StGB does not concern the risk potential of interest in the given context. Anyway, we cannot assume – as it ought to be done according to § 90 Clause 1 StGB – that the sportsman who is engaged in contact sports has agreed to the respective injury of his physical integrity. Providing that he was able to give consent, he has only effectively accepted the appropriate risk but may well have assumed that it will not become a reality. Furthermore, the fact should be added that according to § 90 Clause 1 StGB especially incidents of death which occasionally occur in contact sports are not subject to given consent at all.

448. Therefore, it is considered that the factual injustice of physical injury is not realized in case of injuries which occur as a result of typical risks of established sports due to the lack of objective obligation of due care and diligence.[485] This legal position is relevant for specific contact sports such as boxing, judo, wrestling and similar sports competitions.

449. Beyond the issue of contact sports, this assessment is also relevant for other sports competitions. In terms of criminal law, injuries in risk areas remain irrelevant in sports such as soccer, handball, ice hockey and similar team sports. Only if the risk area is substantially increased a criminal act should be considered.[486]

450. In Styria, a particularly tragic case occurred in rally sport which was even brought to court for criminal assessment. During the international Bosch Super 4-Rally, which was organized in the district of Hartberg and had been approved by the local district administration, a participating rally car skidded off the road in a long left turn, which the rally car pilot tried to take with 170 km/h, and hit a couple of trees. As a consequence, the female co-pilot was fatally injured. On behalf of official experts, the curve was definitely considered to be manageable with up to 175 km/h with a rally car; several participants took this turn with up to 190 km/h. Pilot and co-pilot had already taken part in the rally twice and had acquired the appropriate licences. The LG Graz[487] acquitted the accused driver of the charge of homicide by negligence under particularly dangerous circumstances (§ 81 Clause 1 Z 1 StGB) and explained that due to the joint cooperation of pilot and co-pilot both drivers mutually agreed in equal parts to self-endangerment during the pursuit of rally sport and the distribution of responsibilities in a rally car. Basically, the co-pilot

---

485. *Schütz* in *Höpfel/Ratz* (ed.), Wiener Kommentar zum StGB^2 § 90 Rz 183 (Stand 1.3.2022, rdb.at); cf. furthermore *Hinterhofer*, Die Einwilligung im Strafrecht (1998) 51; *Fuchs/Zerbes,* Österreichisches Strafrecht Allgemeiner Teil I^{11} (2021) 182 f; *Bertel/Schwaighofer/Venier*, Österreichisches Strafrecht Besonderer Teil I^{15} (2020) § 90 Rz 2; *see also Nimmervoll/Stricker* in *Leukauf/Steininger* (ed.), StGB Update 2020 § 90 Rz 18 (Stand 1.2.2020, rdb.at) and cf. regarding the typical sport risk *Hollaender*, Sozialadäquanz und die Grenzen der Strafbarkeit, JSt 2020, 313 (318 f), with reference to extreme sports such as freeriding or extreme climbing *Schwaighofer*, Strafbarkeit bei Selbst- und Fremdgefährdung im Risikosport, in *Büchele/Ganner/ Khakzadeh-Leiler/Mayr/Reissner/Schopper* (ed.), Aktuelle Rechtsfragen des Risiko- und Extremsports (2018) 141.
486. In reference to a skijöring race OGH 8.8.1989 SSt 60/48.
487. LG Graz 5.2.2003, 13 Hr 237/02g.

ignored the risk in the same way as the accused driver, she had considerable responsibility for the races, and the damage which occurred in the end was a consequence of the risk that was jointly taken. The purpose of objectively applied due care and diligence standards – that is the generally binding behavioural requirements to which the legal system demands compliance in order to guarantee protection of physical integrity – does not include those cases in which an individual who is completely capable of his actions and views deliberately and voluntarily puts himself to risk by means of conducting an action which endangers himself and through which he eventually suffers physical harm. Self-endangerment of such a kind as in the given case is not covered by the protective purpose of criminal acts against health and life.

II. Parallel Sports

451. In 'side-by-side sports', criminality is always considered when the offender causes bodily harm to another person in subjectively accusable ways – thus at least negligent – and therefore the illegality of the injurious action may be assumed. The aspect of consent to an immanent risk to injuries in these sports largely recedes due to the fact that such a risk does not present in most relevant cases if the sport is practised in conformity to the rules by all the participants. Therefore, there is definitely no exposure to risk through simple participation in the specific sport.[488] This is especially relevant for collision accidents in skiing which occupy the criminal courts foremost. The central legal aspects often seem to be the lack of normatively effective rules of conduct which may be applied in order to judge unlawfulness. In case of collision accidents in *skiing*, the FIS-Rules are applied which set the standard and which a careful skier ought to follow. Regarding the parallel sport *golf*, it has to be noted that the danger usually derives from hard, flying balls. So, golf players have to comply with the rules of golf. Thereby, they are obliged to ensure that no other person is standing nearby before teeing off.[489] Viewed in this light, the OGH[490] recently affirmed the liability for physical injuries of a third party resulting from negligence of the golf player. The same considerations will probably also apply to injuries caused to other athletes.

452. Nevertheless, from the criminal point of view *potentially dangerous parallel sports* have to be taken into account, thus parallel sports which still include at least a minor risk of injury. If this injury risk is realized, the injurious action can also not be classified as assaults with intent to do bodily injury.[491] However, one case needs to be mentioned – a case presenting a crash in the course of cycling in the slipstream during a training session – which was only accredited by the court in

488. *See* regarding cycling *Flora*, Doping im Radsport – strafrechtliche Konsequenzen, in *Büchele/Ganner/Khakzadeh-Leiler/Mayr/Reissner/Schopper* (ed.), Aktuelle Rechtsfragen im Radsport (2017) 133.
489. Cf. *Hartl*, Verkehrssicherungspflichten und Haftung im Golfsport, Zak 2019, 84.
490. OGH 27.2.2018 Zak 2019, 84 (critically *Hartl*).
491. *See* regarding winter sports off the slopes *Rathgeb/Egger*, Schitour, Variante und Freeriden – Strafrecht 'Abseits der Piste', in *Pilgermair* (ed.), Skisport und Recht (2021) 265.

terms of tort law. More recently, the OGH was again faced with a legal assessment according to tort law. In the already mentioned decision (cf. Part II, §4.I.D.5.), an accident occurred during the break of a sailing regatta. As stated by the court, the participants took over different tasks of the boat crew, so that mutual duties of care and consideration have to be assumed. Based on this, the OGH[492] affirmed the liability of a crew member for slight negligence outside of a competitive situation. Thus, contrary to the quoted decision regarding cycling in the slipstream, the realization of a typical sport risk was denied in the present case.

§3. Criminal Penalties of Doping

453. In the world of sport, the notion has been established that the use of drugs which may artificially enhance the athlete's performance must be prohibited in order to guarantee equal opportunity.[493] However, the issue has to be raised whether doping activities are related to the realization of a criminal offence. This concept may lead to two different aspects: on the one hand, doping substances are verifiably harmful and hazardous to health, and therefore the facts of intentional bodily injury or negligent bodily injury, and in individual situations, even the parallel cases of homicides have to be considered (cf. §3.I). On the other hand, the fact of fraud may be present if the athlete has gained pecuniary advantage due to doping, for example, because of a prize money obtained by fraud (cf. §3.II).

454. § 28 Federal Anti-Doping Act which has replaced the penal provisions of § 5a of the Austrian Drug Act contains a respective criminal offence. According to this regulation, a person who is trafficking prohibited active substances (provided that addictive drugs in the sense of the SMG are excluded), who is using these substances on others, or who is applying methods which are specified in the list of banned methods, which artificially enhance the oxygen transport in the blood (blood doping), or who is applying gene doping on others, ought to be punished. The penalties extend up to imprisonment for five years according to qualification.

455. In contrast to, for example, France or Italy, no criminal offence for self-doping is present in Austrian law. Furthermore, specific regulations for athletes would only be constitutionally questionable under consideration of egalitarian aspects. Moreover, it might be difficult to clearly specify the group of athletes (hobby sportsmen, non-professional athletes, professional athletes) who might classify for the respective criminal offence.[494]

492. OGH 26.11.2020 Zak 2021, 38.

493. *Hagn*, Die rechtliche Beurteilung des Dopings, ÖJZ 1993, 402; *Netrval*, Die Sanktionierung von Doping aus rechtsvergleichender Sicht (Grazer Dissertation 2002); *Markowetz*, Strafrechtliche Probleme des Dopings, JBl 2004, 409.

494. Cf. on the issue *Kornbeck*, Strafbarkeit des Eigendopings und unterstellter Nachholbedarf der USA. Inhaltliche Irrtümer und rechtspolitische Irrwege des US-Repräsentantenhauses bei der Gesetzesvorlage Rodchenkov (H.R.6067), JRP 2019, 1; regarding constitutional aspects *Sautner*, Anti-Doping -Recht. Dopingbekämpfung im Lichte der Bundesverfassung und der Europäischen Menschenrechtskonvention (2019); cf. also *Zeder*, 'Eigendoping' in Österreich strafbar?

I. Doping as Assault or Homicide

456. If the ingestion of doping substances results in damage to health or in death, this fact primarily corresponds to the objective fact of *assault* (§§ 83 ff StGB) or *homicide* (§§ 75 ff StGB). However, the athlete is *not liable to prosecution* himself if he *has taken* the doping substance *himself*, as damage to oneself is not punishable.

457. If a sports physician, a coach or similar attendants give drugs to an athlete without the athlete's knowledge and consent, they are liable to prosecution in case of a subsequent damage to health or death of the very same athlete. However, they can only very rarely be accused of intention to injure or to kill – just by means of dolus eventualis. Hence, in praxi, mainly the offence of *physical injury resulting from negligence* (§ 88 StGB) or *involuntary homicide* (§ 80 StGB) is present.

458. If the athlete *has given his consent* to taking drugs, it has to be examined to which extent the *justification* of § 90 Clause 1 StGB is present. According to this regulation and simply taking its wording into consideration, no justification can be drawn from it for cases of involuntary homicide: § 90 Clause 1 StGB only refers to physical injuries.

459. Regarding the consent to physical injury, it has to be taken into account that the endangerment or the injury (with which the person is compliant) must not be *contra bonos mores.* However, the latter has to be affirmed for doping activities which endanger the health, as these manipulations show no positive purpose or have no positive effect on society.[495] It is self-evident that a consent in the respective sense can only be assumed if it is based on complete and detailed information and clarification of possible health dangers and if it is signed by a person who is able to give consent.

II. Doping as Fraud or Deception

460. The criminal offence of fraud due to doping – especially against organizers of sports events or other athletes – may be present if the athlete who has taken drugs has received a prize which he is not entitled to according to the competition rules.

461. The statement of facts on *fraud* in accordance with § 146 StGB is present if a person performs deceptive actions in order to get rich or in order to benefit a third person, tempting the deceived person to transfer assets which causes him and others pecuniary loss.

Keineswegs!, JRP 2019, 68; thereon *Kornbeck*, Duplik an FritzZeder: Strafbarkeit des Eigendopings, Doping als 'Sportbetrug' und 'präzise völkerrechtliche Vorgaben', JRP 2019, 72.

495. *Markowetz*, JBl 2004, 415; *Netrval*, Doping 177; *Schütz* in WrK^2 § 90 Rz 179.

462. By the year 2020, jurisdiction[496] has affirmed prosecution of doped athletes in the sense of § 146 StGB for the first time. Thereby, it was stated that the fraud may cause a loss to the organizer in terms of both sponsorship money and accommodation costs. Besides the quoted paragraph, the criminal offence can also consist in a deception about the use of a prohibited substance or method (e.g., blood doping) in regard to § 147 Clause 1a StGB (alternative mixed offence).[497] This provision requires that more than minor damage has occurred as a result of one act, and not only after addition of the amounts of several acts.[498]

463. In detail, it is not always unproblematic to recognize the realization of all constituent elements of § 146 StGB regarding criminal acts in doping proceedings. This starts with the requirement for a *deceptive action.* Indeed, during doping control proceedings, it may happen that staff who carry out doping controls manipulate the control by replacing urine samples, etc., which definitely has to be viewed as a deceptive action. However, the athlete who takes part in a competition after having taken drugs is deceiving others regularly (though more implicitly). By means of a silent consent (but often within a licensing process), he has subjected himself explicitly to the competition conditions which forbid doping. Every athlete who participates in a competition under these premises gives the impression of fairness. If it is proven that he has taken drugs, though, a respective act of deception is present.[499] In this context, the OGH[500] recently has pointed out that if the doped cycling athlete is obliged to perform work in return for remuneration two deceptive actions ought to be raised: On the one hand, such an action may be used to establish an employment relationship, on the other hand, doping can also take place while the contract is still in force. Concerning the last situation (doping only during the employment relationship), it is necessary that the obligation to continued payment of wages in the event of a breach of contract has been omitted due to a special agreement towards the contract parties. Apart from this, it is also conceivable that the aggrieved party was induced to refrain from exercising its right of termination because of an error caused by the deception. Thereby, the court[501] holds the view that thus the *causality* of the deceptive act for the transfer of assets is established. The transfer of assets itself constitutes the non-dissolution of the contract and the continued payment of wages.

464. The fact that an *error* has to be caused *for the deceived* is less problematic. Every organizer of sports events can still assume that the athletes who participate in the competition have not taken any drugs; this is valid even though doping cases occur on a regular base and with different accumulation.[502]

496. OGH 23.12.2020 ZWF 2021, 259 (critically *Boyer*).
497. *See* OGH 8.1.2021 ZWF 2021, 259 (*Boyer*).
498. Cf. OGH 27.4.2021 ZWF 2021, 259 (*Boyer*).
499. Cf. *Kirchbach/Sadoghi* in *Höpfel/Ratz* (ed.), Wiener Kommentar zum StGB^2 § 146 Rz 23 (Stand 1.3.2019, rdb.at); *Markowetz,* JBl 2004, 418.
500. OGH 27.4.2021 ZWF 2021, 259 (*Boyer*).
501. OGH 27.4.2021 ZWF 2021, 259 (*Boyer*); in this sense also already OGH 8.1.2021 ZWF 2021, 259 (*Boyer*); thereon affirmative *Hajszan*, JBl 2022, 273 (276).
502. *Hagn*, ÖJZ 1993, 410; *Netrval*, Doping 130; *Markowetz,* JBl 2004, 418.

465. Furthermore, the constituent criminal element of *transfer of assets* on behalf of the deceived is often obvious. The organizer of a sports event – trusting in appropriate participation – has often paid a starting premium, or he pays a prize money to the winner of the competition – trusting in proper and faultless competition.[503] Anyway, in reference to competitors, it is – though controversially – discussed whether the neglect of assertion[504] of the prize money may be considered a respective disposition of assets[505] as the prize money has been paid to the doped competitor.

466. If a *tort of assets* occurs, this loss is evidently located with the competitor who is left empty handed as well as with the organizer who has paid starting premium. The same also applies to the assumption of the costs for overnight stays and the provision of benefits in kind (e.g., skis, poles, bindings and boots).[506] However, if prize money is involved and has already been paid, the legal situation is more problematic. The organizer ought to pay the money, even though he would have to pay it to a sportsman who has not doped. Nevertheless, as the organizer is not obliged to supply benefits to the doped sportsman, as he is affected by the risks of retrospective settlements of transactions (thus, prize money which has been paid wrongly), and as he is now in debt with the true winner, he therefore also suffers a pecuniary loss.[507] In more recent decisions, the OGH[508] followed up on its opinion stated in previous decisions[509] concerning doping and fraud and specified the requirement of a service with economic value with reference to an employment relation. In this constellation, a *tort of assets* may only be assumed if no economically valuable service is rendered by the employee (a professional cycling athlete in the present case). Thus, the value of the service and reward has to be considered. Thereby, regarding doping in professional sports, effects on the sporting and economic environment have to be taken into account. For example, the impact of the exclusion from competitions because of doping or on the athlete's ability to compete and to achieve his athletic goals. Moreover, the consequences of the doping on the image of the employer and the acquisition of financial resources (victim-related factors) should be examined as well. This is accompanied by a case-by-case assessment to answer the question of whether the work performances were individually usable. If not, a damage will occur in the full amount.[510]

467. Besides this, the absence of a claim for repayment under labour law is irrelevant for the occurrence of a pecuniary loss.[511] The mere fact that the remuneration would not have been paid in the event of knowledge of the doping does not mean

503. *Netrval*, Doping 133; *Hagn*, ÖJZ 1993, 410.
504. In regard to the failure to assert a claim as disposal of assets cf. OGH 20.4.1995 JBl 1996, 468 ao.
505. *Markowetz,* JBl 2004, 419.
506. Cf. OGH 23.12.2020 ZWF 2021, 259 (critically *Boyer*) and 8.1.2021 ZWF 2021, 259 (*Boyer*).
507. Cf. *Netrval*, Doping 135; differentiating *Markowetz,* JBl 2004, 419.
508. OGH 27.4.2021 ZWF 2021, 259 (*Boyer*), *see also* OGH 14.9.2021, 14 Os 63/21b; *see* in detail with reference to a pecuniary loss of the employer caused by doping *Hajszan*, JBl 2022, 273 (276 ff).
509. OGH 23.12.2020 and 8.1.2021 ZWF 2021, 259 (*Boyer*).
510. The court came to this conclusion in his first decision OGH 23.12.2020 ZWF 2021, 259 (*Boyer*).
511. OGH 27.4.2021 ZWF 2021, 259 (*Boyer*).

that a pecuniary loss has been incurred. With that in mind the court added that blanket statements regarding the economic worthlessness are not sufficient. Rather, the economic interests of the concretely deceived party under consideration of the above-mentioned individual victim-related factors must be taken into account.[512]

468. However, if the performance is not counterbalanced by an economically valuable consideration, a tort of assets is affirmed with regard to the unilateral pecuniary sacrifice.[513]

469. Finally, concerning the doped athlete's *intention of enrichment*, there is no doubt that the professional athlete tries to gain wealth in regard to the money which is involved in professional sports – it is sufficient that enrichment is – among other aspects – the aim of the deception.[514] For rare cases in which rather low prize money is involved in amateur sport, it may be accepted in individual cases that the athlete was guided towards deceptive doping activities only by his wish for fame.

470. If a doping offence is detected during a doping control in a training session (and not during a control in a competition), it might be possible that – in individual cases – this doping offence gains significance under criminal law and is viewed as *attempted fraud*.[515]

471. Outside of professional sport, in areas in which neither signing bonus nor prize money is paid, only the criminal offence of *deceit* according to § 108 StGB may be applied. However, this would imply that the rights of a third party have been deliberately violated, and this third party will suffer a tort. Nevertheless, this is an offence which may only be prosecuted by means of authorization of the person whose rights have been violated. Beyond that, it is disputable which rights are affected by doping. One aspect that might be considered in regard to this question is the right of the organizer and the participants to the competition and to fairness in the competition.

III. Equestrian Doping

472. (Equestrian) doping is defined as the proceeding of enhancing the performance of a horse by means of respective actions in unfair ways and beyond its natural limits of maximum performance.[516] One of these proceedings may also entail the *administration of performance-enhancing substances*. This kind of doping is only relevant in terms of criminal law as it contains the realization of the offence of fraud

512. OGH 14.9.2021, 14 Os 63/21b.
513. Cf. thereon OGH 8.1.2021 ZWF 2021, 259 (*Boyer*).
514. Cf. *Kienapfel*, Grundriß des österreichischen Strafrechts. Besonderer Teil II^3 (1993) § 146 Rz 205.
515. OGH 23.12.2020 ZWF 2021, 259 (*Boyer*).
516. Cf. *Diz*, Doping im Pferdesport (1985) 33.

only with regard to organizers, competitors and especially participants in bets. For these actions of fraud, the remarks in 2 may well be analogously applied to equestrian sport.

473. One specific aspect in horse races is the fact that *doping on defeat* has to be considered. The main intention behind it is to influence the given situation for bets by means of doping the favourite of the race and limiting its performance. At the same time, high bets are placed on an outsider which naturally leads to higher odds. In this respect, it is evident that the offence of fraud is present.[517]

474. One specific form of doping in equestrian sport is *physical-technical doping*. Examples for this type of doping are surgical procedures on the horse in order to eliminate the sensation of pain, administration of electrical shock in order to drive the horse, but also the preparation of jumping obstacles with nails and picket fences.[518] In regard to these doping practices, it has to be examined to which extent they are considered to be a crime of cruelty against animals under § 222 Clause 1 Z 1 StGB. This statement of fact is given when an animal is deliberately maltreated or is exposed to unnecessary suffering.

475. Any kind of equestrian doping is definitely sanctioned in terms of administrative criminal law (cf. § 5 Clause 2 Z 3, Z 7 and Z 9 TSchG).

---

517. Cf. *Faber/Tillkorn*, Kritische Beobachtungen zum Dopingproblem bei Sportpferden in Deutschland (1977) 614.
518. Cf. *Schreiner*, Sportrechtliche Betrachtung des Pferdedopings (2006) 27.

Part V. Sport and Commerce

476. The following chapter will discuss selected issues of commercial law in connection with sport.[519]

519. *Walter*, Der Schutz von sportlichen Leistungen und Sportveranstaltungen im österreichischen Recht, MR 1995, 206.

Chapter 1. Private Regulation

§1. Sponsoring

477. The *sponsoring contract* is a contract under civil law between a company or business (the sponsor) and an athlete, association or federation (the sponsored).[520] It is the basis of the sponsor's advertising rights to make use of the athlete, the association or the federation, and entitles the sponsor to advertisement for which he has to pay remuneration. Thus, due to the sponsoring contract, the athlete is paid for granting permission to advertisement with him. His sports performance as well as the media suitability of his personality is basic guidance for the respective remuneration.

478. Legal problems may arise if a sponsored federation transfers advertising rights on an event to a sponsor, and the participating athletes are bound by contract to another sponsor. This may lead to collisions such as the *Goldberger* case in the winter of 1994/95. In many cases, the federations try to exclude these athletes from competitions and events, but this procedure is also considered highly questionable due to their monopoly status (cf. the statements on European law). At the very least, the athletes, who create the advertising value of a sports event through their participation in the event, have to receive a proper share of the federation's advertising profits. Anyway, by means of the contract between the federation and the sponsor, the participating athlete is not obliged to advertising performance; this can only be achieved through the consent of the athlete.

479. Organizers of major sporting events such as world or European championships normally sign *exclusive contracts* with sponsors in which they agree to prevent any kind of advertising activities of other businesses or companies in the course of the event. It is a fact that 'Trittbrettfahrer' (entities which try to obtain a marketing platform by fraud, without contractual agreements or advertising remunerations) have tried repeatedly to promote their own products during these major events without any respective sponsoring service. This is called *ambush marketing* (parasite marketing).[521] As the contract between sponsor and organizer can only be effective within the range of the event and for areas which are under the organizer's exclusive control, the prevention of such advertising and promoting activities is

520. *Thiele,* Sponsoring im österreichischen Recht, ecolex-script zu ecolex 1999 H 6, 1; on German law *Vieweg* (ed.), Sponsoring im Sport (1996); *Sengle*, Möglichkeiten und Grenzen des Sportsponsoring am Beispiel der Trikotwerbung im Amateur- und Profifußball (1989); thereon cf. also with further references *Schaubmayr*, Sponsoring im Risiko- und Extremsport in *Büchele/Ganner/Khakzadeh-Leiler/Mayr/Reissner/Schopper* (ed.) Aktuelle Rechtsfragen des Risiko- und Extremsports (2018) 49; *see* regarding the definition of a sponsoring contract VwGH 29.1.2020 DRdA 2021, 35 (critically *Födermayr*) and *Kainz*, Sport-Sponsoring – vertraglicher Leistungsaustausch im Spannungsfeld von Sportlerpersönlichkeit und kommerziellen Interessen, in *Wallentin* (ed.), Fokus Sport – Das Recht (2016) 277.

521. *See* thereon *Spring*, Ambush Marketing – Kreativität gegen Exklusivität?, in *Wallentin* (ed.), Fokus Sport – Das Recht, 165.

legally impossible for areas outside of the organizer's control. However, the usage of the logo for the event is definitely restricted to the authorized sponsors.

§2. Commercial Aspects of Sports Coverage

I. Aspects of Unfair Competition Law

480. While personal rights aspects in connection with the athlete's right to his picture have already been discussed (cf. Part I, §1.III.A.), the following explanations are devoted to *commercial aspects of sports coverage*. In regard to the law of unfair competition, the OGH[522] stated that a media company is not entitled to remove or cover up the advertising of a competitor, who is tied to a sponsoring contract, within the scope of editorial reporting. According to § 1 Clause 1 Z 1 UWG, this constitutes an unfair business practice that is likely to have a detrimental effect on competition.

481. Apart from this, the publication of images of prominent athletes without their consent may also have consequences under the law of unfair competition. In this context, the OGH[523] assessed the use of such images *in connection with self-promotion* of newspaper companies as an infringement of the professional diligence according to § 1 Clause 1 Z 2 UWG. In addition to the lack of public interest, there is also no interest of the athlete in the public commercial advertising. In another decision, the OGH[524] confirmed this legal opinion and added that the use of an athlete's image *in connection with editorial reporting* does not constitute a violation of due care. Thereby, the predominance of sales promotion aspects for the company's own medium has to be taken into account. In view of that, an inadmissible self-promotion is to be assumed if the newspaper adds a daily poster of Austrian national team members during the European football championships without any consent.

482. With regard to the legal situation prior to the amendment of the UWG in 2007, the OGH[525] denied a claim under unfair competition law on the part of the competitor in connection with image reporting without consensus. The purpose of § 78 UrhG is not the assertion of the depicted person's interests by a competitor. Moreover, the law of unfair competition law should not ensure the prosecution of personal rights. In the light of the new jurisdiction on § 1 UWG after the amendment in 2007, the competitor now also has a right to injunctive relief under unfair competition law in addition to the athlete's right according to § 78 UrhG (cf. Part I, §1.III.A) because of the violation of the professional diligence.

---

522. OGH 18.11.2008 EvBl 2009/67 (*Schuhmacher*).
523. OGH 17.9.2014 MR 2014, 314 (*Frauenberger*).
524. OGH 28.3.2017 ecolex 2017, 789 (*Hofmarcher*).
525. OGH 11.3.2008 MR 2008, 123 (*Korn*).

II. Aspects of Intellectual Property Law

483. Apart from considerations under the law of unfair competition, the OLG Wien[526] had also to deal with the matter in the sense of *trademark violations*. In the present case, a bank published a picture of *Marcel Hirscher* depicted with his ski helmet, bearing the logo ('Giebelkreuz') of another bank (the Raiffeisen Group) in an Austrian daily newspaper on the occasion of his ski career end. Based on a *licence contract*, the athlete (respectively, the Austrian Ski Event Company) was entitled to use the Raiffeisen Logo for advertising aspects. Viewed in this light, the court qualified the use as a dual identity and affirmed an injunctive relief of the aggrieved party. Thereto, the OLG Wien stated that although no services or goods were advertised, the defendant had used the logo for itself for advertising purposes in the sense of § 10a Z 5 Trademark Protection Act.

484. In this context, it also has to be noted that the athlete is entitled to remuneration within a *licence agreement* if he permits advertisement with his picture: if the advertisement is placed without his consent, he is entitled to compensation according to standard rates.[527]

§3. Equipment Contract

485. In this contract, a manufacturer of sports equipment supplies an athlete partially or completely with equipment which is necessary for this kind of sport exercise. In return, the athlete agrees to exclusively use the provided equipment. In most cases, this contract is combined with a sponsoring contract which additionally obliges the athlete to be at the manufacturer's disposal for advertising and promoting activities.[528]

§4. Preliminary Termination of Licence and Sponsoring Contracts

486. Recently, the question has been raised time and again to which extent the respective licence or sponsoring contracts may be terminated or modified, if the licensor or the sponsored is accused of *doping offences.* In terms of legal consequences, it has to be differentiated between goal obligation and continuing obligation.

---

526. OLG Wien 21.1.2020 ÖBl 2021, 148 (*Wolfsberger/Zauner*).
527. In reference to a football star OGH 16.2.1982 EvBl 1983/66 = SZ 55/12.
528. In reference to these contracts regarding their classification in social insurance law *Tomandl*, Die sozialversicherungsrechtliche Beurteilung von Sportler-Ausrüsterverträgen, in FS Krejci II (2001) 1735.

I. Goal Obligations

487. The sponsoring contract may, for example, be characterized as a *contract to work* (and thus as a contractual goal obligation) if the athlete only has to provide a single advertising service, for example, a signing session or playing a part in a commercial. In rare cases of an athlete committing a doping offence between the conclusion of the contract and the provision of services, which will – as the individual case may be – completely devaluate the athlete's advertising service or seriously reduce the value of the very same, it has to be questioned whether the sponsor may terminate or modify this contract.

488. *Warranty regulations* are applied when the contract has already been concluded. If this case is present, the secondary warranty remedies of price reduction and especially conversion are at disposal (§ 1167 in connection with §§ 922 et seq., especially § 932 Clause 4 ABGB), particularly as the deficit at hand can definitely neither be improved nor corrected by means of replacement.

489. At the stage prior to contract conclusion, the sponsor is referred to § 920 ABGB, which entitles him to *withdraw from the contract* due to the fact that provision of service is subsequently impossible from fault of the sponsored.

490. Furthermore, sponsors may consider invoking the legal concept of *loss of valid subject matter*. In Austrian law, this clausula rebus sic stantibus is only recognized when a *typical contractual requirement* is omitted. The loss of mere individual requirements does not realize the right to refrain from the contract. In general, a perfect and immaculate sportive image of the sponsored is a typical requirement for the conclusion of contract and is normally assumed by the sponsors.

II. Continuing Obligations

491. In every continuing obligation, the contract can be cancelled by means *of early termination of the contract for cause*, and a contractual exclusion of such a procedure would be *contra bonos mores*. The dogmatic foundation of this termination for cause is the aspect that it is considered unreasonable to sustain such a contractual relation. According to nowadays views, this possible termination also contains the termination due to loss of valid subject matter for continuing obligations.[529]

492. For *licence contracts*, the legal regulations of *rent and lease contracts* – which are closely connected – have to be applied *by analogy* in order to solve the present problem. The regulation of § 1096 ABGB entitles the lessee – in our case

529. *Holzer/Fritzweiler*, Auswirkungen von Dopingverstößen auf Arbeits-, Lizenz- und Sponsorenverträge, in *Fritzweiler* (ed.), Doping – Sanktionen, Beweise, Ansprüche (2000) 71 ff.

the licensee – to discontinue or reduce his service in return if the lease object – here the licence – turns out to be partly or completely unusable without any fault on his part.

§5. Other Problems in Sport Concerning Commercial Law

493. The central *media marketing* of sports events might not only be questionable in terms of European law but also in regard to national antitrust law.[530]

494. The *exclusive allocation of TV broadcasting rights* to a telecommunication business in Germany has resulted in the fact that competitors are at least legally entitled to short-term reports in the length of normally ninety seconds.[531]

495. The Austrian Supreme Courts also had to deal with the matter of the right to short-term reports. At the time, the national football league had marketed the broadcasting rights for their league matches to a pay-per-view channel. The Austrian Broadcasting Corporation (ORF), which had been excluded, called the BKS based on § 5 Fernseh-ExklusivrechteG,[532] in order to assert its claim to short-term reports. The BKS' decision[533] was challenged in the administrative court, and the latter decided that the ORF is entitled to broadcast reports on each football match for the length of at least ninety seconds.[534] All the appeals which were filed with the administrative court against this decision were dismissed and rejected due to lack of relevant constitutional issue.[535] Besides this, the VwGH[536] has recently denied a distortion of competition through the acquisition of the broadcasting rights for the UEFA Champions League matches. According to the court, it is justified if the ORF acquires broadcasting rights at a higher price. After all, unlike private broadcasters, the ORF can count on higher advertising revenues.

496. Between associations and federations, there is a dispute on who is entitled to the *marketing of league matches*. In many cases, the federations occupy this right.

497. The central issue is the term 'organizer'. According to German law,[537] the term 'organizer' is used for whoever carries organizational and financial responsibility for a sports event, bears the operating risk, and is thus entitled to organize and market this event. Frequently, this concept applies to the association which organizes the event. However, if a sports federation has made considerable efforts and

530. Cf. German Bundeskartellamt 2.9.1994 SpuRt 1995, 118; Swiss Richteramt III Bern 22.9.1994 and Appellationsh of Bern 14.11.1994 SpuRt 1995, 30.
531. Cf. in addition dBVerfG 17.2.1998 SpuRt 1998, 116.
532. BGBl I 2001/85.
533. BKS 11.11.2004, 611.003/0035/2004.
534. VwGH 17.6.2005, 2005/04/0034.
535. VfGH 30.11.2004, B 1317/04; 14.1.2005, B 1599/04.
536. *See* VwGH 19.6.2018 RZ 2018, 237.
537. Cf. dBGH 19.6.1956 GRUR 1956, 515; 18.12.1959 GRUR 1960, 273.

their competition or event has developed into an extraordinary marketable product, the aspect of joint organizer may be considered.[538]

498. A relevant source of revenues for the sports associations is the trade with *merchandise*. The copying of legally protected logos or emblems by third parties without holding a licence violates the law (§ 1 UWG), and is thus illegal.[539] The association may ask for an injunction and may also claim compensation (cf. regarding the use of a logos in media coverage §5.II).

499. So-called *sports bets* have developed an enormous economic relevance. In contrast to § 1274 ABGB these betting debts are enforceable.[540] However, the organizers of sports events are definitely not entitled to receive a share from bets on results of their event ('Wettrecht').[541] Nevertheless, the fact that sports bets are legally permitted also has shown negative consequences for sport. It has led to the problem that time and again, people have tried to manipulate sports results in order to fraudulently gain profits from bets. Thus, referees and football players of the German National Football League, for example, have been bribed. Tennis has also been repeatedly under suspicion of betting manipulations.

538. In reference to TV broadcasting rights for home matches of the European Cup dBGH 11.12.1997 SpuRt 1998, 28; cf. furthermore *Walter*, MR 1995, 206.
539. OGH 17.9.1996 SpuRt 1998, 154.
540. OGH 30.10.1998 JAP 1999/2000, 33.
541. *Marhold/Friedrich*, Zur Existenz eines Wettrechts und die wettbewerbsrechtlichen Folgen seiner Vereinbarung, in *Karollus/Achatz/Jabornegg* (Hrsg), Aktuelle Rechtsfragen des Fußballsports (2000) 35.

Part VI. Sport and Covid

Introduction

500. The emergence of the coronavirus in February 2020 had a significant impact on the economic and social life, including sports. In addition to banning spectators from events, athletes themselves were also often prevented from practising sports. In addition to total bans, the practice of sport was also permitted under several restrictions. Therefore, in further sequence, the issued governmental measures and some resulting legal consequences are to be examined.

§1. Governmental Measures

501. Initially, the governmental COVID-19 measures were based on provisions of the Austrian Epidemic Law Act (EpiG).[542]

502. Later, a situation-adequate legal framework consisting of various acts and directives was conceived.[543] So, the COVID-19 Measures Act (COVID-19-MG)[544] was enacted in March 2020 including several ordinance authorizations to the responsible federal minister in order to ensure a more specific regulation according to the respective pandemic situation. The quoted statute enabled the establishment of general, nationwide *entry bans for business premises*, on the one hand, and for *certain places* on the other hand.[545] Based on this act, two ordinances were issued at the beginning: One prohibited the entry of public places in general,[546] while the other one[547] referred to entering operations of trade and service, sport and leisure facilities.

542. BGBl 1950/186.
543. Cf. thereon the compilation in *Resch* (ed.), Das Corona-Handbuch: Österreichs Rechtspraxis zur aktuellen Lage: Überblick über die COVID-19-Sondergesetzgebung[1.04] (Stand 29.1.2021, rdb.at) and with accordance to the initial legal framework *Leissler*, EpidemieG und COVID-19-MaßnahmenG: Maßnahmen
und Entschädigungen, ecolex 2020, 286 (287 f).
544. BGBl I 2020/12; *see Leissler*, ecolex 2020, 286.
545. The COVID-19-MG (cf. BGBl I 2021/204) is still, presumably until the end of June 2023, in force. However, the wording has been concretized in the meantime (e.g., bans on entry for retirement homes, exit regulations, regulations on the use of means of transport, etc.).
546. BGBl II 2020/98; cf. on the illegality of this general entry ban VfGH 14.7.2020 VfSlg 20.398.
547. BGBl II 2020/96; *see* on the illegality of the ordinance due to the non-documentation of the decision bases and an unequal treatment of comprised operations VfGH 14.7.2020 VfSlg 20.399.

503. Due to the need for rapid action in a dynamic crisis situation, the governmental measures are only valid for a short period of time, and some of them have already expired or have been revised.[548] With that in mind, issues will be discussed without explicit reference to certain COVID-19 provisions in the following sections.

I. Prohibition of Sports Events

504. The football stadiums that are otherwise packed with fans remained empty during the beginning of the COVID-19 crisis. Athletes had to settle for virtual support *(ghost games*). Thereby, bans and restrictions on events with larger crowds were initially based on § 15 EpiG in order to grant protection against the spread of notifiable diseases. In the beginning, the district authorities were instructed by means of decrees to prohibit certain events (e.g., outdoor events with more than 500 people and indoor ones with more than 100).[549] Then, prohibitions were enacted with directives, based on the quoted provision. To that, the VfGH[550] deemed provisions to be unlawful because the minister did again not adequately document the basis for his decision.

505. Apart from this, special temporary governmental ordinances were issued on the basis of the COVID-19-MG.[551] So, for example, the prohibition of events with more than ten people[552] or the authorization requirement of events.[553] In this context, the wording of the ordinances has been controversially discussed, e.g., regarding the question of whether athletes or referees are comprised of the mentioned number of persons.[554]

506. In the following, two issues concerning the prohibition of sports events deserve consideration: The *refunding of ticket prices* and the *impossibility of performance* on the part of the athlete (*see* §1.IV.C and §1.IV.D).

548. *See*, for example, regarding a relaxation of the measures (COVID-19-LV) BGBl II 2020/197.
549. Decree of 10.3.2020, No. 2020-0.172.682; decree of 1.4.2020, No. 2020-0.201.688 ('Ostererlass') or decree of 6.4.2020, No. 2020-0.221.712 with which the often criticized 'Ostererlass' was finally removed.
550. VfGH 1.10.2020, V 428/2020.
551. *See* in this sense § 50 Clause 20 EpiG in the version of BGBl I 2022/131 according to which § 15 EpiG no longer applies to prohibitions of gatherings because of COVID-19; thereon *Keisler/ Hummelbrunner*, Epidemierecht, in *Resch* (ed.), Das Corona-Handbuch: Österreichs Rechtspraxis zur aktuellen Lage[1.06] Rz 57/2 (Stand 1.7.2021, rdb.at).
552. § 10 COVID-19-LV BGBl II 2020/197.
553. § 10 Clause 4 COVID-19-LV BGBl II 2020/231; cf. in more detail *Klose*, COVID-19 und Veranstaltungen, ZfG 2020, 129 and regarding regulations according to further provisions in detail *Feik*, Neuerungen beim COVID-19-Veranstaltungsbegriff, ZVG 2021, 196.
554. In this sense *Brodil*, Wer beim Sport noch zuschauen darf, Die Presse 2020/32/01.

II. Prohibition and Restriction on Entry

507. Initially, entry bans were enacted on the basis of § 20 EpiG. According to § 20 Clause 1 EpiG, the closure of *operations in certain industries*, which entail a particular risk for the spread of diseases mentioned by law, is enabled *for certain areas*. The basic prerequisite thereby is that the maintenance of the operation would cause serious danger to the employees themselves and to the public in general. Thereafter, COVID-19 was also included in the group of notifiable diseases by an ordinance.[555] Within the field of winter sports après ski locals in general should be noted in this context.[556] Besides this *cable car operations* in Kitzbühl were initially closed based on this provision.[557]

508. On the contrary, based on § 20 Clause 2 EpiG, the operation of *individual commercial enterprises* with a fixed place of business can be restricted or closed by the district authority under the above-mentioned prerequisites. Apart from this, the quoted provision enables the enactment of a *ban on entry for persons*, who got in contact with sick people. While closures in terms of area are enabled in the sense of Clause 1 by way of an ordinance, Clause 2 refers to individual measures concerning single operations (e.g., a single après ski bar) and single contact persons enacted with notifications.[558]

509. Regarding *means of public transport*, such as ships in general, rafts and railways § 26 EpiG has to be considered.[559] However, this provision generally refers to the measures of the EpiG (e.g. § 20 of the act). Thereby, an ordinance should only determine in what manner and by which organs the operation of public transport institutions ought to be regulated. In this context, the question has to be raised whether cable car operations may also be comprised of a ban enacted in the sense of § 26 EpiG. This has been acknowledged by the regional administrative court of Vorarlberg.[560] After all, the subsumption of cable car operations could also be supported by the demonstrative enumeration in the wording.

510. As already mentioned above, the measures were later enacted by ordinances of the responsible federal minister on the basis of the COVID-19-MG. So, for example, the ban on entering the skiing resort Bludenz in Vorarlberg.[561] Apart

555. BGBl II 2020/74 in connection with § 20 Clause 4 EpiG.
556. *See* thereon regarding the après ski local Kitzloch (causa Ischgl) *Fister*, Öffentlich – rechtliche Betrachtungen zum Fall Ischgl, AnwBl 2022, 21 with further considerations according the prerequisites of § 20 EpiG.
557. *See* in detail *Müller*, Schisport in Krisenzeiten: Die COVID-19-Maßnahmen betreffend Seilbahnbetriebe aus verwaltungs- und verfassungsrechtlicher Sicht, in *Pilgermair* (ed.), Skisport und Recht (2021) 95 (102).
558. Cf. on the systematic of § 20 EpiG VwGH 24.2.2021 ARD 6761/6/2021.
559. *See* thereon according the admissibility of a prohibition to enter a shipping company: LVwG of Vienna 29.1.2020, VGW-101/092/863/2021.
560. LVwG of Vorarlberg 27.1.2021, LVwG-408-138/2020-R7; *see also* in this context opposing an illegality of an entry ban regarding a cable car operation in Salzburg VfGH 17.3.2022, V 125/2022.
561. LVwG of Vorarlberg 5.11.2020 ARD 6729/9/2020.

from this, health and fitness studios were also affected by the ban on entering the customer area of operations.[562] The same counts for cable car operators.

511. While these considerations refer primarily to the *hobby sport* field, exemption clauses are relevant in *professional sports*. In this sense, the bans on entering non-public sports facilities were not applied to sportsman, who practise their sporting activity professionally, generate income from it and have already participated in international competitions. This circumstance gains also significance for players, coaches and trainers in the highest division of the Austrian football league. They were also entitled to enter sport facilities in order to train in small groups up to six people.[563] Besides this, the practice of sports was still eligible in non-public open-air areas, where a distance of at least 2m is maintained during the typical practice of the sport.[564] The latter constellation was, for example, relevant with regard to tennis. However, the closed sports facility could only be entered in order to get to the open-air area; besides, changing clothes in dressing rooms was not allowed. Due to the impossibility of compliance with the minimum distance, playing football was not eligible anyway.

512. Besides total prohibitions of access, skiers were later, for example, granted access if they are wearing an FFP2 mask in closed cable cars and access areas; the entering of sporting facilities was, e.g., possible against the presentation of a 3-G-certificate. In this context, the Austrian Constitutional Court[565] has affirmed the compliance with the constitution.

III. Restriction on Traffic

513. In order to prevent the spread of a notifiable disease, § 24 EpiG constitutes the possibility to enact *restrictions on traffic for the residents* in epidemic areas by the responsible district authority. Thereby, reference should be made again to the causa Ischgl, where the access to and departure from the famous skiing place was prohibited. A departure chaos among vacationers was the consequence.[566]

514. Besides this, regarding infected persons *quarantine measures* in accordance with § 7 EpiG can be enacted by notification. Currently, these strict quarantine measures are displaced by traffic restrictions according to the recent COVID-19-ordinance,[567] which is based on the newly inserted § 7b EpiG.[568] Thereby, the practising of sports remains also possible for infected persons as long as they wear a FFP2 face mask.[569]

---

562. *See*, for example, LVwG of Vienna 28.12.2020, VGW-101/032/13993/2020.
563. Cf. e.g. § 8 Clause 2 COVID-19-LV BGBl II 2020/197.
564. Cf. § 8 Clause 3 COVID-19-LV BGBl II 2020/197.
565. VfGH 3.12.2021 CaS 2022, 68.
566. Cf. in more detail *Fister*, AnwBl 2022, 21 (26 ff).
567. Cf. the COVID-19 Traffic Restriction Regulation (COVID-19-VbV), BGBl II 2022/295.
568. *See* thereon BGBl I 2022/89.
569. In detail § 3 COVID-19-VbV.

IV. Selected Consequences of the Governmental Measures

A. Compensation for Loss on Earnings

515. First of all, it should be noted that the provisions of the EpiG have remained in force despite the enactment of the COVID-19-MG. In the view of § 32 EpiG, the people mentioned are entitled to receive compensation for the loss of earnings incurred as a result of the acquisition limitation. Thereby, the basic prerequisite is that the issued measures are listed in the quoted provision. This especially applies to prohibitions and restrictions on entry in regard to § 20 EpiG, to restrictions on traffic (cf. § 24 EpiG) and to quarantine measures according to § 7 EpiG.

516. Apart from this, a special legal assessment comes to the fore concerning *cable car operations*. In this context, the regional administrative court of Vorarlberg[570] opposed a compensation for loss on earnings caused by measures determined in § 26 EpiG. As stated by the court, the quoted provision is not listed in § 32 EpiG. On the contrary, the VfGH[571] noticed an unequal treatment on the differentiation between measures based on §§ 20 and 26 EpiG. At that, the Constitutional Court held the view that closures of public transportation operations are only regulated separately due to their special relevance in society. Nevertheless, regarding the issued measures, reference should be made to § 20 EpiG so that compensation with accordance to § 32 EpiG is to be granted.

517. Besides these considerations, if prohibitions and restrictions are enacted on the basis of the COVID-19-MG, the question comes to the fore whether compensations according to the EpiG still remain possible. After all, the special law does not entail any compensation clause. This problem has occupied many courts.[572] Finally, the VfGH[573] affirmed the constitutional compliance of the missing compensation because of alternative measures and rescue packages (e.g., the fixed cost subsidy).[574] In this context, reference should be especially made to the '*Sportbonus*'. So, the federal minister takes over part of the membership fees in order to provide financial support to non-profit sports associations to recruit new or win back lost members.[575]

---

570. LVwG of Vorarlberg 27.1.2021, LVwG-408-138/2020-R7.
571. VfGH 5.10.2021 ZVR 2022, 60; 29.11.2021 E 3639/2021.
572. Among others LVwG of Vorarlberg 27.1.2021, LVwG-408-138/2020-R7 and LVwG of Vienna 28.12.2020, VGW-101/032/13993/2020.
573. VfGH 14.7.2020 VfSlg 20.397.
574. Thereby § 13 Clause 2 and 3 COVID-19-MG BGBl I 2022/103 regulate that the provisions of the EpiG basically remain in force. However, this does not apply to regulations according closures of operations if a special COVID-19 ordinance is enacted; cf. also *Obereder*, Die Bedeutung von § 13 Abs 2 COVID-19-MG für Rechtsakte gem § 20 EpiG und deren Vergütung gem § 32 EpiG, ZVG 2022, 75.
575. *See* § 14 Clause 1 Z 9 in connection with § 5 Clause 4 BSFG; for more details cf. information on the homepage https://www.sportbonus.at/de/Startseite.

518. Viewed in this light, the VwGH[576] denied several claims in accordance with § 32 EpiG.

519. Furthermore, it has to be noted that this court[577] also denied a claim of an enterprise operating in the management of a stadium and in the organization of sports events. Thereby, it has been stated that the indirect impact due to a ban on events cannot be equated with a case according to § 20 EpiG.

B. Cancellation or Reduction of Lease

520. Due to the governmental measures, some business operations stood still or could not be used the same way as before (especially in the onsite service sector). As a consequence, sales and revenue decreased. In the sense of § 1104 ABGB, no lease or rent has to be paid if the existing object becomes unusable because of extraordinary events expressly mentioned in the law. The wording also includes epidemics. The question of whether the provision is applied in the COVID-19 crisis has already been addressed by jurisdiction and jurisprudence.[578] As stated by the OGH,[579] the unusability of business objects because of governmental COVID-19-measures can be summarized under the provision. However, the termination of the contract is not caused thereby. The court[580] followed up on these considerations in another decision concerning the operator of a fitness studio. In addition, the OGH held the view that there is no obligation to switch to an online offer (for example, offering nutrition supplements or fitness clothes) instead. Besides this, the tenant is not obliged to pass the given fixed cost subsidy on to the lessor. Nevertheless, a subsequent adjustment by the funding agency (COFAG) remains possible. However, according to jurisdiction,[581] an impairment of contractual use through governmental measures is necessary. A decline of revenue because of other reasons, such as lower travel activity due to a risk of infection, constitutes by contrast a typical corporate risk.

---

576. VwGH 24.2.2021 ARD 6761/6/2021 and 16.11.2021 ecolex 2022, 172; *see also Obereder*, Warum Betretungsverbote für Betriebsstätten nach dem COVID 19-MG keinen Vergütungsanspruch vermitteln, ZVG 2021, 424.
577. VwGH 9.2.2022, Ro 2021/03/0019.
578. *See* thereon *Edelhauser*, Bestandrechtliche Folgen der COVID-19-Pandemie, ÖJZ 2020, 341; *Ehgartner/Weichbold*, COVID-19: Mietzinsminderung für Geschäftsräume?, wbl 2020, 250; *Lovrek*, COVID-19: Auswirkungen auf Bestandverträge, ZIK 2020, 1; in more detail *Laimer/ Schickmair*, Ausgewählte zivilrechtliche Probleme in der COVID-19-Krise, in *Resch* (ed.), Das Corona-Handbuch: Österreichs Rechtspraxis zur aktuellen Lage[1.06] (Stand 1.7.2021, rdb.at).
579. Cf. regarding a tanning salon OGH 21.10.2021 JBl 2022, 40.
580. OGH 13.12.2021 wobl 2022, 104; *see* in this sense before OGH 25.11.2021 immolex 2022, 45 (*Rainer*); cf. regarding the obligation of a restaurant to establish a take-away service OGH 25.1.2022, 8 Ob 131/21d and 19.5.2022, 3 Ob 36/22y.
581. *See* with reference to a travel agency OGH 24.3.2022 wobl 2022, 214; cf. also OGH 24.3.2022, 3 Ob 209/21p: *Fadinger/Seeber,* Neue OGH-Entscheidungen zeigen Grenzen der Mietzinsminderung aufgrund von COVID-19 auf, wobl 2022, 207.

521. In cases where the object can still be used partly (residual use), the lease or rent is only reduced in accordance with § 1105 ABGB.[582] In this context, further prerequisites have to be considered regarding lease contracts, e.g., fixed-term contract up to one year (cf. § 1105 ABGB). Due to the fact that lease contracts for sporting facilities (e.g., football stadiums) are usually concluded for a long period of time,[583] the application of the quoted provision has to be negated in most cases.

C. Legal Consequences under Labour Law

522. Under the given context also relevant questions regarding the *impossibility of professional sports performance* due to governmental measures ought to be raised. Thereby, the existing § 1155 ABGB (cf. Part III, Chapter 1, §1.III.D) was supplemented by a Clause 3.[584] According to this provision, work preventions because of issued measures were assigned to the sphere of the employer and therefore caused an obligation to continued payment of wages. Nevertheless, leave and compensatory time had to be used up in the case of impossibility upon request of the employer. However, this special provision expired by the end of 2020 – from then on general regulations are applied again. Nevertheless, this does not change the assignment to the employers' sphere and thus the obligation to continued payment of wages.

523. Regarding infected athletes, regulations of work preventions due to illnesses are applied. For sportsman in quarantine without being ill other important reasons for the absence are relevant (cf. § 8 Abs 3 AngG and § 1154b Abs 5 ABGB).[585] Under the aspect of labour law, the relationship between a claim according to § 32 EpiG and the continued payment of wages has been discussed controversially.[586]

524. While these considerations are merely relevant for athletes working in an employment relation (*see* Part III, Chapter 1, §1.III), regulations regarding contracts for work might also be taken into account. On the contrary, sportsmen working on the basis of a free contract of service are not comprised by the provision.

582. With reference to restaurants and coffee houses OGH 25.1.2022, 8 Ob 131/21d; 29.3.2022, 4 Ob 218/21v.
583. *See*, for example, the extension of the lease contract for the stadium of the Austrian football association Admira until the year 2043 https://sport.orf.at/stories/3059481/ (30.8.2022).
584. BGBl I 2020/16.
585. Cf. also *Gerhartl*, Erbringung von Arbeitsleistungen durch infizierte Arbeitnehmer, RdW 2022, 412 (413); *see* in general regarding COVID-19 *Drs*, Arbeitnehmerseitige Dienstverhinderung und Urlaub, in *Resch* (ed.), Das Corona-Handbuch: Österreichs Rechtspraxis zur aktuellen Lage[1.06] (Stand 1.7.2021, rdb.at) and *Dullinger*, COVID-19-bedingte Dienstverhinderung in der Arbeitnehmersphäre, ZAS 2021, 12.
586. *See* with reference to different opinions *Resch*, Verhältnis Vergütung nach Epidemiegesetz zur arbeitsrechtlichen Entgeltfortzahlung, ecolex 2021, 285.

525. In the light of social law, it has to be mentioned that the *compensations for travel expenses* (cf. Part III, Chapter 1, §1, III.E.4.a) can also be paid non-contributory even when no training and competitions take place. This will be relevant for home training and such sessions via videoconference.[587]

D. Compensation for Ticket Holders

526. In this context, the question comes to the fore whether the holders of tickets to sports events will be refunded the ticket price. Regarding the conclusion of an individual contract, jurisprudence[588] holds the view that regulations according to *contracts for work* are applied (e.g., for day skiers).

527. Apart from this, if a sports event was cancelled due to the pandemic situation in 2020,2021, and in the first half of 2022, the organizer can give a voucher for the amount to be refunded to the visitor or participant with accordance to the issued *Art, Culture and Sports Protection Act*[589] (KuKuSpoSiG). The quoted law was enacted in order to protect the organizer of events from insolvency.[590] Besides this, this solution also applies to season ticket holders (e.g., for football games), whereby the partly impossibility leads to a reduction of the price.[591] However, a voucher can anyway be issued up to a maximum amount of 70 Euro and above remuneration must be refunded in cash. As stated by jurisdiction,[592] this also applies to multi-day events for every single day.

§2. Sports Associations Measures

528. As already mentioned above, sports events could also be held under restrictions. Thereby, the sports associations were obliged to take specific measures (e.g., entrance controls) as defined by the authority. Besides this, the elaboration of a specific *prevention concept* is required in certain cases. This concept should include, e.g., rules of conduct for athletes, coaches and trainers, specifications for training

587. Cf. *Lidauer*, Beitragsrecht, in *Resch* (ed.), Das Corona-Handbuch: Österreichs Rechtspraxis zur aktuellen Lage[1.06] Rz 31/1 (Stand 1.7.2021, rdb.at).
588. *See* thereon regarding § 1168 ABGB *Laimer/Schickmair* in *Resch*, zivilrechtliche Probleme[1.06] Rz 46.
589. BGBl I 2020/40; *see* in general *Kriegner*, Kunst, Kultur, Sport: Gutscheine statt Entgeltrückzahlung, VbR 2020, 124 and *Gelbmann*, COVID-19-Fälle aus der verbraucherrechtlichen Praxis, VbR 2021, 156.
590. OGH 22.2.2022, 6 Ob 235/21h; *see* regarding the application to ticket brokers OGH 27.4.2022, OGH 9 Ob 8/22z.
591. In this sense § 1 Clause 6 KuKuSpoSiG and *Laimer/Schickmair* in *Resch*, zivilrechtliche Probleme[1.06] Rz 48; *see also* regarding ski tickets *Bergmayr/Reheis*, 'Faire' Lösung? – Saison- und Jahreskarten in Zeiten von COVID-19, ZVR 2021, 40.
592. *See* regarding a three day festival OGH 12.10.2021 Zak 2022, 15 and 19.10.2021 ecolex 2022, 199; cf. in detail the compilation in § 1 KuKuSpoSiG.

and competition infrastructure and, for example, a hygiene and cleaning plan.[593] In doing so, an undercutting of the mentioned minimum distance in the field of professional team sports was, for example, possible, at the beginning of the pandemic. In this context, the BSO has issued general and sport-specific recommendations for safe sports operations.[594]

593. Cf. initially § 15 Clause 2 EpiG BGBl I 2020/104, then § 8 Clause 3 COVID-19-LV BGBl II 2020/207; later such a concept was also necessary regarding events with more than 100 people according to § 10 COVID-19-LV, BGBl I 2020/231; now provisions are mentioned in the Basic Measures Ordinance, BGBl II 2022/156 regarding gatherings with more than five hundred people; *see* thereon in general *Gerhartl*, COVID-19: Präventionskonzept und Beauftragter, ARD 6767/4/2021.

594. Cf. various documents on the homepage *Sport Austria*, Handlungsempfehlungen für Sportvereine und Sportstättenbetreiber, https://www.sportaustria.at/de/schwerpunkte/mitgliederservice/informationen-zum-coronavirus/handlungsempfehlungen-fuer-sportvereine-und-sportstaettenbetreiber/ (29.8.2022).

Selected Bibliography

Andeßner/Schmid (ed.), Finanzen im Sportverein. Handbuch zur Finanzierung, Besteuerung und Rechnungslegung (1997).

Dörner/Holzer, Ein Betriebsschitag, DRdA 1990, 372.

Drs, Arbeitnehmerseitige Dienstverhinderung und Urlaub, in *Resch* (ed.), Das Corona-Handbuch: Österreichs Rechtspraxis zur aktuellen Lage[1.06] (Stand 1.7.2021, rdb.at).

Ebner, Allgemeines steuerliches Gemeinnützigkeitsrecht, in *Ebner/Hammerl/Oberhuber* (ed.), Die Besteuerung der Vereine: Handbuch für die Praxis, Beratung und Wissenschaft[11] (2022).

Eisenberger, Ist der ÖSV immun gegen Bosman? Der 'Fall Goldberger' im Lichte des Gemeinschaftsrechts, RdW 1997, 643.

Ermacora, Öffnung der Forststraßen für das Mountainbiken – Juristische und politische Aspekte der Freigabe von Forststraßen aus Sicht des Alpenvereins, ZVR 2016, 528.

Fritzweiler/Pfister/Summerer, Praxishandbuch Sportrecht[4] (2020).

Gelbmann, Die Organe des ideellen Vereins, JAP 2003/2004, 86.

Gitter, Sport und gesetzliche Unfallversicherung, DRdA 1991, 17.

Grünberger, Steuerfibel für Sportvereine (1992).

Gschöpf, Haftung bei Verstoß gegen Sportregeln (2000).

Hagn, Die rechtliche Beurteilung des Dopings, ÖJZ 1993, 402.

Hammerl, Wirtschaftliche Tätigkeiten von Vereinen, in *Ebner/Hammerl/Oberhuber* (ed.), Die Besteuerung der Vereine: Handbuch für die Praxis, Beratung und Wissenschaft[11] (2022).

Haybäck, Aktuelle Rechtsentwicklung zum Bildnisschutz nach § 78 UrhG, wbl 2020, 53.

Hinteregger, Felsklettern und Grundeigentum, ZVR 2000, 116.

dies (ed.), Trendsportarten und Wegerecht (2005).

Holzer, Arbeits- und sozialversicherungsrechtliche Konsequenzen der Mitarbeit von Vereinsmitgliedern im Rahmen wirtschaftlicher Vereinstätigkeit, in *Korinek/Krejci* (ed.), Der Verein als Unternehmer (1988) 347.

ders, Der Fall Bosman und der österreichische Sport, DRdA 1996, 197.

ders, Freigabe eines Eishockeyprofis durch einstweilige Verfügung des Arbeits- und Sozialgerichts, DRdA 1996, 528.

ders, Die Rechtsstellung von Trainern aus arbeitsrechtlicher Sicht nach österreichischer und deutscher Rechtslage, in *Dury* (ed.), Der Trainer und das Recht (1997) 37.

Holzer/Reissner, Die Rechtsstellung von Berufssportlern aus Staaten mit einem EU-Assoziationsabkommen in Österreich, ASoK 2001, 42.
dies, Zur arbeitsrechtlichen Gleichbehandlungspflicht in EU-Assoziationsabkommen, DRdA 2003, 476.
Karollus/Achatz/Jabornegg (ed.), Aktuelle Rechtsfragen des Fußballsports (2000).
Keisler/Hummelbrunner, Epidemierecht, in *Resch* (ed.), Das Corona-Handbuch: Österreichs Rechtspraxis zur aktuellen Lage[1.06] (Stand 1.7.2021, rdb.at).
König, Sind Schiedsabreden auf den CAS/TAS wirksam? SpuRt 2004, 137.
König/Fischer, Ausbildungskosten – Rückersatz eines Leistungssportlers bei Vereinswechsel, in FS Dittrich (2000) 465.
Koziol/Welser, Grundriss des bürgerlichen Rechts I[15] (2018).
Krejci, Neuer Start der Vereinsrechtsreform? RdW 2001, 206.
Krogmann, Sport und Europarecht (2001).
Laimer/Schickmair, Ausgewählte zivilrechtliche Probleme in der COVID-19-Krise, in *Resch* (ed.), Das Corona-Handbuch: Österreichs Rechtspraxis zur aktuellen Lage[1.06] (Stand 1.7.2021, rdb.at).
Löschnigg/Reiff in *Löschnigg/Melzer* (ed.), Angestelltengesetz I[11] (2021) § 1.
Mahler-Hutter, Der Sachverständige für Schisport. Kollisionen – FIS-Regeln, in *Pilgermair* (ed.), Skisport und Recht (2021) 195.
Malaniuk, Österreichisches Bergsportrecht[2] (2000).
Markowetz, Haftungsrechtliche Ansprüche im Zusammenhang mit Doping, ÖJZ 2004, 407.
ders, Strafrechtliche Probleme des Dopings, JBl 2004, 409.
Müller, Schisport in Krisenzeiten: Die COVID-19-Maßnahmen betreffend Seilbahnbetriebe aus verwaltungs- und verfassungsrechtlicher Sicht, in *Pilgermair* (ed.), Skisport und Recht (2021) 95.
Netzle, Das Internationale Sport-Schiedsgericht in Lausanne. Zusammensetzung, Zuständigkeit und Verfahren, in *Röhricht* (ed.), Sportgerichtsbarkeit (1997) 9.
Neumayr, Wintersport und Wegfreiheit im Bergland, in *Pilgermair* (ed.), Skisport und Recht (2021) 373.
Pepelnik, Zur historischen Entwicklung der Wegefreiheit im ForstG – Unter besonderer Berücksichtigung des Befahrens des Waldes mit Fahrrädern, ZVR 2016, 514.
Pfister, Die Doping-Rechtsprechung des TAS, SpuRt 2000, 133.
Pichler/Holzer, Handbuch des österreichischen Skirechts (1987).
Rechberger/Frauenberger, Der Verein als ‘Richter’, ecolex 1994, 5.
Reissner, Austritt eines Fußballtrainers auf Grund von Mobbing, DRdA 2005, 277.
ders, Lern- und Übungsbuch Arbeitsrecht[6] (2020).
Resch, Europarechtliche Fragen zur Ausbildungsentschädigung, Transfersystem und dem Recht des Spielers auf Freigabe, DRdA 2004, 87.
Rummel, Privates Vereinsrecht im Konflikt zwischen Autonomie und rechtlicher Kontrolle, in FS Strasser (1983) 813.
Seebacher, Haftungsfragen bei Körperverletzung im Sport (1997).
Schellner, Neue Selbstständige gemäß § 2 Abs 1 Z 4 GSVG bei Einzelsportarten, ASoK 2000, 210.

Schrammel, Das Verhältnis des Berufssportlers insbesondere auch des Einzelsportlers zum Verband unter besonderer Berücksichtigung der sozialrechtlichen Stellung, in *Grundei/Karollus* (ed.), Berufssportrecht IX (2020) 1.

Schwaighofer, Schutzbekleidung und Mitverschulden im Sport (2019).

Strein, Die Auswirkungen des EG-Rechts auf den Sport, SpuRt 1998, 4.

Strohmayer, Die sozialversicherungsrechtliche Stellung von Sportlern, in *Grundei/Karollus* (ed.), Berufssportrecht IX (2020) 23.

Thöny, Sind Nationalmannschaften noch zu retten? JBl 1998, 627.

Wagner/Ecker, Tourengehen auf Skipisten – Eine rechtliche Analyse zur Entgelterhebung für Naturkonsum, RdU 2018, 225.

Walter, Der Schutz von sportlichen Leistungen und Sportveranstaltungen im österreichischen Recht, MR 1995, 206.

Weber/Cach, Ausschluss von Vereinsmitgliedern aus wichtigem Grund – Dogmatische Grundlage und ausgewählte verfahrensrechtliche Fragen, GesRZ 2018, 224.

Wyler, Die Schiedsabrede im Sport, in *Röhricht* (ed.), Sportsgerichtsbarkeit (1997) 43.

Selected Bibliography

Index

The numbers here refer to paragraph numbers.

Index

www.ingramcontent.com/pod-product-compliance
Ingram Content Group UK Ltd.
Pitfield, Milton Keynes, MK11 3LW, UK
UKHW020144290926
15471UKWH00004B/694

9 789403 523767